Martin McDonagh

"Is McDonagh to be considered a self-consciously postmodern parodist, an ethical satirist or an anarchic cultural bother-boy? This volume of new, informed, and well-argued essays will enable readers to make up their own minds."

Nicholas Grene, *Trinity College Dublin*

"These lucid, informed and perceptive essays convincingly articulate the global reach of McDonagh's plays and establish him as a world dramatist."

Anthony Roche, *University College Dublin*

This book represents the first collection of original critical material on Martin McDonagh, one of the most celebrated young playwrights of the last decade. Credited with reinvigorating contemporary Irish drama, his dark, despairing comedies have been performed extensively both on Broadway and in the West End, culminating in an Olivier Award for *The Pillowman* and an Academy Award for his short film *Six Shooter*.

In *Martin McDonagh: A Casebook*, Richard Rankin Russell brings together a variety of theoretical perspectives – from globalisation to the gothic – to survey McDonagh's plays in unprecedented critical depth. Specially commissioned essays cover topics such as identity politics, the shadow of violence and the role of Catholicism in the work of this most precocious of contemporary dramatists.

Contributors: Marion Castleberry, Brian Cliff, Joan Fitzpatrick Dean, Maria Doyle, Laura Eldred, José Lanters, Patrick Lonergan, Stephanie Pocock, Richard Rankin Russell, Karen Vandevelde.

Richard Rankin Russell is Associate Professor of English at Baylor University, Texas. His essays on modern playwrights have appeared in *Eire-Ireland*, *Comparative Drama*, *New Hibernia Review*, *Modern Drama* and *Journal of Modern Literature*.

Casebooks on Modern Dramatists
Kimball King, *General Editor*

Martin McDonagh
A Casebook

Edited by Richard Rankin Russell

Routledge
Taylor & Francis Group

NEW YORK AND LONDON

First published 2007
by Routledge
711 Third Ave, New York, NY 10017

Simultaneously published in the USA and Canada
by Routledge
2 Park Square, Milton Park, Abingdon, Oxon OX14 4RN

*Routledge is an imprint of the Taylor & Francis Group,
an informa business*

First issued in paperback 2012

Transferred to Digital Printing 2009

© 2007 Taylor & Francis Group, LLC

Typeset in Sabon by Graphicraft Limited, Hong Kong

British Library Cataloguing in Publication Data
A catalogue record for this book is available
from the British Library

Library of Congress Cataloging in Publication Data
Martin McDonagh : a casebook / editor, Richard Rankin Russell.
p. cm. – (Casebooks on modern dramatists)
Includes bibliographical references and index.
1. McDonagh, Martin—Criticism and interpretation. I. Russell, Richard Rankin.
PR6063.C377Z75 2007
822′.914—dc22
2007019056

ISBN13: 978-0-415-97765-4 (hbk)
ISBN13: 978-0-415-54168-8 (pbk)
ISBN13: 978-0-203-93585-9 (ebk)

Contents

Notes on contributors

Marion Castleberry is Professor of Theatre and Chair of Graduate Theatre Studies at Baylor University in Texas. A Horton Foote expert, he is Founding President of the Horton Foote Society and has published extensively on that playwright, including an edition of Foote's essays entitled *Horton Foote: The Genesis of an American Playwright* (2004). He is also Artistic Director of the American Actors Company and co-founder of the Horton Foote American Playwrights Festival. His most recent directing credit was for the Off-Broadway production of Horton Foote's *The Traveling Lady* (2006), which was nominated for a Drama Desk Award for Best Revival of a Play.

Brian Cliff is currently a lecturer in Irish Studies in the School of English at Trinity College, Dublin. He has also taught at Montclair State University, Emory University, and the Georgia Institute of Technology. His primary research is in Irish culture and literature, and he has published and presented on Irish theatre history and on authors including Paul Muldoon, Frank McGuinness, Emma Donoghue, and Anne Enright. His current book project is "Border Writing: Community and Contemporary Irish Literature." He has also co-edited (with Éibhear Walshe) a collection of essays, *Representing the Troubles: Texts and Images, 1970–2000* (2004).

Joan FitzPatrick Dean is Distinguished Teaching Professor of English at the University of Missouri-Kansas City, where she teaches drama and modern British, American, and Irish literature. Her books include *Riot And Great Anger: Stage Censorship in Twentieth-Century Ireland* (2004) and *Dancing at Lughnasa* (2003).

Maria Doyle is Associate Professor of English at the University of West Georgia where she teaches drama and Irish studies. She has published in venues including *Theatre Journal*, *Modern Drama*, and *New Hibernia Review* on playwrights such as Marina Carr, Conor McPherson, and Stewart Parker and is currently writing a book on Marina Carr's drama.

Laura Eldred is an assistant Professor of English at Lebanon Valley College in Pennsylvania. She was previously a Post-Doctoral Fellow at the University of North Carolina at Chapel Hill, where she earned her Ph.D. in English Literature under Weldon Thornton. Her essay, "Martin McDonagh's Blend of Tradition and Horrific Innovation" appeared in *The Theatre of Martin McDonagh: A World of Savage Stories* (2006), and she has published other articles on authors such as Salman Rushdie, Arundhati Roy, and Patrick McCabe.

José Lanters is Professor of English at the University of Wisconsin-Milwaukee, where she also serves on the advisory and curriculum committees of the Center for Celtic Studies. She has published widely on Irish fiction and drama, including the books *Missed Understandings: A Study of Stage Adaptations of James Joyce* (1988) and *Unauthorized Versions: Irish Menippean Satire, 1919–1952* (2000).

Patrick Lonergan lectures in the English Department at the National University of Ireland in Galway. He edits the "Books" section of *Irish Theatre Magazine* and regularly reviews theater in the West of Ireland for *The Irish Times*. He has published several essays on Martin McDonagh and is currently writing a book on globalization and Irish theater.

Stephanie Pocock earned her M.A. in English literature at Baylor University, where Richard Rankin Russell directed her Master's thesis on Ibsen and Caryl Churchill. An article on Churchill's play, *Light Shining on Buckinghamshire*, drawn from that thesis, was published in *Modern Drama* in 2007. Miss Pocock is currently a Ph.D. candidate in English literature at the University of Notre Dame.

Richard Rankin Russell is Associate Professor of English at Baylor University in Texas. His essays on the dramatists Stewart Parker, Marina Carr, Brian Friel, Gary Mitchell, and Tom Stoppard have appeared in *Eire-Ireland*, *Comparative Drama*, *New Hibernia Review*, *Modern Drama*, and *Journal of Modern Literature*, respectively.

Karen Vandevelde took her Ph.D. from the National University of Ireland at Galway and has taught there and at the University of Limerick. She currently is Research Policy Advisor at Ghent University (Belgium) in the Department of Research Affairs. Her book, *The Alternative Dramatic Revival in Ireland*, 1897–1913, was published 2005, and she has published articles on Irish drama in a variety of journals.

Abbreviations

The following is a list of plays by Martin McDonagh and their abbreviations used parenthetically throughout these essays. Full publication information is given in the individual bibliographies following each essay.

BQLOP   *The Beauty Queen of Leenane and Other Plays (A Skull in Connemara, The Lonesome West)*

Plays 1   *Plays 1 (The Beauty Queen of Leenane, A Skull in Connemara, The Lonesome West)*

TC   *The Cripple of Inishmaan*

TL   *The Lieutenant of Inishmore*

TP   *The Pillowman*

General Editor's note

Routledge is pleased to present *Martin McDonagh: A Casebook*, as McDonagh is one of the twentieth and twenty-first centuries' most promising young Irish playwrights. Born in England of Irish parents, McDonagh has written prolifically for the stage. He is best known for his Leenane trilogy, his Aran Islands trilogy, and the Olivier prize-winning 2004 play, *The Pillowman*. Critics have noticed curious combinations of Synge, Mamet and Pinter in McDonagh's writing style, to which I would add Sam Shepard. (I am thinking of the multiple cans of peas in McDonagh's *The Cripple of Inishmaan*.) However, it is safe to say that McDonagh represents modern Ireland uniquely and combines traditional lyrical beauty with violence and ironic humor.

Appropriately, this volume is edited by Richard Rankin Russell, an associate professor at Baylor University, who is quickly becoming a major scholar of Irish studies. While Russell's specialty is contemporary Irish drama, he is adept at earlier Irish drama, too, as his recent articles have proven.

Kimball King
General Editor

Introduction

In 1994, an unemployed young London-born man of Irish descent, Martin McDonagh, wrote the drafts of seven plays in nine months, the entirety of his dramatic corpus to date (O'Toole, "A Mind in Connemara" 44). While he has insisted that he will never write another play, that remains to be seen, and the existing plays offer a series of challenges to traditional theatrical expectations—in Ireland and abroad. McDonagh's dramas refuse to conform to any lingering stereotypical notions of Irish identity as bucolic or nationalistic. In his rise to fame, however, he has deliberately courted another Irish stereotype—the pugnacious, drunken "Paddy"—most notably when he told Sean Connery to "fuck off" after Connery warned him and his brother John McDonagh to be quiet during the London *Evening Standard* Theatre Awards ceremony in November 1996, a ceremony at which McDonagh received the Most Promising Playwright Prize (O'Toole, "A Mind in Connemara" 45). One is reminded of Brendan Behan's drunken, bumbling interview on the BBC Panorama program with Malcolm Muggeridge in 1956. Although Behan did not even curse and mumbled many of his answers, he quickly helped make the incident an anarchist critique of the staid London establishment. McDonagh has more explicitly claimed to endorse such a viewpoint, telling Fintan O'Toole in interview that his rejection of the cult of sentimentality for dead "martyrs" of the Irish Republican Army in the 1970s and 1980s was based on his immersion in punk rock music such as the Sex Pistols and the Pogues: "I was always coming from a left-wing or pacifist or anarchist angle that started with punk, and which was against all nationalisms" (O'Toole, "A Mind in Connemara" 42).[1]

McDonagh's general contrariness may well have helped generate his dramatic conflicts, many of which feature characters who argue endlessly over petty objects and rehash old arguments with disturbing ferocity, perhaps none more so than the brothers Coleman and Valene Connor in *The Lonesome West* (1997). Anthony Roche has shown how such arguments in McDonagh may have their roots in Irish dramatic antecedents such as Lady Gregory's short play, *The Workhouse Ward* (1908), which features two older male characters divided, yet bound together by fighting ("Re-Working

The Workhouse Ward"). Such quarrelsome companionship typifies many of the relationships between pairs of characters in McDonagh's plays, such as Maureen and her mother Mag in *The Beauty Queen of Leenane* (1996), McDonagh's first play to be performed, and between Katurian and his brother Michal in *The Pillowman* (2003), his most recent play to be staged. In fact, it is difficult to imagine a Martin McDonagh drama without such relationships.

Partly because McDonagh's plays regularly feature routine violence, they have engendered great critical controversy from the start. Critics have argued over his representations of the elusive, abstract invention that is "Irishness," discussed whether or not he endorses the violence he depicts, and wondered whether or not his work has any real artistic merit. Fintan O'Toole, the prominent Irish drama critic for *The Irish Times*, has long defended McDonagh in a series of reviews and articles that note how his plays such as *The Beauty Queen of Leenane* successfully blend elements of "pre-modern" and "postmodern" Ireland and "the trivial and the tragic" in an effort to offer a clearer picture of western contemporary Ireland partly imagined by McDonagh ("*The Beauty Queen of Leenane*" 379, 381). For example, in his 1996 review of *Beauty Queen*, O'Toole suggests that "The 1950s is laid over the 1990s, giving the play's apparent realism the ghostly, dizzying feel of a superimposed photograph. All the elements that make up the picture are real, but their combined effect is one that questions the very idea of reality" ("*The Beauty Queen of Leenane*" 379–80). Such an effect creates a surrealism that suffuses McDonagh's plays and immerses his audience in an ambiguous world seemingly bereft of morality.

Audiences naturally look for an anchor in the topsy-turvy world of McDonagh's plays and he gives them one in his theory of theater, which is simplicity itself. He has repeatedly noted, in the relatively rare interviews that he has given, that the essence of his art is storytelling, a concern he shares with important earlier Irish dramatists such as W. B. Yeats, John Synge, Lady Gregory, and others. For instance, in a 2005 interview with Jesse McKinley for *The New York Times*, McDonagh explains that he views the theater as "a box to tell a story in, basically," adding, "And that's a beautiful thing" (quoted in McKinley N. pag.).

McDonagh grew up in both the Elephant and Castle area of south London and nearby Camberwell in a working-class family and was raised by a father from Connemara and a mother from Sligo. He spent six weeks every summer in his childhood with his father's family in Connemara, in western Ireland, and the Irish-inflected English he heard there spoken by his relatives and locals served as the catalyst for his playwriting. He told Dominic Cavendish in 2001 that "Writing in an Irish idiom freed me up as a writer. Until then, my dialogue was a poor imitation of Pinter and Mamet. I used to try and write stories set in London, but it was just too close to home. Now I've shaken off those influences, I can move back" (quoted in Cavendish N. pag.). The idiom spoken in all of McDonagh's plays except *The Pillowman* immediately reminded critics of the Irish-English dialect in John Synge's dramas from the early twentieth century, but McDonagh is cosmopolitan in his literary and dramatic influences, having cited Jose Luis Borges, Vladimir Nabokov, David Mamet, and Harold Pinter as exemplars (O'Toole, "A Mind in Connemara" 43, 44). He was so influenced, in fact, by Mamet and Pinter, that he turned to Ireland and this dialect in part to disguise the influences of these two dramatic giants upon him.

But Irish playwrights, especially Synge, in his exploration of lonely locales in the western area of the republic, have clearly influenced McDonagh. Shaun Richards has even argued that McDonagh's success is predicated upon his successful intertextual engagement with Synge's plays, particularly *The Playboy of the Western World* ("'The Outpouring of a Morbid, Unhealthy Mind'"). Not only influential for later writers such as McDonagh, Synge's dramatic evocation of the strange blend of tragedy and comedy in the daily lives of inhabitants of the Aran Islands in the 1890s has also proven uncannily prescient for understanding changes to the very genre of drama in the second half of the twentieth century.

One of the critical commonplaces about drama after World War Two concerns its inherently mixed nature. David L. Hirst, for example, notes that post-war tragicomedy is comprised of a "bewildering variety of theatrical idioms [. . .]" (121). It is this genre that is perhaps most suited to appreciating the continuing dilemma of being human in our complex and fragmentary world, as Beckett, perhaps most memorably of all contemporary playwrights, has shown. Being able to laugh at the most grotesque representations of cruelty onstage, for example, ideally serves not to trivialize the cruelty, but to recognize it and yet reject its power over us. McDonagh has admitted that "I walk that line between comedy and cruelty because I think one illuminates the other. And yeah, I tend to push things as far as I can because I think you can see things more clearly through exaggeration than through reality" (quoted in O'Hagan 24). The often uneasy laughter that attends productions of McDonagh's plays testifies to the audience's discomfort with such a strategy, but it is a strategy with far more of an ethical force than is sometimes admitted in discussions of the playwright's work.

The evolving criticism on many contemporary plays eventually shows their underlying ethical aims, but even sophisticated critics can refuse to recognize this authorial strategy in plays by authors such as McDonagh that present such persistent violence so forcefully. Hirst argues that "The strength of modern drama resides chiefly in its discovery of fresh theatrical structures which serve a serious ethical and social purpose" (128). A significant strand of criticism of Martin McDonagh's work, however, refuses to believe that there is any unifying ethic behind the plays: for example, Nicholas Grene, writing on *The Beauty Queen of Leenane*'s project of demythologizing Ireland, argues that "With a mother like Mag, with a home like Leenane, matricide is all but justified" (47).[2] And yet, as Richards has shown, McDonagh shares with John Synge, M. J. Molloy, and Tom Murphy a concern to highlight "the economic desolation of the west [of Ireland] and [explore] its negative impact on the lives of his characters" (253). By destroying stereotypical views of western Ireland as an area populated by happy peasants and alerting audiences to the continuing poverty endemic in certain segments of the West despite the rise of the Celtic Tiger, McDonagh's plays set in that area enact a vital ethical function. Additionally, by holding a mirror up to his audience and showing us the lack of limits to our breathless fascination with violence and cruelty, McDonagh shows us that we desire to watch others' discomfort and even laugh at it, a point made by several of the essays collected here.[3]

The present volume of essays subtly explores previously unrecognized dimensions of McDonagh's drama and persistently questions many previous interpretations of his work. They are remarkable for both their sustained attention to the text of the plays themselves and to critical questions that arise from careful readings of McDonagh's drama through various theoretical lenses. Collectively, these essays demonstrate that far from being settled, the issues raised by Martin McDonagh are vitally important to both our understanding of contemporary drama and for appreciating the complexity of being human in an increasingly chaotic world.

In the opening essay, Jose Lanters draws on her previous work dealing with Irish Menippean satire to articulate a new way of reading McDonagh's drama: as postmodern satire. Postmodern satire, as she argues, views metanarratives with skepticism and tends to destabilize them, characteristics that account for the varied responses to McDonagh's work. Through her interpretation of the signifying maneuvers of the various narratives in *The Pillowman*, Lanters leads us to a new appreciation of how McDonagh parodies and deconstructs the "Irishness" of his five plays set in Ireland.

Joan Dean's essay on McDonagh's stagecraft explores the surprisingly conventional theatrical tropes that the playwright often deploys, such as a character's sudden reappearance from the dead, in order to subvert audience expectations and highlight his works' performative nature. Although his dramaturgy may be conventional, Dean argues that McDonagh's manipulation of timeless stage gimmicks generates epistemological uncertainty on the part of his characters. Even when two endings are possible, as in the conclusion of *The Lieutenant of Inishmore*, McDonagh offers his audiences unexpected satisfaction and closure after overturning a series of stereotypes about the Irish and the West of Ireland.

Several of the contributors attend primarily to one play, in the process illuminating heretofore unrecognized elements of McDonagh's work. For example, Marion Castleberry, a playwright, director, and theater professor, shows how McDonagh creates comedy in *The Beauty Queen of Leenane* by variously juxtaposing the mundane and the shocking and featuring characters who obsess over trivial things in the midst of cruel conversations. Castleberry references the ground-breaking work of Vivian Mercier in *The Irish Comic Tradition* (1962) and for good reason: McDonagh's comic blending of the macabre, grotesque, and fantasy connects him to the oral and written Irish comic tradition from its oral roots through its twentieth-century manifestations.[4]

Catholicism, long a favorite whipping boy for a range of Irish writers, figures prominently in McDonagh's work, but critics have either dismissed it as mere background or played down any sense of the transcendent associated with it in analyses of McDonagh's work. Stephanie Pocock, however, explains here that the character of Father Welsh in *The Lonesome West* is actually far more humane and moral than critics have generally suggested in spite of his ineptitude and choice to take his own life. Pocock argues that the heart of this under-valued play lies in McDonagh's approving treatment of his sacrificial priest, a treatment that places McDonagh in a long line of Irish writers such as George Moore and James Joyce who, despite disdain for the Catholic Church in its institutionalized form, have nonetheless offered up similarly sympathetic priest characters in their fiction.

The work of any author that stands the test of time finally surmounts its immediate physical setting and attains a universality. Karen Vandevelde shows how several Flemish and Dutch adaptations of McDonagh's *The Leenane Trilogy* overcome language barriers and communicate a different set of meanings to their continental audiences than those conveyed by the original, more realistic production by Irish director Garry Hynes with the Druid and Royal Court theater companies. Vandevelde suggests that the re-ordering of crucial scenes across *The Leenane Trilogy* and the resulting four-hour production emphasize a contemporary European dramatic focus on ambiguity and meta-theatricality, qualities that are latent in McDonagh's scripts.

Maria Doyle's essay explores a series of McDonagh's plays that employ violence in unexpected ways and with unexpected consequences for audience perception. Visceral scenes such as the drug dealer hanging by his ankles in the opening of *The Lieutenant of Inishmore* draw audiences in by their immediacy, an immediacy that film, McDonagh's most influential source, cannot achieve. Doyle draws on conventions inherent to the Grand Guignol and on the searingly intimate violence of contemporary British playwright Sarah Kane's *Blasted* to demonstrate how McDonagh both borrows from these exemplars and, at times, inverts them to manipulate audience expectations about violence, implicating us in the process, an inherently ethical maneuver.

While several contributors touch upon McDonagh's love of film, Laura Eldred compellingly explains the influence of the horror film in particular upon McDonagh's drama, especially by assessing that genre's creation and subsequent destruction of monsters. She shows that McDonagh often creates monsters but then leads the audience or reader into sympathy for them, rather than killing them, subverting the monster's destruction we have been conditioned to expect by our own viewing of horror films. McDonagh's sympathetic monsters, such as Maureen in *The Beauty Queen of Leenane* and Padraic in *The Lieutenant of Inishmore*, refuse to conform to stereotypical, romantic constructions of Irish national identity that obtained during the nadir of Irish nationalism under former leader Eamon de Valera and, somewhat disturbingly, offer counter-narratives to a neatly defined nationalist history. Like Doyle, Eldred suggests how the audience is thus indicted in McDonagh's dramatic depictions of violence as we reveal our own bloodlust.

Brian Cliff, in his contribution, shows that *The Pillowman*, McDonagh's least Irish play, inscribes a narrative of potential redemption into a text that is suffused with the torture of adults and children as well as murder. Cliff carefully surveys this strange play's performance history in locales ranging from London to New York to Japan, unfolds its intricate plot, and subtly discusses its critical reception before showing how many of these responses misinterpret the play's conclusion, suggesting its real emphasis is on unexpected grace in the form of the policeman Ariel's salvaging of the writer Katurian's stories.

One of the great pleasures in editing a collection of essays is the ability to include contributions that would normally not be published in journals for reasons of length. The final essay in the collection, by Patrick Lonergan, an expert on both McDonagh and globalism and its cultural impact, is a masterly survey of the inspirations for McDonagh's drama from a variety of sources around the world, including American, Australian, and English soap operas, American movies directed by Quentin Tarantino, and the British movie *Shallow Grave*. He lucidly and convincingly details these influences and traces their impact on McDonagh's corpus by carefully explaining how his use of a peripheral Irish idiom—his use of a recognizable rural Irish dialect and setting—generates the marked mobility of his plays across national boundaries. The result of this process has resulted in a conceptual authenticity instantly recognizable in its cultural sources, which now replaces the typically authentic aura of the live stage production. Lonergan's essay gestures toward the movement, openness, and freedom implicit in McDonagh's work and serves as a fitting conclusion to a collection celebrating a body of work that continues to travel well.

Notes

1 See John Waters's essay "The Irish Mummy" for a thoughtful brief exploration of McDonagh's plays through the music of the Pogues. Waters suggests that McDonagh shares the Pogues' attitude of both connection to and distance from Ireland and that this status creates the curious blend of "loathing and pride, attachment and rejection, assault and embrace" common to their respective art:

"The Pogues, by virtue of profound connections with Ireland had access to the culture without necessarily being hidebound by its various paralyzing elements. Being mainly outsiders in the sense of being removed by a generation and a stretch of water, they achieved a detachment which enabled them to see something we all knew but could not speak. In a sense, their removal allowed them to participate in the organic growth of the culture in a more authentic manner than if they had fully belonged. So it is with Martin McDonagh" (31, 31–32).

2 See, too, the far angrier response from Vic Merriman, in his essays "Decolonization Postponed: The Theatre of Tiger Trash" and "Settling for More: Excess and Success in Contemporary Irish Drama." In the first essay, Merriman argues that McDonagh's first four stage plays "stage a sustained dystopic vision of a land of gratuitous violence, craven money-grubbing and crass amorality. No loyalty, either communal, personal or familial can survive in this arid landscape. Death, affection, responsibility appear as meaningless intrusions in the self-obsessed orbits of child-adults" (273). See Richards's "'The Outpouring of a Morbid, Unhealthy Mind'" for a penetrating refutation of Merriman's argument. The second Merriman essay generally recycles the essential argument of the first essay, often *verbatim.*

3 For a compelling moral reading of McDonagh's most controversial play, *The Lieutenant of Inishmore*, see Catherine Rees's essay, "The Good, the Bad, and the Ugly." Rees argues that McDonagh is following Synge in part by "writing within this classical Irish tradition of the idyllic, pastoral countryside, while savagely attacking the sentimentality of the terrorist movement as a noble response to 'the love of one's land' by employing the overt and dramatic tactics of the London playwrights of the late 1990s, the so-called 'in yer face' British drama. It is this combination of dramatic styles which makes *The Lieutenant* so hard for critics" (30). Rees's essay explicitly critiques the claim made by Mary Luckhurst in her essay, "Martin McDonagh's *Lieutenant of Inishmore*: Selling (-Out) to the English," that the outdated constructs of rural Ireland in that play pander to English critics' continuing stereotypes of Ireland and the Irish mainly to generate more money for McDonagh.

4 Anthony Roche was the first critic to suggest that Mercier's conception of "'the Irish comic tradition,' in particular elements of satire, the macabre, and the grotesque" is helpful to understanding McDonagh's drama. See his "Re-Working *The Workhouse Ward*" 173.

References

Cavendish, Dominic. "He's back, and only half as arrogant." *Daily Telegraph* 6 Apr. 2001. N. pag. 21 Apr. 2006 <http://www.telegraph.co.uk/arts/main.jhtml?xml=arts/2001/04/06/bthing.xml>.

Druids, Dudes and Beauty Queens: The Changing Face of Irish Theatre. Ed. Dermot Bolger. Dublin: New Island, 2001.

Grene, Nicholas. "Ireland in Two Minds: Martin McDonagh and Conor McPherson." *Yearbook of English Studies* 35 (2005): 298–311.

Hirst, David L. *Tragicomedy.* The Critical Idiom: 43. London: Methuen, 1984.

Luckhurst, Mary. "Martin McDonagh's *Lieutenant of Inishmore*: Selling (-Out) to the English." *Contemporary Theatre Review* 14.4 (2004): 34–41.

McKinley, Jesse. "Suffer the Little Children." *The New York Times* 3 Apr. 2005. N. pag. 3 Apr. 2005 <http://www.nytimes.com/2005/04/03/theater/newsand features/03mcki.html>.

Merriman, Vic. "Decolonisation Postponed: The Theatre of Tiger Trash." *Irish University Review* 29.2 (1999): 305–17. Rpt. in *The Theatre of Martin McDonagh: A World of Savage Stories* 264–80.

—— "Settling for More: Excess and Success in Contemporary Irish Drama." *Druids, Dudes and Beauty Queens* 55–71.

O'Hagan, Sean. "The wild west." *Guardian* 24 Mar. 2001: 24.

O'Toole, Fintan. "*The Beauty Queen of Leenane*." *The Irish Times* 6 Feb. 1996. Rpt. in *The Theatre of Martin McDonagh: A World of Savage Stories* 379–81.

—— "A Mind in Connemara: The Savage World of Martin McDonagh." *New Yorker* 6 Mar. 2006: 40–47.

Rees, Catherine. "The Good, the Bad, and the Ugly: The Politics of Morality in Martin McDonagh's *The Lieutenant of Inishmore*." *New Theatre Quarterly* 21.1 (Feb. 2005): 28–33.

Richards, Shaun. "'The Outpouring of a Morbid, Unhealthy Mind': The Critical Condition of Synge and McDonagh." *Irish University Review* 33.1–2 (Spring/Summer 2003): 201–14.

Roche, Anthony. "Re-working *The Workhouse Ward*: McDonagh, Beckett, and Gregory." Spec. issue on Lady Gregory. *Irish University Review* 34.1–2 (Spring/Summer 2002): 171–84.

The Theatre of Martin McDonagh: A World of Savage Stories. Ed. Lilian Chambers and Eamonn Jordan. Dublin: Carysfort Press, 2006.

Waters, John. "The Irish Mummy: The Plays and Purpose of Martin McDonagh." *Druids, Dudes and Beauty Queens* 30–54.

1 The identity politics of Martin McDonagh

José Lanters

Martin McDonagh has been accused by his most hostile critics of writing shallow soap operas and, in his "Irish" plays, of trivializing Irish politics and perpetuating Irish stereotypes. Writing in the *Independent*, Paul Taylor calls *The Pillowman* "mere entertainment" written by a playwright with "a disturbingly defective moral sense" (N. pag.) Vera Lustig terms his rural Irish tragicomedies "empty," and accuses McDonagh of misogyny: "The men [. . .] are naturalistic creations; while the women are painted in crude brush-strokes" (42). Mary Luckhurst bluntly argues that McDonagh "relies on monolithic, prejudicial constructs of rural Ireland to generate himself an income" (35), and objects to the "orgy of random violence" in *The Lieutenant of Inishmore*, perpetrated by characters who are "*all* psychopathic morons" incapable of "meaningful political discussion" (36 emphasis in original). However, I will argue that it is precisely through the erasure of boundaries between the trivial and the profound, the fragmentation of identity, and the radical destabilization of traditional norms and values, including those relating to gender and sexuality, that McDonagh's postmodern plays engage satirically with the foundations of Irish nationalism. Jean-François Lyotard has argued that in contemporary society and culture, "[t]he grand narrative has lost its credibility" (37). Postmodern satire rejects and discredits metanarratives, and focuses instead on the radical contingencies of what Lyotard calls *petites histoires* or "*petits récits*" (60): small-scale fictions that are always situational and preliminary. In doing so, postmodern satire exposes the inadequacies of all categories, and indeed of language itself, not (just) as an act of nihilism, but as a way of critiquing the ideology of bourgeois society and the nation state.

The point Stanley Fish makes about irony—that it is "a risky business because one cannot at all be certain that readers will be directed to the ironic meanings one intends" (181)—holds particularly true for McDonagh's satire: some audience members see his depictions of Ireland as negative representations of the "real thing," others interpret them as grotesque parodies of stale clichés about the nation and its inhabitants, while still others regard them romantically as the quintessence of Irishness. One female audience member reportedly called *The Beauty Queen of Leenane* "disgusting. I've never seen anything so racist" (quoted in Tymoczko 16), while Richard Harris saw nothing more in the play than "Irish cliché after Irish cliché" (quoted in Dening, "The Wordsmith of Camberwell" N. pag.). A *Village Voice* reviewer called McDonagh's islanders "updated stage Oirishmen" (quoted in Mulkerns N. pag.), whereas the *World of Hibernia* found in McDonagh's work something "quintessentially Irish—a dark humor that is both sad and uplifting; a story embodied by a furtive, yet honest imagination; and the ability to poeticize language in a manner that is the culmination of centuries of telling a good story" (Adam 70). Fish argues that no text is inherently ironic: both irony and literalness are interpretive ways of reading that occur in "a history in the course of which realities and anchors have been established, although it is always possible, and indeed inevitable, that they will have to be established again." Such a state of affairs may be distressing to some, "because it seems to doom us to an infinite regress of unstable interpretations; but one can just as easily say that it graces us with an endless succession of interpretive certainties, a reassuring sequence in which one set of obvious and indisputable facts gives way to another" (196).

Many cultural critics have noted that postmodernism is often equated with the depoliticization of art and the absence of a historical perspective. Originating in and responding to the age of mechanical reproduction, postmodern satire has as its primary characteristic a skepticism toward metanarratives of any kind. Moral and political foundations are radically destabilized in postmodern texts, which blur the line between mimetic representation and the medium's inability to point to anything beyond itself. Characters in such texts are shallow and egotistical, cognitively dysfunctional, and unable to tell truth from lies. Because such satire always implicates itself in the destabilizing process, its irony is often, in Kevin Dettmar's words, "completely unmarked [...] (which, of course, then begs the question of whether it is in fact ironic)" (86). For these reasons, it has been argued that "a cultural stance that operates through the destabilizing of the concepts of positionality, identity, and referentiality creates perhaps insurmountable problems when we try to determine the focus, direction, and purpose of its satirical operation" (Alberti xx). This principle of destabilization explains the widely divergent reactions to McDonagh's work. Rather than being "apolitical," such postmodern dramatic satire,[1] questions the very bases on which political decisions are made by heightening "our awareness of the radically contingent nature of every choice we make" (Dettmar 104).

The Pillowman, the third play McDonagh wrote, "but the first he regarded as good" (O'Toole, "Nowhere Man" N. pag.), was written before the "Irish" plays yet subsequently revised and is his most recent play to premiere in production, in 2003. It deals specifically with the question of signification and interpretation. How is meaning created and by whom? How does "surface" relate to "symbol"? In addressing such fundamentals, the work provides a context in which the "Irishness" of McDonagh's

"Irish" plays can be understood. Katurian's dilemma in *The Pillowman* is also that of McDonagh, and of his audience: can a writer "just tell stories" (*petites histoires*) for mere "private" entertainment, or do those stories always end up acquiring unintended (political) meaning, simply by virtue of being out of the author's hands and in the public sphere? To what extent is an author responsible for what others "do" with his stories once they are "out there"? In 1997, McDonagh told Fintan O'Toole: "I'm not into any kind of definition, any kind of -ism, politically, socially, religiously, all that stuff," while also admitting that "anything you believe socially or politically will come through even though I try to avoid it as much as I can. My instinct is to always hide my social or political beliefs but it's natural for something to come out" ("Nowhere Man" N. pag.). In *The Pillowman*, Katurian makes a similar claim. Echoing McDonagh's own public statements, the character maintains that he is entirely apolitical and that he aims at avoiding "meaning" anything beyond the surface of the narrative: "No axe to grind, no anything to grind. No social anything whatsoever. [. . .] [U]nless something political came in by accident, or something that *seemed* political came in, in which case show me where it is. Show me where the bastard is. I'll take it straight out. Fucking burn it. You know"? (*TP* 7–8).

McDonagh (and Katurian) refuse to be held responsible for the consequences of their stories' release into the public sphere. McDonagh has made this artistic disavowal explicitly: "I don't think that Martin Scorsese can be held responsible because John Hinckley saw *Taxi Driver* many times and became obsessed with Jodie Foster" (quoted in Pacheco E29). Such abrogation of responsibility is a way of acknowledging that meaning is not inherent in a text but is rather constructed by readers on the basis of what they bring to it by way of context, similar to the way a detective solves a problem by interpreting clues, as in *The Pillowman*:

Tupolski:　The father. [. . .] He represents something, does he?

Katurian:　He represents a bad father. He *is* a bad father. How do you mean, "represents"? [. . .] All the story says, I think, is the father treats the little girl badly. You can draw your own conclusions. [. . .]

Tupolski:　And the first conclusion we are drawing is exactly how many stories have you got "a little girl is treated badly," or "a little boy is treated badly"? [. . .]

Katurian:　But that isn't saying anything, I'm not trying to say anything . . . [. . .] What, are you trying to say that I'm trying to say that the children represent something? [. . .] That the children represent The People, or something?

Ariet:　(*approaching*) "I am trying to say." He's putting words into my fucking mouth now, "I am trying to say," let alone draw our own fucking conclusions. . . . (*TP* 10–12)

Katurian here suggests that his stories, his *petites histoires*, mean only one thing. But that position assumes there is a stable, straightforward relationship between signifier and signified, created by the author, that can be transmitted intact to a listener.

When Katurian is placed into the position of listening to Tupolski's story, however, their roles are reversed, and it is Katurian who searches for clues and desires to know the author's intentions:

Katurian: (*pause*) So the old man *meant* for the deaf boy to catch the plane?
Tupolski: Yeah.
Katurian: Oh.
Tupolski: What, didn't you get that?
Katurian: No, I just thought the boy happened to catch it, like it was an accident.
Tupolski: No. No, the old man wanted to save the boy. That's why he threw the plane. [...]
Katurian: I think it could've been more clear. (90–91)

Katurian's initial conviction that "'The *only* duty of a storyteller is to tell a story'" (7) holds true only when he speaks from the writer's position; when he speaks from the point of view of the audience, his attitude is closer to that of Tupolski, who explains: "All this story is to me, this story is a pointer. [...] It is saying to me, on the surface I am saying this, but underneath the surface I am saying this other thing" (18–19). Within the context of the satire, neither position can be taken at face value: Tupolski is a detective searching for clues to arrive at "the truth" about a murder case, but he is also, as he tells Katurian, "a high-ranking police officer in a totalitarian fucking dictatorship. What are you doing taking my word about anything?" (23). And Katurian's attempts to understand his brother's motivations by relying on what Michal tells him are contradicted by his own guiding motto: "First rule of storytelling. 'Don't believe everything you read in the papers'" (40). The only mystery to which McDonagh's plays provide clues is that of signification itself.

Indeterminacy is a fundamental characteristic of postmodernism that "include[s] all manner of ambiguities, ruptures, and displacements, affecting knowledge and society" (Hassan 168). *The Pillowman* is set in an unspecified totalitarian dictatorship, whose location could be anywhere between the Czech Republic, Poland, Serbia, and Armenia. National "identity" is problematized: McDonagh provides a number of signifiers which, to an audience well versed in current events and recent history, present themselves as potential clues to a political mystery. However, given that the play premiered more than a decade after the fall of the Berlin wall, the free-floating signifiers do not "add up" to form a reality; they cannot be definitively attached to a signified. The material presents itself as a parody

or a reproduction of no original: the play is "something-esque" (*TP* 18),
but the "something" is indeterminate (Kafka's influence is present, as is
Pinter's and that of the Brothers Grimm, but the references remain elliptical).
The text fits Baudrillard's definition of a simulacrum: "The real [...] is
no longer anything but operational. In fact, it is no longer really the real,
because no imaginary envelops it anymore. It is a hyperreal, produced
from a radiating synthesis of combinatory models in a hyperspace without
atmosphere" (2).

Like national identity, the individual identities of the play's characters
dissolve in a language game of associations and connections whose measure
is "the intertextuality of all life" (Hassan 172). Katurian Katurian Katurian's
initials are KKK, but what do they signify? That Katurian's parents were
"funny people" (*TP* 8), as he explains to Tupolski? Do the initials evoke
the Ku Klux Klan and therefore suggest Katurian's sinister intentions? Or
do they merely signify mindless repetition, and therefore evoke postmodern
concepts like simulacrum and endless reproduction? Is it significant that
Tupolski's partner Ariel shares a name with controversial former Israeli
prime minister Ariel Sharon, or with the imprisoned spirit of Shakespeare's
play *The Tempest*, or with a particular rebel angel of Milton's *Paradise
Lost*? The politics, McDonagh might say, are accidental; the puzzle, Katurian
would say, has no solution, although "the idea is you should wonder what
the solution is, but the truth is there is no solution [...]" (17). What
counts is not the answer to these questions, but the act of speculation
itself: how interpretations are arrived at, why we ask these questions, and
what we hope to achieve by them.

In addition to parodically referencing "high" literature (Kafka, Synge,
Beckett, Pinter, and others), McDonagh's plays are also "something-esque"
in that they draw on television soap operas, westerns, detective dramas,
and fairy tales. The frame of reference of such popular genres is generic
rather than mimetic, in that elements within popular texts are measured
against the codes, formulas, and conventions of the genre to which they
belong, which depend on suspense, unexpected plot turns, and heightened
emotions—all of which are pushed to extremes by the postmodern parodist, leading to often extreme juxtapositions of violence and cruelty coupled
with sentimentalism and farcical humor. As commercial products, popular
genres are instrumental in disseminating the norms and values (relating to
law and order, love, wealth, etc.) embedded in the metanarratives by which
bourgeois society maintains itself. The postmodern parodic exploitation of
these stereotypes (in which the priest is corrupt and ineffectual, the love
interest cynical, the family dysfunctional, etc.) exposes the formulas as
formulas and the metanarratives as linguistic constructs (see Bertens and
D'haen 80–91).

As part of this project, McDonagh's Irish plays disrupt and question
cultural constructions of "Irishness" by subjecting their most cloying popular
manifestations to violent parody. McDonagh grew up in a London Irish

neighborhood where "his mother listened to the ballads of the Irish singer Delia Murphy" (O' Toole, "A Mind in Connemara" 41), who represented, for that generation, "the importance of re-establishing cultural identity after the devastating period of Civil War in Ireland and the many years of English colonisation. The songs that Delia sang were decidedly Irish, many nationalistic and characterised by a strong sing-a-long ballad style" (quoted in Kiernan).[2] Irish folk singer Liam Clancy concurs:

> I grew up in the height of what could be called The National Inferior-
> ity Complex in Ireland. Irish people were very sensitive to the "pig-in-
> the-parlour," "dirty Irish" image, and they even became ashamed of
> their own music and songs. [. . .] Delia Murphy [. . .] gave all of us
> a feeling of confidence and a feeling of value that there was something
> to our own traditions, [. . .] there was no need to be ashamed [. . .],
> because she wasn't. (quoted in Kiernan)

In Delia Murphy's signature song "The Spinning Wheel," a blind old woman, "crooning, and moaning, and drowsily knitting," dozes off to the monotonous sound of the turning reel, while her granddaughter steals away with her lover to "rove in the grove, while the moon's shining brightly" (Waller N. pag.). In *The Beauty Queen of Leenane*, Pato refers to Delia Murphy's "creepy oul voice" and calls "The Spinning Wheel" a "creepy oul song": "They don't write songs like that anymore. Thank Christ," he comments (*BQLOP* 33). In the play, the plot of the song is gruesomely distorted as Mag, a much more cunning old woman than the drowsy grandmother, is murdered by her daughter Maureen after Mag has taunted her with her unconsummated one-night affair with a neighbor.

The kind of iconoclasm that distorts "The Spinning Wheel" also informs *A Skull in Connemara*, where two drunken men wielding mallets smash the disinterred bones of the dead to the tune of Dana's "All Kinds of Everything." In her day, the 1970 Eurovision Song Contest winner and her syrupy song, now re-classified as "[m]usic to hammer dead fellas to" (*BQLOP* 143), represented the epitome of Irish female wholesomeness. The obsession of the characters in all of McDonagh's plays with cultural ephemera and with tourism, exemplified by the "*touristy-looking*" tea towel in Mag's kitchen in *Beauty Queen* with the phony Irish blessing embroidered on it (*BQLOP* 3), functions as both a symptom and a cri-tique of how nationalism manifests and perpetuates itself in commodified form through popular culture.

As I have argued elsewhere, in McDonagh's plays, "social and moral conventions become mere games to play: they have certain superficial formal rules that can be followed and abandoned at will" (Lanters 218). If the nation is, as Benedict Anderson argues, "an imagined community" distinguished from others only by the style in which it is imagined (6), then identity, too, including national identity, is a set of conventions, and hence a commodity that can be traded and exploited. In a society "in which discrepant worlds are generally available on a market basis, [. . .] [t]here will be an increasingly general consciousness of the relativity of *all* worlds, including one's own. [. . .] It follows that one's own institutionalized conduct may be apprehended as a 'role' from which one may detach oneself" (Berger and Luckmann 192, emphasis in original). The running gag in *The Cripple of Inishmaan*—that "Ireland mustn't be such a bad place, so, if the Yanks want to come here to do their filming" (*TC* 13), and "if French fellas want to live in Ireland" (13), and "if coloured fellas want to come to Ireland" (25), and "if German fellas want to come to Ireland" (37), and "if sharks want to come to Ireland" (55), and "if cripple fellas turn down Hollywood to come to Ireland" (63)—suggests that the country's value is not inherent (the country is great and therefore it attracts tourists), but must be gauged in terms of its potential to attract visitors (tourists come here and therefore the country is great).

Because "Ireland" is a commodity, Irish history and culture consist of a set of signifiers—empty phrases and conventions—that can be combined at will, as in a game. Not anchored in any actuality, the phrases and conventions themselves come to stand for "Irishness." When Helen and Bartley in *The Cripple of Inishmaan* play "England versus Ireland," Helen, as "England," breaks three eggs on Bartley's head, giving him "a lesson about Irish history." When Bartley complains, Helen admonishes him by saying that there will be "worse casualties than eggy hair before Ireland's a nation once again, Bartley McCormick" (51). Irish history and identity are a game and there is no identity beyond the expression and performance of identity; historical and cultural constructs cannot be detached from the linguistic contour that frames them.

Billy's Hollywood screen test in *The Cripple of Inishmaan* captures the linguistic parameters that spell "Irishness," when he describes himself, within his role, as "An Irishman! (*Pause.*) *Just* an Irishman. With a decent heart on him, and a decent head on him, and a decent spirit not broken by a century's hunger and a lifetime's oppression!" (52–53, emphasis in original). Upon his return to Inishmaan, Billy makes fun of these "arse-faced lines," which he calls a "rake of shite," remembering that they "had me singing the fecking 'Croppy Boy' then" (63). The enactment of Irishness here, as well as in the film *Man of Aran*, which Helen calls "[a] pile of fecking shite" (61), is ridiculed as phony by characters in a play that itself has been castigated by some critics as being the epitome of phony Irishness. The screen and the film, as copies of copies of no original "Irishness," question the notions of authenticity and identity—key terms in the discourse of Irish nationalism.

The Lieutenant of Inishmore is McDonagh's most "political" play, although the politics, he claims, emerged at a later stage, since his original intention had been to write about gangsters rather than terrorists. Once the plot was set, however, McDonagh claims, "I was trying to write a play that would get me killed" (quoted in O'Toole, "A Mind in Connemara" 45). One has to be wary of taking a satirist's word for anything, even outside the boundaries of his work; after all, the satirist's business is to erase boundaries and categories, to blur the distinction between reality and fiction, and to undermine all forms of authoritativeness, including his own. Satirists therefore frequently deny their political intentions and suggest they are "just" writing stories. On the other hand, they may make grandiose claims, as when McDonagh argues that he has written a "brave" play with which he put his life on the line, while terming those who initially declined to stage it "cowards." Not that he believed he would actually die: "At the time I was writing it, telling my friends about it, I was aiming to be the Irish Salman Rushdie. And he's still alive" (quoted in Dening, "The scribe of Kilburn" N. pag.). In other words, rather than executing an authentic political act, McDonagh was performing a script that had already been written, enacted, and safely completed by Salman Rushdie. In *The Pillowman*, Katurian is described by Tupolski as "lily-livered and subservient on the one hand, yet vaguely sarcastic and provocative on the other" (*TP* 14), a description that can also be applied to McDonagh himself. McDonagh has been accused of trivializing a serious issue, endangering the peace process, and presenting material too close to the bone for victims of real atrocities, while others have castigated the castigators for failing to see his satirical intent. If there is a message at all, it is that the truth is not out there.[3]

In 1988, Theo D'haen contended that the self-conscious use of Irish history in Desmond Hogan's postmodernist novel *A Curious Street* posited Irish history "not as a 'true' legitimation for refound unity and wholeness, but as a verbal construct projected upon the Irish past." With this novel, D'haen went on to argue, "Hogan destroys the idea, typical for a previous generation of Modernist Irish writers, that literature is in itself a useful means for the creation of national unity" (84). While that may be the case in fiction, on the Irish stage, that connection between art and national identity has been much more resistant to being dislodged. Christopher Murray's book *Twentieth-Century Irish Drama: Mirror Up to Nation* (1997), which was completed around the time when McDonagh burst upon the theatrical scene, starts from the assumption that "in the Irish historical experience drama [. . .] and theatre [. . .] were both instrumental in defining and sustaining national consciousness" (3), and concludes that "[t]he more problematic and fragmented identity becomes the greater the need for imagery of wholeness. [. . .] The dream is always waiting to be fulfilled; the nation is always awaiting completion" (246–7). Ondřej Pilný, however, argues that "McDonagh's plays progressively satirise the pervasive concern of Irish theatre discourse with the issue of Irish identity, simply by offering an absurd, degenerated picture as a version of 'what the Irish are like'" (228). I would contend that McDonagh's satire is more sophisticated than that in its deconstruction of the very notion of "identity" itself.

Martin McDonagh's drama undermines and destabilizes the very foundational elements of Irish nationalism, beginning with the nuclear family (the private sphere) and extending to the public institutions of the state and the church. Kathryn Conrad has noted that the position of the nuclear family (and hence of women) in Ireland, as enshrined in the 1937 constitution, is intimately bound up with the ideology of Irish nationalism: "If the [family] cell is stable, so too are the social institutions built upon it, and one can present to the world one's capacity to rule. Instabilities must therefore be constructed and treated as foreign—not only to the family, not only to one's political position, but also to the nation as a whole" (10). Gender and sexuality cannot be contained within familial or national borders: "Any identity category [other than Irish] potentially troubles the national border by threatening the primacy of national identity," but especially homosexuality because it questions "the coherence of all identity categories" and "does not fit neatly within the discourse of bourgeois nationalism, since it threatens the reproduction of the heterosexual family cell that serves as the foundation of the nation-state" (21). Consequently, the discourse of Irish nationalism has excluded homosexuality or branded it as foreign and corrupting.

In McDonagh's Irish plays, nationalism is satirized precisely through the fragmentation of the nuclear family and the destabilization of the "fixed" categories of gender and sexual identity. For example, a mother and daughter torment each other until murder ensues; two brothers are locked in an interminable fight, having murdered their father; a husband cannot remember if he murdered his wife; crippled children are abandoned and ridiculed; and fathers, lovers, and neighbors are threatened and murdered for the sake of a cat. In all these works, agents of the state and the Church are alienated from or corrupted by the system they represent: the priest is drunk and suicidal; the policeman is ineffectual and frustrated. The family unit has imploded and the authorities are powerless because the boundaries between the public and the private spheres are eroded as traditional family loyalties are replaced by self-interested greed and cruelty, and authority figures reveal themselves as isolated and pathetic individuals. In these plays, the dismantling of the family unit and the representatives of the nation state moves beyond the general postmodern cynicism toward all meta-narratives in its active critique of Irish nationalist politics.

In his 1997 interview with Fintan O'Toole, McDonagh stated: "I was never any sort of nationalist. It always struck me as kind of dumb, any kind of pride in the place you happen to be born in" (quoted in O'Toole, "Nowhere Man" N. pag.). Nationalism, however, was all around him when he grew up: "Like most southern Irish people, the community I grew up in were republican-leaning Catholics" (quoted in Dening, "The scribe of Kilburn" N. pag.). After the controversy over the staging of *The Lieutenant of Inishmore*, McDonagh told another interviewer: "I chose the INLA because I come from a republican Catholic background and I think

it's worthwhile to attack your own side first" (quoted in Rosenthal N. pag.).
The plot of *The Lieutenant of Inishmore* revolves around a terrorist named
Padraic and his cat, Wee Thomas. Padraic has just decided to form a
splinter group of the INLA, itself a splinter group of the IRA—a detail that
functions as an indicator of the play's use of fragmentation as a satirical
device. Since "[a]ny identity category potentially troubles the national border
by threatening the primacy of national identity" (Conrad 21), McDonagh's
play satirizes Irish nationalist identity politics by foregrounding and prob-
lematizing the gender and sexual identity of its characters, and by interrogat-
ing the republican exclusionary attitude toward women and homosexuals.
The statements that highlight these issues in the play are Padraic's assertion that "[t]here's no boy-preferers involved in Irish terrorism" (*TL* 33),
and "[w]e don't be letting girls in the INLA. No. Unless pretty girls" (35).

One way in which McDonagh destabilizes general assumptions about
the connection between political violence and masculinity in many of his
plays is by simultaneously pointing up the (homo)erotic potential of all-
male violence, thereby also troubling the distinction between love and hate
and undercutting the machismo of tribal warfare. The entire plot of *The
Lonesome West* revolves around a feud between two brothers (a broad but
convenient metaphor for civil war or tribal conflict), who agree about
nothing except that fighting "does show you care" (*BQLOP* 256).[4] In
addition to tormenting each other, both brothers enjoy reading women's
magazines, a sure sign, according to Coleman, of being "a fecking gayboy"
(228). In *The Cripple of Inishmaan*, local gossip Johnnypateenmike reports
that a feud has broken out between childhood friends Pat Brennan and
Jack Ellery over a hostile encounter between their pets, a cat and a goose.
When the animals are found killed, Johnny fears that the feud between
their owners will escalate, because "we can all put two and two together"
(*TC* 41), only to discover that the two men were seen by a child "kissing
the faces off each other in a haybarn" (72). Apparently clues do not add
up so easily after all. The pets, it turns out, were killed by Helen, a girl
with a penchant for violence.

McDonagh's female characters such as Helen—foul-mouthed, tough girls
and hard-drinking, selfish old women—"rely on the inversion of [...]
better-known character types: the comely young rural maiden [...], and
the kindly, wise and benign matriarch" (Dean 64). In addition, these characters often flirt with "scandalous" forms of behavior like prostitution. In
The Lonesome West, Girleen—whose real name is Mary, like "the mammy
of Our Lord" (*BQLOP* 215)—says she is "tinkering with the idea" of
"charging for entry," causing Father Welsh to cry out in exasperation,
"Isn't it enough for a girl going round flogging poteen, not to go talking of
whoring herself on top of it"?! (180). In *The Cripple of Inishmaan*, Helen
trades kisses for favors with Babbybobby, four film directors (who turn
out to be stable-boys), and an actor, and possibly exchanges more than
kisses with the egg-man. The prostitute's trading of her sexuality in the

public sphere transgresses the boundaries set for women by the nationalist construction of Irishness, which seeks to contain and hide female sexuality within the private realm of marriage and family.

Patrick Lonergan reads McDonagh's treatment of gender and sexuality in *The Lieutenant of Inishmore* as a comment on the Irish theatrical trope that "sexual dysfunction and confusion about sexual identity are symbolic of the inherent futility of republican violence." Instead, he argues, through Padraic and Mairead's love affair, "terrorist violence is shown not to impede sexual expression but to facilitate it," as the audience is made to realize "that they will assume that terrorists are sexual failures, while sympathizing with a heroine's attempts to gain the love of a man who does not seem to notice her" (75). My own reading of McDonagh's use of sexuality and gender is based on Judith Butler's contention that identities are "*fabrications* manufactured and sustained through corporeal signs and other discursive means" (136 emphasis in original); McDonagh's game with signifiers emanates from an awareness that the characteristics categorizing gender difference are "instituted and inscribed on the surface of bodies" (136). The treatment of gender in *The Lieutenant of Inishmore* is less a reversal of cultural norms than it is an interrogation of the very operations of cultural normativity and its consequences.

In this view, every form of identity (personal, national, gender) is a performance; indeed, to paraphrase Butler, there is no identity behind the expressions of identity: "identity is performatively constituted by the very 'expressions' that are said to be its results" (25). Of all the plays, *The Cripple of Inishmaan* goes furthest in taking the notion of performativity to its logical conclusion by depicting every act as a re-enactment of no original. The "Aran Islanders" of McDonagh's play perform the parts of "Aran Islanders" in Robert Flaherty's film, a copy of which they subsequently watch in the course of the play. The "real" film they watch (*Man of Aran*) was billed as a documentary of "real" life on Aran featuring "real" Aran Islanders, but contains scenes that had no counterpart in the lives of the islanders on the Inishmore of 1934. The "Aran Islanders" of McDonagh's play reject the "Aran Islanders" of Flaherty's film as bogus, even as their own status as characters in *The Cripple* is no more "real" than that of the actors in *Man of Aran*. In Hollywood, a real cripple cannot play a cripple as well as a non-crippled actor, says Cripple Billy, the "real" cripple, who was played in the play's original production by the perfectly able-bodied Ruaidhri Conroy. The "stage-Irish" scene later scoffed at by Billy and Bartley is no more or less "stage Irish" than the Ireland that passes for reality in McDonagh's play. Billy pretends to have tuberculosis (TB) so he can pretend to have TB in a film, only to find that he has TB in the (pretend) world of McDonagh's play. It comes as no surprise to hear Helen claim that the shark in *Man of Aran* was not real, but a pretend shark, a part performed not by an actor in a shark suit, but by "a tall fella in a grey donkey jacket" (*TC* 61). Mammy's conclusion, "All that fuss o'er a fella in a grey donkey jacket. I don't know" (61), recalls Davey's question at the end of *The Lieutenant of Inishmore*: "So who the feck is this fecking cat? [. . .] So all this terror has been for absolutely nothing"? (68). In McDonagh's plays, animals most effectively expose the imagined and constructed nature of human forms of identity.

A central trope of Irish nationalist rhetoric identifies the nation as woman: Mother Ireland, the Poor Old Woman, and so on. As Conrad points out, "The desire to get the land back has been written as a male desire, and women have been written as the object of that desire by their metaphorization as the land itself. Within this system of desire and representation, women are perpetually locked in a passive position; they are the country that men occupy" (56). In *The Lieutenant of Inishmore*, Padraic's love interest, Mairead, has close-cropped hair, wears army trousers, and is a crack shot with her air rifle. When she uses that rifle to blind the terrorists Brendan and Joey, they argue with each other as to whether the perpetrator was "a boy with lipstick" or "a girl with no boobs" (*TL* 51). Padraic is troubled by Mairead's fluid gender identity and her desire to join his terrorist splinter group and advises her: "Be staying home, now, and marry some nice fella. Let your hair grow out a tadeen and some fella's bound to be looking twice at you some day, and if you learn how to cook and sew too, sure, that'd double your chances. Maybe treble" (36). Within seconds of saying this, however, Padraic himself is kissing Mairead, in spite of the combat trousers and the "shocking" hair (33). Padraic himself, we learn elsewhere, used to wear a "girly scarf" when he was a boy, although he crippled his cousin for laughing at him for it (7). The fluidity and instability of gender and sexuality here signify "the fluidity and incoherence of *identity*," and hence the fact that "all identity categories and allegiances are inherently unstable," and therefore also "the social, economic, and political structures built upon those categories" (Conrad 32, emphasis in original).

As a further illustration of this instability of identity categories, Davey, the boy accused by Padraic of killing his cat, rides his mammy's pink bicycle and is afraid to admit he likes cats "because if I went around saying it they'd call me an outright gayboy, and they do enough of that with me hairstyle" (*TL* 18). "Mad" Padraic has no such qualms about being a cat lover:

Padraic: I will plod on, I know, but no sense to it will there be with Thomas gone. No longer will his smiling eyes be there in the back of me head, egging me on, saying, "This is for me and for Ireland, Padraic. Remember that," as I'd lob a bomb at a pub, or be shooting a builder. Me whole world's gone, and he'll never be coming back to me. (44)

If loving his cat makes Padraic a "gayboy" in the eyes of some, this perception is heightened by the fact that his male cat occupies the position traditionally held by the woman: "for me and for Ireland." The implied ambiguity of Padraic's sexuality may also be encoded in his name, which echoes that of another Irish rebel, Padraig Pearse. According to Susan Harris, in order for Irish nationalists to be able to respect Pearse's sacrifice for the Irish republican cause, they "must either ignore/deny his sexuality or separate it completely from his political life" (144–45). The same is true of Roger Casement. In McDonagh's play, the cat loved by Mairead and characterized by Davey as "a snooty little bitch" (*TL* 20), is called Sir Roger, "a funny name for a cat," according to Donny (25), although Padraic recognizes it as the name of "that oul poof" (65). Conrad argues that, as in the case of Pearse, "[f]or Irish nationalists to accept that Casement was an 'Irish patriot'—and, particularly, to claim him as a martyr—required that his homosexuality be pushed back into the closet or denied" (27). Accepting mixed identity allegiances, such as gay republican or female terrorist, "threatens to expose and destabilize everyone and everything" (33), which is exactly McDonagh's satirical objective.

By placing cats over people in their affections, the most violent characters in the play, Padraic and Mairead, breach the boundaries between humans and animals in a grotesque fashion that exposes the misguided nature of their obsession and the constructedness of signification. The felines in *The Lieutenant of Inishmore* have the personal and political aspirations of their owners projected upon them and thus become carriers of meaning, at the same time that such signifying practices are undermined by the absurdity of the device. This absurd reversal of priorities is illustrated by the fact that Sir Roger's "funny name" invests the hapless animal with republican significance and hence gives Mairead a reason to kill on his behalf, whereas Joey implies that the INLA needed no such political motivation and blew up Airey Neave "just because he ha[d] a funny name" (*TL* 29).

At the same time that "gayboy" cat-lover Padraic is falling in love with butch cat-lover Mairead, Donny and Davey are desperately trying to hide the death of Padraic's black cat, Wee Thomas, by covering Mairead's orange cat, Sir Roger, in black shoe polish. Padraic discovers the ruse and kills Sir Roger as an impostor, whereupon Mairead, once she finds out what has happened to her cat, kills Padraic. Sir Roger masquerading as Wee Thomas ends up as a bundle of conflicting identity markers. He contradicts himself in terms of his species and gender (an anthropomorphized male cat who is also a "bitch"), race (an orange cat pretending to be a black cat), politics (an Orange-Unionist cat pretending to be a republican cat), and sexual orientation (a gay cat pretending to be a straight cat); and if "Wee Thomas" is read as a version of "Tommy," we can also add a British soldier to this Irish mix.[5] Having killed Sir Roger, Padraic digs up Wee Thomas and sits stroking his "headless, dirt-soiled body" (55). At the end of the play, after Padraic's death, the real Thomas returns home alive: neither Padraic nor Donny or Davey had been able to tell the difference between the real pet and the unidentified stray that caused all the play's commotion. Wee Thomas had simply been out having a good time:

Davey: So all this terror has been for absolutely nothing?
Donny: It has!
Davey: All because that fecker was after his hole? Four dead fellas, two
           dead cats . . . me hairstyle ruined! Have I missed anything?
Donny: Your sister broken-hearted. [. . .] All me shoe polish gone. (68)

The erasure of hierarchical difference—dead men are on a par with a
ruined hairstyle and shoe polish—suggests the randomness of all categories. Even the play's ending is random and depends on whether the live cat
used in the production will eat or ignore the Frosties it is offered. The ultimate plot twist reveals identity as arbitrary and exposes identity politics
as an instrument used by interest groups to perpetuate themselves and
their ideologies.

At the end of *The Lieutenant of Inishmore*, the stage is strewn with
body parts and corpses as a visual and physical reminder of the disintegration that is the consequence of the postmodernist's distrust of totality:
"fragments are all he pretends to trust" (Hassan 168). Mary Douglas has
remarked that "the body is a model that can stand for any bounded
system. Its boundaries can represent any boundaries which are threatened
or precarious" (quoted in Butler 132). The bloody carnage, the physical
breaking up and shattering of the bodies of cats and humans, is the theatrical equivalent of the disintegration of the textual infrastructure in narrative Menippean satire. Much like Menippean satire, postmodern satire
such as McDonagh's drama reduces social and philosophical categories
and hierarchies to the common level of the body, at which level they are—
often literally—exploded. As a game with boundaries, this type of satire
undermines any stable category by constantly shifting its position, juxtaposing violent extremes and excluding a "middle ground" of compromise,
creating "a distinctive open-endedness, which resists both comic and tragic
forms of resolution and closure" (Palmeri 4). Things fall apart, literally,
not because the center cannot hold, but because there is no center. As
such, "postmodern satire rarely finds a positive voice of rejuvenation to
provide alternative visions for situations that have been satirically criticized as unfavorable" (Beard 287). To do so, indeed, would be counter-
productive: the questions asked by such satire are ultimate questions about
the very nature of signification itself.

Notes

1 Narrative Menippean satire relies on parody, sharp contrasts and incongruous
  juxtapositions, hierarchical leveling, scandal scenes, and inversion to create an
  inconclusive stand-off between opposing perspectives that leaves meaning unre-
  solved and readers suspended between conflicting interpretations.
2 Kiernan is Murphy's granddaughter.
3 The motto of the popular television program *The X-Files* was "the truth is
  out there."

4 Father Welsh's attempt to reconcile Coleman and Valene takes the form of a common strategy for ethnic conflict resolution: "It is not surprising that interventions to halt ethnic conflict, and subsequent attempts at long-term peacemaking, often posit a revisiting of the history of each side and an acceptance of responsibility for the past actions of one's own community" (Roe *et al.* 122).

5 "Wee" in McDonagh always has overtones of "urine"—as in the boys caught "weeing in the churchyard" by Mary in *A Skull in Connemara* (*BQLOP* 90), or the drunk who "[d]rowned on wee" in Mairtin's story in that same play (141). In that sense, Wee Thomas also serves as the "piss-taker" of *The Lieutenant of Inishmore*.

References

Adam, Michelle. "A Stage for the Irish." *World of Hibernia* 6.1 (2000): 70.

Alberti, John. "Introduction." *Leaving Springfield* xi–xxxii.

Anderson, Benedict. *Imagined Communities: Reflections on the Origin and Spread of Nationalism*. Rev. ed. London and New York: Verso, 1991.

Baudrillard, Jean. *Simulacra and Simulation*. Trans. Sheila Faria Glaser. Ann Arbor: U of Michigan P, 1994.

Beard, Duncan Stuart. "Local Satire with a Global Reach: Ethnic Stereotyping and Cross-Cultural Conflict in *The Simpsons*." *Leaving Springfield* 273–91.

Berger, Peter L., and Thomas Luckmann. *The Social Construction of Reality*. Harmondsworth, UK: Penguin, 1971.

Bertens, Hans, and Theo D'haen. *Het postmodernisme in de literatuur*. Amsterdam: Synthese, 1988.

Butler, Judith. *Gender Trouble: Feminism and the Subversion of Identity*. New York: Routledge, 1990.

Conrad, Kathryn. *Locked in the Family Cell: Gender, Sexuality and Political Agency in Irish National Discourse*. Madison: U of Wisconsin P, 2004.

Dean, Joan FitzPatrick. "Tales Told by Martin McDonagh." *Nua: Studies in Contemporary Irish Writing* 3.1–2 (2002): 57–68.

Dening, Penelope. "The scribe of Kilburn." *Irish Times* 18 Apr. 2001. N. pag. 25 Jan. 2006 <http://www.ireland.com/newspaper/features/2001/0418/archive.01041800079.html>.

———. "The Wordsmith of Camberwell." *Irish Times* 8 July 1997. N. pag. 8 July 1997 <http://www.irish-times.com/irish-times/paper/1997/0708/fea7.htm>.

Dettmar, Kevin. "Countercultural Literacy: Learning Irony with *The Simpsons*." *Leaving Springfield* 85–106.

D'haen, Theo. "Desmond Hogan and Ireland's Postmodern Past." *History and Violence in Anglo-Irish Literature*. Ed. Joris Duytschaever and Geert Lernout. Amsterdam: Rodopi, 1988. 79–84.

Fish, Stanley. "Short People Got No Reason to Live: Reading Irony." *Doing What Comes Naturally: Change, Rhetoric, and the Practice of Theory in Literary and Legal Studies*. Durham and London: Duke UP, 1989. 180–96.

Harris, Susan Cannon. *Gender and Modern Irish Drama*. Bloomington and Indianapolis: Indiana UP, 2002.

Hassan, Ihab. *The Postmodern Turn: Essays in Postmodern Theory and Culture*. Columbus: Ohio State UP, 1987.

Kiernan, Carol. "Ireland's Ballad Queen: Delia Murphy, Her Life and Music, a Woman for the Times." 1 Feb. 2006 N. pag. <http://www.irishheritage.net/durack.htm>.

Lanters, José. "Playwrights of the Western World: Synge, Murphy, McDonagh." *A Century of Irish Drama: Widening the Stage*. Ed. Stephen Watt, Eileen Morgan, and Shakir Mustafa. Bloomington and Indianapolis: Indiana UP, 2000. 204–22.

Leaving Springfield: The Simpsons and the Possibility of Oppositional Culture. Ed. John Alberti. Detroit: Wayne State UP, 2004.

Lonergan, Patrick. "Too Dangerous to Be Done? Martin McDonagh's *Lieutenant of Inishmore*." *Irish Studies Review* 13.1 (2005): 65–78.

Luckhurst, Mary. "Martin McDonagh's *Lieutenant of Inishmore*: Selling (-Out) to the English." *Contemporary Theatre Review* 14.4 (2004): 34–41.

Lustig, Vera. "Ireland's Cottage Industry." *New Statesman* 25 July 1997: 42.

Lyotard, Jean-François. *The Postmodern Condition: A Report on Knowledge*. Trans. Geoff Bennington and Brian Massumi. Minneapolis: U of Minnesota P, 1989.

McDonagh, Martin. *The Beauty Queen of Leenane and Other Plays (A Skull in Connemara and The Lonesome West)*. New York: Vintage, 1998.

——. *The Cripple of Inishmaan*. London: Methuen, 1997.

——. *The Lieutenant of Inishmore*. London: Methuen, 2001.

——. *The Pillowman*. London: Faber, 2003.

Mulkerns, Helena. "McDonagh Play Gets Mixed Reaction." *Irish Times* 9 Apr. 1998. N. pag. 9 Apr. 1998 <http://www.irish-times.com/irish-times/paper/1998/0409/hom19.html>.

Murray, Christopher. *Twentieth-Century Irish Drama: Mirror up to Nation*. Manchester and New York: Manchester UP, 1997.

O'Toole, Fintan. "A Mind in Connemara." *New Yorker* 6 Mar. 2006: 40–47.

——. "Nowhere Man." *Irish Times* 26 Apr. 1997. N. pag. 26 Apr. 1997 <http://www.irish-times.com/irish-times/paper/1997/0426/fea1.htm>.

Pacheco, Patrick. "Laughing Matters." *Los Angeles Times* 22 May 2005: E29.

Palmeri, Frank. *Satire in Narrative: Petronius, Swift, Gibbon, Melville, and Pynchon*. Austin: U of Texas P, 1990.

Pilny, Ondrej. "Martin McDonagh: Parody? Satire? Complacency"? *Irish Studies Review* 12.1 (2004): 225–32.

Roe, Mícheál D., William Pegg, Kim Hodges, and Rebecca A. Trimm. "Forgiving the Other Side: Social Identity and Ethnic Memories in Northern Ireland." *Politics and Performance in Contemporary Northern Ireland*. Ed. John P. Harrington and Elizabeth J. Mitchell. Amherst: U of Massachusetts P, 1999. 122–56.

Rosenthal, Daniel. "How to Slay 'em in the Isles." *Independent* 11 Apr. 2001. N. pag. 25 Jan. 2006 <http://enjoyment.independent.co.uk/theatre/features/article238733.ece>.

Taylor, Paul. Rev. of *The Pillowman*. Cottesloe Theatre, NT, London." *Independent* 17 Nov. 2003. N. pag. 25 Jan. 2006 <http://enjoyment.independent.co.uk/theatre/reviews/article78798.ece>.

Tymoczko, Maria. "A Theatre of Complicity." *Irish Literary Supplement* 16.2 (1997): 16.

Waller, John Francis. "The Spinning Wheel." *Anthology of Irish Verse*. Ed. Padraic Colum. New York: Boni and Liveright, 1922. N. pag. Bartleby.com, 2001. 12 Aug. 2006 <http://www.bartleby.com/250/>.

2 Martin McDonagh's stagecraft

Joan FitzPatrick Dean

If Martin McDonagh had taken this idea to a writing workshop, he'd have been told "We don't write plays like that anymore."

(Hynes 204)

In the final moments of Martin McDonagh's play, *The Lieutenant of Inishmore*, a cat named Wee Thomas saunters on stage. The audience gasps at this moment as it races to re-adjust its expectations and anticipate how the cat's presence may re-shape a play very near its end. All of the play's action emanates from a single premise: the death of this animal. The cat's entrance is a startling moment, but also a strangely familiar one in Irish drama. Bringing presumably dead characters to life on stage has proved such a durable theatrical ploy for Irish playwrights that it has reached the level of dramatic trope. Even in 1913 Cornelius Weygandt referred to it as "a very old motive [motif], and familiar in the meliorized form that made it known to the theatre in 'Conn the Shaughraun' (1875) [*sic*]. Before that, Crofton Croker had given it currency in 'The Corpse Watches,' among those outside of the circles in which it was a familiar folk-story" (Weygandt 168). Indeed, when Dion Boucicault's *The Shaughraun* toured Australia, audiences were invited to "Come and see a real Irish wake." Oscar Wilde brought Jack Worthing's supposedly dead wicked brother Ernest on stage in Act Two of *The Importance of Being Earnest* (1895). Synge had the death-feigning Dan Burke sit up in his deathbed to confront the stranger his young wife invited into their home in *In the Shadow of the Glen* (1903). Four years later, the storied, bloodied but still very much alive father of Christy Mahon arrived at the O'Flaherty shebeen to undo the reputation of his son in *The Playboy of the Western World* (1907). The title of Thomas Kilroy's *The Death and Resurrection of Mr. Roche* (1968) foretells a more recent iteration of this "very old motive."

The Lieutenant of Inishmore is not McDonagh's only play to feature this trope. In *A Skull in Connemara*, Mick O'Dowd writes out his confession of killing Mairtin Hanlon. As the audience grapples with the disquieting revelation that one of only four characters has murdered another of those four characters in what is a very funny play, "*MAIRTIN enters behind [MARY], somewhat concussed, a big bloody crack down the centre of his forehead, dripping onto his shirt*" (*BQLOP* 157). At the very moment that Mick's signed confession goes up in smoke, the audience revises its understanding of the action, delights in Mairtin's gruesome appearance, and resumes its laughter.

Perhaps the most bizarre appearance from the dead in McDonagh's corpus occurs in *The Pillowman* when the supposedly murdered mute child appears on stage. Not only is the little girl covered with fluorescent green paint, which does not inspire relief or warmth, but also, her presence forces the characters and audience to re-examine the conclusions they have reached about the central character Katurian's involvement in the alleged child murders.

None of these entrances is as stunning as the entrance of the supposedly dead Cripple Billy Claven in *The Cripple of Inishmaan*. In scene three, the audience, like Babbybobby, believes that the letter from Dr. McSharry giving Billy only three months to live was accurate and authentic. Like Babbybobby, the audience enjoys learning Billy's sad secret, which privileges the audience by placing it at an advantage over other characters. A cliché-ridden deathbed monologue in which Billy laments "dying in a one-dollar rooming-house, without a mother to wipe the cold sweat off me, nor a father to curse God o'er the death of me, nor a colleen fair to weep tears o'er the still body of me" (*TC* 52) clinches belief in his demise. Once the islanders' viewing of *Man of Aran* is complete, however, the stage directions tell us that "*KATE pulls back the sheet, revealing BILLY, alive and well*" (61). Moreover, Billy's apparent resurrection is only the first of many reversals that mark the end of *The Cripple*.

McDonagh's Wee Thomas in *The Lieutenant of Inishmore* has the distinction being a cat in this company of dead men walking. With the exception of Jean-Claude van Itallie's 1993 adaptation of Mikhail Bulgahov's *The Master and Margarita*, there just are not many cats in theater history. Any theatrical director will tell you that animals on stage are problematic: they are unpredictable creatures with scripts of their own. Wee Thomas is a real, living, unleashed cat. But it is also a trained animal, rehearsed and scripted to perform a part. The same might be said of McDonagh's characters: they are rooted in the familiar, but enact highly performative roles.

All of these moments are thrilling, theatrical *tours de force* that delight the audience. McDonagh's plays are driven by venerable dramatic strategies, perhaps even more familiar in internationally syndicated television programming than in Irish drama. McDonagh has repeatedly asserted that while he saw very few stage plays before writing his own, his television viewing was extensive. In 1997, for example, after winning the *Evening Standard* award and having four plays running in London simultaneously, he told an interviewer for *The New York Times*, "My life is staying at home and watching TV. It really is. I sleep a lot" (quoted in Lyman 18).

Like their precedents in Boucicault and Synge or on the television drama *The Sullivans*, all four entrances just iterated simultaneously negate conclusions that the audience and characters have reached and thereby expose the audience's gullibility—the ease, facility, and even eagerness with which it believes what it is told. McDonagh ruthlessly exploits the audience's willingness to suspend its disbelief and to accept, with his characters, a version of truth, especially one that endows it with knowledge not universally shared. That is, after all, one of the reasons that audiences come to the theater (or watch television).

McDonagh's commercial success rests on his uncanny skills as a playwright, especially his deft manipulation of multiple and shifting dramatic illusions within a largely conventional, representational dramaturgy. Cows might explode, as in his film *Six Shooter* (2005); they do not do so surrealistically or impressionistically, however, but logically and realistically. McDonagh's remarkable popularity, now well documented and sustained for more than a decade in scores of countries and dozens of languages, owes much to his prodigious deployment of venerable performative and comic techniques. As Clare Wallace observes, while McDonagh's plays "continually draw attention to the genres, themes and stereotypes they quote, formally they are highly conservative dramas" (37).

One of the features that distinguishes McDonagh from many of his Irish and British contemporaries is an unremittingly comic, anti-*avant-garde* dramaturgy. McDonagh relies upon tightly structured scenes that create audience suspense and build to cliff-hanging, shocking, sometimes violent, and hilarious blackouts. His stagecraft fuses graphic violence with the time-honored strategies that recall the mechanistic clockwork of the nineteenth-century, well-made play. He is especially fond of those dramatic clichés, such as mistaken identity, hidden truths, running gags, mysterious secrets, misdirected letters, sudden reversals, lost lockets, undying revenge, and which fuel the breakneck momentum of farce. These ploys are hardly unique to the stage drama about which McDonagh knew so little when writing his plays; they are even more prevalent in television sit-coms and soap operas. In ways that some critics have described as postmodern, McDonagh plays on audience familiarity with dramatic conventions not only to subvert and invert ideas about stage reality, comedy, and Ireland and the Irish, but also to acknowledge and to exploit theatrical artifice. His inventive adaptation of comic strategies and his aggressive manipulation of audience expectations create a self-reflexivity that exposes the performative nature of his plays.

The dramaturgy in the five published Irish plays is remarkably consistent from play to play and reflects the fact that they were all written in an intensely productive nine months in 1994–95 (O'Toole, "A Mind in Connemara" 44). At their core, McDonagh's Irish plays rely on consistent inversion of types, clichés, and all manner of audience expectations regarding Ireland, specifically the West of Ireland, and its inhabitants. *The*

Pillowman, which was revised in 2001 (46), departs from Irish themes to focus on the nature, freedom, and responsibility of the artist, but it too overtly deploys familiar good cop/bad cop types (only to invert them) and relies heavily on performative storytelling.

Within the plays in *The Leenane Trilogy*, there is also a striking consistency since they are bound together in time and place: Mag Folan's burial in *The Beauty Queen of Leenane* takes place a month before the annual autumn grave clearings begin in *A Skull in Connemara*; Tom Hanlon's disinterment and theft of Oona's body precipitates his suicide, the second of three funerals Coleman and Valene attend in *The Lonesome West*. These are McDonagh's leanest, most economical plays: each brings only four characters on stage. Although there are scenes outside the domestic interiors—in the parish cemetery and at a lakeside bench, for instance—the set design required remains the familiar rural Connemara cottage. These are the most self-contained, the most domestic of McDonagh's plays. With the exception of Father Welsh, the characters in *The Leenane Trilogy* have known all of the other characters their entire lives. As Ray Dooley tells Mag Folan in *Beauty Queen*, "It's only a million times you've seen me the past twenty years" (*BQLOP* 13).

Not only is the isolation of the individuals within the family most acute in *The Leenane Trilogy*, but also so is the recourse to references to a pervasive and banal mass culture. Ray Dooley interrupts his conversation with Mag when he "stops and watches TV a moment" (13). Brand names like Complan and Kimberley biscuits become running jokes in *Beauty Queen*. *A Skull in Connemara* is littered with references to American television police programs from the 1970s and 1980s—*Petrocelli*, *Quincy*, *McMillan and Wife*, *Hill Street Blues*, *Starsky and Hutch*—that have inspired Tom Hanlon's hopes for advancement in the Garda ranks. When the character Valene in *The Lonesome West* tries to understand Father Welsh's explanation of the Catholic Church's teaching on suicide, he can do so only with reference to *Alias Smith and Jones*. These incongruous references to popular culture place *The Leenane Trilogy* in the period immediately before the economic boom, known as the Celtic Tiger, which dates from the mid-1990s.[1] McDonagh retains the insularity of the West, but rejects its association with purity or authenticity. The West may still be a lonesome place and a closed world, but it is also saturated by globalized media that characters embrace and, in fact, take as their moral compass.

Both of the published plays in the projected Aran Islands trilogy are more specifically dated and bound to events beyond the Aran Islands. For example, *The Cripple of Inishmaan*, the only Irish play not set in the 1990s, spans several months in the mid-1930s beginning with Robert Flaherty's filming of *Man of Aran* (1934). Its settings are far less claustrophobic than those of the other plays: the primary domestic interior is not the cottage kitchen but an often-busy shop, as well as the island shore, Mammy O'Dougal's bedroom, the church hall, and a Hollywood hotel room. *The Lieutenant of Inishmore* is also tied to a specific time: "*circa 1993*" (*TL* 3), five years before the Good Friday Agreement in Northern Ireland. Both of the Aran plays offer many more characters than do those from *The Leenane Trilogy*: nine in *The Cripple* and eight in *The Lieutenant*.

The Pillowman departs from the Irish environment, but its dramaturgy is comparable even though it reflects and refracts the play's thematic emphasis on the nature and limits, privileges and responsibilities, morality and immortality of art. In *The Pillowman* the writer Katurian enunciates a straightforward aesthetic that consistently echoes McDonagh's comments on playwriting. That aesthetic foregrounds narrative, discounts the polemical and autobiographical, and re-asserts the Aristotelian structural principles of recognition and reversal. The narrative imperative, which dominates the Irish plays, is summarized when Katurian tells Tupolski: "A great man once said, 'the first [or only] duty of the storyteller is to tell a story'" (*TP* 7). By appearing to quote directly, Katurian repeats this central idea four times in a single speech so that he might get its wording just right. Tupolski, too, later refers to it. As often as the last eleven words of that sentence are quoted by reviewers, no one has identified who the great man is, but his sentiment comes very close to McDonagh's own. Shortly before the premiere of his first play in 1996, he said, "I have always felt that the story element was the most important dimension" (quoted in O'Connell 23), an idea reinforced by his 2002 assertion that "None of my plays are especially accurate pictures [. . .] they're all just stories" (quoted in Hoggard 10).

Katurian amplifies the primacy of narrative by telling Tupolski that he has "no axe to grind" (*TP* 7); "I don't have themes" (16); and "I'm not trying to tell you anything" (17). Later, Katurian tells Ariel: "I kind of hate any writing that's even vaguely autobiographical. I think people who only write about what they know only write about what they know because they're too fucking stupid to make anything up" (76). As little as the plot and characters of *The Pillowman* have to do with McDonagh's own autobiography, Katurian's comments on writing are wholly consistent with what McDonagh has said about his own writing. In 1997 McDonagh told Fintan O'Toole "My instinct is to always hide my social or political beliefs but it's natural for something to come out" (quoted in O'Toole, "Nowhere Man" 1). Shortly before the 2001 opening of *The Lieutenant of Inishmore*, he told the *Guardian* "I'm not trying to solve anything" (quoted in O'Hagan 35).

Katurian's narrative focus on the "twist" (*TP* 22, 28, *passim*) corroborates McDonagh's own belief that "a play should be a thrill like a fantastic rollercoaster" (quoted in Weston 74). Like McDonagh's rollercoaster, Katurian's twist evokes the Aristotelian principle of recognition, "a change from ignorance to knowledge" (*Aristotle on the Art of Poetry* 36). The dominant and pervasive dramatic strategy in most plays is the initial withholding and subsequent revelation of information. Usually, as in Sophocles' *Oedipus Rex*, the audience has at least as much, if not more, knowledge than characters involved in the developing action. From this privileged position, the audience can anticipate what Aristotle's *Poetics* describes as "the best form of recognition"—one coincident with a reversal (36).

Stage pretense in all its multivalent forms—disguise, irony, joking, deception, play-acting, practice, kidding, lying, or even pretending to be dead—plays these levels of knowledge against one another. In McDonagh's drama, pretense travels under many different guises. For instance, in *The Lieutenant of Inishmore*, a tabby cat is badly covered with black shoe polish. When Maureen, in *Beauty Queen*, catches her mother denying that Ray left a message for her, she levels this accusation: "The lies of you. [. . .] Arsing me around, eh? Interfering with my life again"? (*BQLOP* 21–2). In *The Lonesome West*, although (or perhaps because) seventeen-year-old Girleen Kelleher is in love with Father Welsh, she says shocking things in front of him. When he takes her literally, she explains, "I'm only codding you, Father" (*BQLOP* 182).[2] When Girleen announces she is pregnant, she clarifies for his benefit "I'm not really" (183). Similarly, Billy apologizes to Babbybobby for having "codded" him with the forged doctor's letter in *The Cripple of Inishmaan* (*TC* 66). Finally, Michal admits to Katurian that when he swore to Katurian that he did not kill the children "I was kind of playing a trick on ya" (*TP* 48). These shocking revelations and their reversals are the carefully designed scaffolds on which McDonagh builds his rollercoasters.

Within a conventional representational dramaturgy, these stage pretenses generate epistemological uncertainties that underpin all of McDonagh's plays, not least because so many of his characters are convincing, sometimes pathological, liars. Virtually all of McDonagh's characters harbor secrets and perpetrate deceptions. In *A Skull in Connemara*, when asked if he actually breaks up the bones he disinters and dumps them in the slurry, Mick answers, "Oh, maybe it's true now, and maybe it isn't at all" (*BQLOP* 99). When Michal says he told Ariel the truth, Katurian asks "Which particular truth"? (*TP* 51). Katurian explains one dimension of the epistemological dilemma, one routinely encountered by McDonagh's audiences, to his mentally challenged brother as the common basis for storytelling and police interrogations:

Katurian: This is just like storytelling. [. . .] A man comes into a room, says to another man, "Your mother's dead." What do we know? Do we know that the second man's mother is dead? [. . .] No, we don't. [. . .] All we know is that a man has come into a room and said to another man, "Your mother's dead." That is all we know. First rule of storytelling. "Don't believe everything you read in the papers." (39–40)

The truth Michal told his interrogator, that Katurian's stories inspired the children's murders, is thus flatly denied by Katurian.

In a world suffused with pretense, McDonagh's five published Irish plays employ a chronological, suspense-driven narrative through a representational dramaturgy in which the audience experiences multiple reversals. Drawing deeply, freely, and selectively on stereotypical images of the West of Ireland, McDonagh plays on the disparity between the stereotypes brought by the audience and the reality created on stage. Writing about a pre-Celtic Tiger Ireland, McDonagh taps the economic realities, such as emigration, unemployment, and late marriage, all well-documented by historians, sociologists, and creative writers, to create realistic narratives and to instill a similarly realistic horizon of expectations in his audience.

Subject to systematic subversion and inversion are the platitudes about Ireland passed on from Young Ireland through the Literary Revival to *Bord Fáilte* (the Irish Tourist Board): its populace as eloquent, witty, well-spoken; its West as an unspoiled refuge from the "the filthy modern tide"; its ethos as a devotional, Catholic (or, alternatively, as repressed and priest-ridden); its people as spiritually rich but materially impoverished. McDonagh's West of Ireland conforms to and reinforces some unflattering stereotypes: there are few economic opportunities and little money; sex is a decided rarity; and good food equally scarce. Widowers fondly recall their dead wives' inability to prepare even the simplest fare: Mick wistfully remembers Oona's horrible scrambled eggs; Babbybobby laments his beloved Annie's inability to cook jam roly-polies. The domestic monument that Valene installs as symbolic of his dominance of Coleman is a huge orange stove in which no meal, but only Valene's plastic religious figurines, is ever cooked. Salaried employment is associated almost exclusively with emigration. Few characters have jobs and those who do are hardly successful at what they do: Father Welsh commits suicide over his failure to provide any moral guidance; Garda Thomas Hanlon has no respect for the law; Billy's aunts, Kate and Eileen, run a shop that stocks little besides peas, sweeties, and, on occasion, eggs.

Moreover, McDonagh's Irish characters talk about junk food as much as they do about bad television programming and are better informed about both than about Catholicism or Irish history. The pieties of Irish nationalism and Irish history are reduced to a cliché or a pet's name. In *The Lieutenant of Inishmore*, McDonagh's terrorists regularly lapse into parodies of the Irish nationalistic tradition of speeches from the dock. This performative, practiced oratory interrupts the flow of largely realistic dialogue and becomes another running joke. The INLA terrorists who come to assassinate Padraic lament his limited understanding of their cause: "[I]t isn't only for the school kids and the oul fellas and the babes unborn we're freeing Ireland. No. It's for the junkies, the thieves and the drug pushers too!" (*TL* 29). Similarly, Padraic echoes former Taoiseach (Prime Minister of Ireland) Eamon de Valera's 1943 St. Patrick's Day speech in conflating his love of country and of cats: "Ah, Mairead. Y'know, all I ever wanted was an Ireland free. Free for kids to run and play. Free for fellas and lasses to dance and sing. Free for cats to roam about without being clanked in the brains with a handgun" (60). The treatment of Irish history is not simply riddled with misinformation, but systematically ridicules the cherished pieties of Irish republicanism. Joey, the INLA man who loves animals, tells his comrades: "There's no guts in cat battering. That sounds like something the feckin' British'd do. Round up some poor Irish cats and give them a blast in the back as the poor devils were trying to get away, like on Bloody Sunday" (28). This co-option of republican rhetoric is deployed to advance any argument from tolerating drug dealers to loving cats.

Evoking republican rhetoric is only one linguistic strategy that establishes a superficial veneer of Irish authenticity. McDonagh's most effective use of Hiberno-English and a specifically Galwegian dialect does not ask the audience to recognize its Irish-language word order or lexicon in isolated instances, but reiterates a distinctive syntax and phraseology to develop running jokes that anyone, in any careful translation, can recognize. A Londoner by birth, upbringing, and accent, McDonagh adeptly uses the cadences and nuances of the Galway dialect and localized cultural allusions. With repetition these highly idiomatic allusions and speech patterns become increasingly comic. The Leenane plays teem with specific references to localized brand names: Kimberley biscuits, Tayto crisps, Complan. In *A Skull in Connemara*, for instance, the phrase "pure drink-driving," which carries the implication that the driver, although he may have murdered people, including his wife, in car accidents, is beyond blame because he was incapacitated by drunkenness, appears repeatedly. Perhaps the most memorable and successful examples occur in *The Cripple of Inishmaan* when characters reassure each other that "Ireland mustn't be such a bad place, so, if the Yanks want to come to Ireland to do their filming" (*TC* 8 and 13; first by Johnny and then Bartley) and that "if French fellas" and "if coloured fellas" and "if German fellas" and "if sharks want to come to [or live in] Ireland" (Helen, 13; Bobby, 25; Mammy, 37; Johnny, 55), and "if cripple fellas turn down Hollywood to come to Ireland" (Bartley, 63). Not only is the distinctive intensifier "so" dropped into the sentence at a syntactically surprising point, but five different characters, including a ninety-year old alcoholic woman, also employ it.

In a reversal of audience expectations that the stereotypical Irish are celebrated for their eloquence and verbal dexterity, however, McDonagh's characters often struggle with language. Especially when referring to any matter even vaguely related to human sexuality, the characters' lack of vocabulary forces them into ludicrous locutions such as the euphemistic "boy-preferrer" (*TL* 33), or "virgin feckin' gayboy" (192), the oxymoronic "king of the virgins" (195), or Father Welsh's pleonastic "you feckin' fecker ya" in *The Lonesome West* (*BQLOP* 197).

The often-frantic narrative pace of McDonagh's plays also undermines the myth of the West of Ireland as unspoiled by the hectic pace of modern culture, a place where nothing much happens. The plays in *The Leenane*

Trilogy are less motivated by a particular event (such as the filming of an American movie or the presumed death of a cat in *The Cripple* or *The Lieutenant*) than by deeply entrenched, but trivial grudges, feuds, resentments, and anger. For example, Coleman Connor, one of the two quarrelsome brothers in *The Lonesome West*, bitterly claims that Maryjohnny has "owed me the price of a pint since nineteen-seventy-fecking-seven. It's always tomorrow with that bitch. I don't care if she does have Alzheimer's" (*BQLOP* 171). Ray Dooley in *Beauty Queen* still mourns the loss of his swing-ball set ten years ago. These trivial events belong to the distant past, but loom large in the characters' sexless, sterile lives. Characters snipe at one another, picking fights, squabbling, goading one another in an infantile and infantilizing fashion.

The most controversial subversion of Irish stereotypes, however, involves McDonagh's female characters. Old women, traditionally thought to be kindly, genial, and long-suffering, might actually be so, as are Kate and Eileen Osbourne in *The Cripple*. But elsewhere, in place of long-suffering mothers, McDonagh creates a fearful array of crusty and often hard-drinking, selfish old women: Mag Folan in *Beauty Queen*, Maryjohnny Rafferty in *A Skull in Connemara*, and Mammy in *The Cripple*. Rather than being respected in their families and communities, most of their relatives wish these matriarchs, all widows, dead or try (sometimes successfully) to kill them. Both Johnnypateenmike, who has been trying to kill his mother with drink for decades, and Maureen, who succeeds in killing Mag, tell their mothers how much they look forward to seeing them dead in their coffins.

Instead of comely young maidens who might be dancing at de Valera's crossroads in his naïve version of a bucolic, Catholic Ireland, McDonagh imagines attractive, tough-talking young women. Slippy Helen in *The Cripple of Inishmaan*, Girleen Kelleher in *The Lonesome West*, and Mairead Claven, the title character in *The Lieutenant of Inishmore*, are "awful fierce" (*TC* 24), assertive young women who variously talk candidly about being molested by priests, prostituting themselves to an array of neighbors, and blinding livestock. If Father Welsh's under-twelves girl footballers, all of whom are sent off in their last match, are any indication, the next generation of Irish women will be no less fierce. Gender expectations are analogously destabilized among males by Donny's pink bicycle or Coleman's and Valene's penchant for what are typically described as women's magazines (*Bella* and *Take a Break*).

McDonagh's manipulation of audience expectations and Irish stereotypes places him not only in the mainstream of comic playwrights, but also of Irish playwrights. The history of Irish drama can be effectively told in terms of the subversion and inversion rather than the reaffirmation of character types ranging from the nineteenth-century stage Irishman through the idealized West of Ireland peasant to the winsome Irish colleen. Dion Boucicault's plays transformed the stage Irishman from buffoon to hero in the nineteenth century. Later, the great controversies of the first decade of the twentieth century often stemmed from outrage over John Synge's representations of oft-idealized characters, especially women, from the West of Ireland. O'Casey's irreverent depiction of Dubliners during the Easter Rising in *The Plough and the Stars* (1926) provoked disdain, disorder, and civil disobedience. Similar cases can be made for characters created by some of the most influential twentieth-century Irish dramatists: Samuel Beckett, Frank McGuinness, Tom Murphy, Thomas Kilroy, and Marina Carr.

The screening of *Man of Aran* in *The Cripple* offers an historical perspective on how consciously constructed and deeply contested the images of Ireland have been. In the 1930s, Robert J. Flaherty, an American documentary maker, came to the Aran Islands armed with Irish-American ancestry and a reading of Synge's plays and *The Aran Islands*. Even in its day, Flaherty's documentary filmmaking was widely recognized as less than disinterested.[3] McDonagh pits mutually exclusive images—Flaherty's idealized, heroic types—and his own anti-romantic, comic ones against one another. McDonagh's islanders refuse to suspend their disbelief to enter Flaherty's "documentary" narrative and instead offer derisively hilarious comments. They find Flaherty's epic battle with a shark tedious and his islanders unfamiliar. What outsiders like Flaherty see as authentic, such as Aran sweaters, and invest with symbolic and sentimental meaning, become the object of mockery.[4] To Helen, Flaherty's fishermen are "wet fellas with awful jumpers on them" (*TC* 60).

The screening of *Man of Aran* is the most intertextual of McDonagh's many presentational set pieces. With three exceptions in *The Pillowman*, these set pieces are diegetically accommodated in the logical action of the play; that is, they are seen and heard by other characters and integrated into the representational texture of the chronological narrative. Yet another presentational technique is the dictation or reading of letters by Pato in *Beauty Queen* and by Father Welsh in *A Skull in Connemara*. Delivered as monologues, letter-dictation is governed by the same assumption as the soliloquy: that the character speaks without pretense and says what he believes to be the truth.

McDonagh's most memorable presentational set pieces are structured around confession and storytelling. Moving toward recognition or the discovery of identity, his plays progress toward the catharsis of confession and, with it, the revelation of some long-kept secret. Confession is, of course, a sacrament in Catholic religion, one that Catholic children experience from a very young age. From *The Confession of Saint Patrick* (*c.* AD 450), through Stephen Dedalus's confession in James Joyce's *Bildungsroman*, *A Portrait of the Artist as a Young Man* (1916), to Bernard MacLaverty's novel *The Anatomy School* (2001), confession looms large in Irish literature. The words "confess" and "confession" appear repeatedly in *A Skull in Connemara* as Maryjohnny and Thomas try to extract from Mick an admission that he murdered Oona. When he finally writes out a confession for them, Mick confesses to something he has not done, that is, killing Mairtin. Epistemological uncertainty, Mick's belief that he has done something that he in fact has not, then cues the entrance of the supposedly dead Mairtin.

Furthermore, the climactic scene of *The Lonesome West* is structured around a series of revelations in the form of confessions. For Coleman, confession is "the good thing about being Catholic. You can shoot your dad in the head and it doesn't matter at all" (*BQLOP* 240). Father Welsh's letter urges Valene and Coleman to adopt a secular version of confession:

> Couldn't the both of ye, now, go stepping back and be making a listeen of all the things about the other that do get on ye're nerves, and the wrongs the other has done all down through the years that you still hold against him, and be reading them lists out, and be discussing them openly, and be taking a deep breath then and be forgiving each other them wrongs, no matter what they may be. (223)

The final scene of this play travesties confession as a therapeutic tool, let alone a sacrament. Valene and Coleman compete in "a great oul game [of] [. . .] apologizing" (239) that circles back to the refrains "I do accept your apology so" (238 and *passim*) and the phrase, or variations on it, "I'm taking a step back" (246 and *passim*). The performative glee that the brothers take in the game is evident when Coleman announces, "Okay, it's my go. I'm winning" (244). Later Valene invites Coleman to "Try and top" his confession about Alison and Coleman obliges with a story about his cutting off the ears of Valene's dog when he was younger (249–50).

Storytelling, a familiar trope in Irish drama from Lady Gregory's day through Conor McPherson's, affords even greater opportunities for performativity in McDonagh's drama. The island storyteller in *The Cripple*, Johnnypateenmike, for instance, carefully clears the ground for his three pieces of news in the first scene of *The Cripple* by insisting on the respectful attention of his listeners. He boasts of "me fine oratory skills" (*TC* 8) and resents any interruption of his presentation of his report.

While variants of storytelling figure in most of the plays, it dominates *The Pillowman*. The nine stories embedded in *The Pillowman* are presented with increasing performativity. The first, "The Little Apple Men," is merely summarized by Tupolski and Ariel. Tupolski paraphrases the second, "The Tale of the Three Gibbet Crossroads," as he reads through it. When Tupolski orders Katurian to stand and read the third, "The Tale of the Town on the River," the stage directions call for a heightened performativity as Katurian "*reads the story, enjoying his own words, its details and its twists*" (*TP* 21). In fact, this is the only story that is actually read rather than retold. This increasing performativity foregrounds the act of storytelling and invites the audience to see Katurian as a self-conscious artist.

The second scene takes Katurian out of the police interrogation room to another time and another place in the first of the play's three departures from a representational dramaturgy arrivals and into a presentational realm. Katurian narrates and plays the character of little Kat by acting out in "The Writer and the Writer's Brother." The performance of "The Little Jesus" in Act Two, scene two employs the same presentational format, as a play-within-the-play, with Katurian narrating (although not reading) as well as playing a part in the enacted story. Act Two begins with Michal's attempt to recite "The Little Green Pig" to drown out the sounds of his brother being tortured. When they are together, Katurian tells Michal two stories: "The Pillowman" and "The Little Green Pig." Michal urges Katurian not just to tell but also to perform them: "Do your mouth smiley like the Pillowman's mouth is" (45); for the second story Katurian will use a "*piggy voice*" (65).

Tupolski's story, "The Story of the Little Deaf Boy on the Big Long Railroad Tracks. In China" (87), reveals all the plodding contrivance that Katurian's stories avoid. From its clumsy title through the fact that Katurian does not understand that the wise old man in the tower has designed and flown the paper airplane to save the child, Tupolski's story is a feeble fiction. More than any of Katurian's well-honed narratives, it resembles Ariel's fantasy, in which the community's children will honor and love him for protecting them.[5]

In the conclusion of *The Pillowman* "the dead Katurian" again narrates a "footnote to a story" (102), whereby Michal is willing to suffer all that he has for the sake of Katurian's stories that Ariel preserves in his police file, "which would have ruined the writer's fashionably downbeat ending, but was somehow [. . .] somehow [. . .] more in keeping with the spirit of the thing" (104). As Werner Huber points out, the final story and "The Writer and the Writer's Brother" are both followed by a truer or more accurate version. For Huber, the last of Katurian's lines, "an added alternative ending destabilizes for good the relationship between the story (as signifier) and the violent deed (as signified) [. . .] *The Pillowman* comes across as an illustration of Jacques Derrida's concept of *différance*, the deferral of stable meaning, in this case the deferred validation and continuous revision of the direction taken by action units and plot structures" ("From Leenane to Kamenice" 290). As often as McDonagh may revive presumably dead characters, others do indeed die, producing, at least for the audience, finality.

An even more manipulative set-piece appears in scene seven of *The Cripple of Inishmaan*. Represented on stage is "*a squalid Hollywood hotel room*" (*TC* 52), where Billy plays out the maudlin clichés of the lonely, dying Irish emigrant. The scene's sentimentality is allowed to percolate in the audience until Billy emerges from behind the impromptu screen in the church hall to denounce "the arse-faced lines they had me reading for them" (63). Having dispelled the illusion of his death created in the previous scene as only the rehearsal for a screen test, Billy goes on to create another illusion: "wasn't the reason I returned that I couldn't bear to be parted from ye any longer? Didn't I take me screen test not a month ago and have the Yanks say to me the part was mine"? (63). This account is no less sentimental, scripted, and contrived than the rehearsal for his screen test. And it is just as false. The next scene reveals that the part was not his; he is not healthy and has come home to die.

The end of *The Cripple* perhaps best exemplifies McDonagh's rollercoaster of reversals. In the last two scenes, the audience and characters are given to believe variously that Billy has died of tuberculosis in Hollywood; that Billy did not die and was successful in Hollywood, but returned because he loves Inishmaan and its people; that Billy failed in Hollywood; that Billy has TB; that Billy's parents killed themselves for the insurance benefit to pay for his care; that Billy's parents tried to drown Billy but that Johnnypateenmike rescued him and paid his medical expenses; that Billy is going to drown himself; that Billy and Helen will go out walking. Despite Billy's tuberculosis and imminent death, *The Cripple* ends at this moment, perhaps the happiest in the play.

In *The Pillowman*, Katurian is no less discerning in believing what he has been told than are McDonagh's paying audiences. Despite his own familiarity with the storyteller's methods, Katurian is just as eager to believe anything that will help him, his brother, and later his stories, survive. Tupolski alerts Katurian to his epistemological vulnerability by warning him in the play's first scene, "I am a high-ranking police officer in a totalitarian fucking dictatorship. What are you doing taking my word about anything"? (*TP* 23). Katurian, however, accepts Tupolski's promise that Michal will not be harmed, then later believes that Ariel tortured Michal. He also believes his brother when Michal swears that he did not kill the children. Then he accepts as true Michal's confession that he killed three children. Like the audience, he tries to understand the situation on the basis of the information he has. But Ariel has not tortured Michal. Michal enacted Katurian's stories in an effort to see if they really were far-fetched. Even Michal's confession is not entirely true. Michal did not stage "The Little Jesus" with the third child, but "The Little Green Pig." The confusion of these two stories results in one of the play's most bizarre moments: the presentational intrudes on the representational when the supposedly dead little mute girl now painted green appears on stage.

After Michal admits that he did murder the children, Katurian sets out his priorities: "If they came to me right now and said, 'We're going to burn two out of three of you—you, you brother, or your stories,' I'd have them burn you first, I'd have them burn me second, and I'd have it be the stories they saved" (53). By the end of the play, Katurian makes a poorly disguised effort to ingratiate himself with Tupolski in the hopes that the "good cop" will save his stories. The play's final twist is that whereas Tupolski would destroy the stories, the hitherto thuggish, bad cop Ariel preserves them. The audience thus has to be prepared to believe not only the worst about McDonagh's characters, but also the best as well: that Johnny rescued Billy; that Mick loved Oona; that Pato wanted to marry Maureen and care for Mag; that Helen will go out walking with Billy.

Perhaps the most aggressive challenge McDonagh offers his audience concerns genre. Comedy, of course, was long thought to be an inferior dramatic genre to tragedy. No less simplistically, critics sometimes define comedy and tragedy on the basis of the play's conclusion, tragedies ending, in George Steiner's formulation, "badly," and comedies ending happily (3). Northrop Frye's seminal description of ameliorative comedy saw the characters move away from order into chaos and return to an improved order (163–86). Mikhail Bakhtin linked comedy with the suspension of hierarchical order and authoritarian structures during a period of carnival (70–106).

McDonagh's comedies do not take place during a suspension of order, but in a violent, unpredictable normalcy. Having lost sight of, openly abandoned, or never known traditional ethical or moral codes such as those associated with Catholicism, McDonagh's Irish characters obsess over trivial standards, such as grammatical niceties and childhood grudges. His audiences are often complicit in accepting McDonagh's comic premises. There is no practice of routine disinterment, even in the rockiest terrain in Connemara, for example, and Leenane is not the murder capital of Europe.

Although the setting of the Irish plays might fuel the presumption that traditional values pertain, the prevailing ethos is no ethos at all. As many critics have observed, McDonagh creates a space that is consistently unbalanced and unpredictable. In 1998, Joseph Feeney described McDonagh's plays as characterized by "an unstable postmodernism" (29). That same year, Fintan O'Toole wrote that *The Leenane Trilogy* and *The Cripple* "are set in a place that has all but collapsed. This is a world where meanings have been lost" ("Shadows over Ireland" 18). Similarly, Patrick Lonergan argues, "*The Lieutenant of Inishmore* presents audiences with a world in which morality is disturbingly confused" (73). In the Irish plays the very idea of order, let alone epistemological stability, is as dubious as it is in the totalitarian dictatorship of *The Pillowman*.

What is distinctly anti-*avant-garde* in McDonagh's dramaturgy concerns the degree of closure he provides in his conclusions, principally through death: nearly half the characters in *The Pillowman*, the film *Six Shooter*, and *The Lieutenant of Inishmore* die; three funerals punctuate *The Lonesome West*; Maureen murders her mother and goes mad in *Beauty Queen*; Billy will soon die. Only *A Skull in Connemara* has no death and then only because Mick's attempt to kill Mairtin is unsuccessful. Although "a dead Katurian" narrates the coda in *The Pillowman*, he is, like his brother, father, mother, and two young children, dead. Audiences, however, and most reviewers, embrace McDonagh's invitation to accept closure, perhaps the most contrived of his dramatic illusions. What the audience takes from the theater is a sense of finality and satisfaction that corroborates its understanding of a realistic comic dramaturgy.

The ending of *The Lieutenant of Inishmore*, McDonagh's most political and, in the author's own judgment, moralistic play, anticipates two possibilities: that the cat might choose to eat Frosties or not. In either case, closure is at hand; the audience will not be left adrift. If the former ending obtains, Donny will say, "Didn't I tell you he likes Frosties, Davey"? but if the latter, Davey will say, "He doesn't like Frosties at all, Donny" (*TL* 69). Either will serve as a curtain line to confirm Davey's recognition and the play's moral that "all this terror has been for absolutely nothing" (68).

Notes

1 In *The Lonesome West*, Coleman dates the plays to 1993 when he admits to diluting Valene's poteen for ten years: "You haven't tasted full-strength poteen since nineteen eighty-fecking-three" (*BQLOP* 246).
2 On the instability created by "codding," see Werner Huber, "The Plays of Martin McDonagh" 563–64.
3 See, for instance, Hugh Gray, "Robert Flaherty and the Naturalistic Documentary": "Because he is an artist and not just a reporter, he places effect, dramatic values, and emotional impact above what might be called literal accuracy, and this brings us to a major criticism of Flaherty's work in which the word 'fake' plays a part" (42).
4 For an anthropological analysis of Aran Islanders' attitudes to *Man of Aran* see John Messenger, "Literary vs. Scientific Interpretations of Cultural Reality in the Aran Islands of Eire."
5 The four principal characters all imagine themselves as pillowmen. Katurian uses a pillow to kill his parents and, by doing so, to rescue his brother. Ariel killed his father the same way and fantasizes about a retirement in which he will be honored for protecting children. Tupolski's story emblematizes his attempt to rescue children in danger. Michal, whose motives are less obvious, says that "The Pillowman" was his "favourite" story and that the title character "reminds me a lot of me" (*TP* 52).

References

Aristotle. *Aristotle on the Art of Poetry*. Ed. Lane Cooper. New York: Ginn, 1913.
Bakhtin, Mikhail. *Rabelais and His World*. Trans. Helene Iswolsky. Cambridge, MA: MIT P, 1968.
Feeney, Joseph, S.J. "Martin McDonagh: Dramatist of the West." *Studies* 87.345 (1998): 24–32.
Frye, Northrop. *Anatomy of Criticism: Four Essays*. Princeton: Princeton UP, 1957.
Gray, Hugh. "Robert Flaherty and the Naturalistic Documentary." *Hollywood Quarterly* 5 (Autumn 1950): 41–48.
Hoggard, Liz. "Playboy of the West End World." *Independent Magazine* 15 June 2002: 10–12.

Huber, Werner. "From Leenane to Kamenice: The De-Hibernicising of Martin McDonagh"? *Literary Views on Post-Wall Europe: Essays in Honour of Uwe Böker.* Ed. Christoph Houswitschka, Ines Detmers, Anna-Christina Giovano-poulos, Edith Hallberg, and Annette Pankratz. Trier: Wissenschaftlicher Verlag Trier, 2005. 283–94.

——. "The Plays of Martin McDonagh." *Twentieth-Century Theatre and Drama in English: Festschrift for Heinz Kosok.* Ed. Jürgen Kamm. Trier: Wissenschaftlicher Verlag Trier, 2005. 555–71.

Hynes, Garry. "Garry Hynes in Conversation with Cathy Leeney." *Theatre Talk: Voices of Irish Theatre Practitioners.* Ed. Lilian Chambers, Ger FitzGibbon, Eamonn Jordan, Dan Farrelly, and Cathy Leeney. Dublin: Carysfort P, 2003. 195–212.

Lonergan, Patrick. "'Too Dangerous to Be Done'? Martin McDonagh's *Lieutenant of Inishmore.*" *Irish Studies Review* 13.1 (Feb. 2005): 65–78.

Lyman, Rick. "Most Promising (and Grating) Playwright." *New York Times Sunday Magazine* 25 Jan. 1998: 16–19.

McDonagh, Martin. *The Beauty Queen of Leenane and Other Plays (A Skull in Connemara and The Lonesome West).* New York: Vintage, 1998.

——. *The Cripple of Inishmaan.* London: Methuen, 1997.

——. *The Lieutenant of Inishmore.* London: Methuen, 2001.

——. *The Pillowman.* London: Faber, 2003.

Messenger, John. "Literary vs. Scientific Interpretations of Cultural Reality in the Aran Islands of Eire." *Ethnohistory* 11 (1964): 41–55.

O'Connell, Jeff. "New Druid Playwright is a 'Natural.'" *Galway Advertiser* 11 Jan. 1996: 23.

O'Hagan, Sean. "The wild west." *Guardian Weekend* 24 Mar. 2001: 33–36.

O'Toole, Fintan. "A Mind in Connemara." *New Yorker* 6 Mar. 2006: 40–47.

——. "Nowhere Man." *Irish Times* 26 Apr. 1997, Weekend: 1.

——. "Shadows over Ireland." *American Theatre* July/Aug. 1998: 16–19.

Steiner, George. *The Death of Tragedy.* New York: Hill and Wang, 1961.

Wallace, Clare. "'Pastiche Soup,'" Bad Taste, Biting Irony and Martin McDonagh." *Litteraria Pragensia* 15.29 (2005): 3–38.

Weygandt, Cornelius. *Irish Plays and Playwrights.* New York: Houghton Mifflin, 1913.

Weston, Alannah. "Starlife." *Daily Telegraph Magazine* 12 July 1997: 74.

3 Comedy and violence in *The Beauty Queen of Leenane*

Marion Castleberry

Ireland's most celebrated playwrights—Samuel Beckett, Sean O'Casey, and John Millington Synge—have all delighted in creating laughter in darkness and finding humor in the pain and torture of living. In their comedy, laughter is never very far from tears. Much of contemporary Irish drama seems to follow this same tradition of using comedy to explore the darker side of the human experience. This is certainly true of the plays of Martin McDonagh, the most celebrated Irish playwright of the last decade. "I walk that line between comedy and cruelty," McDonagh declares, "because I think one illuminates the other":

> And yeah, I tend to push things as far as I can because I think you can see things more clearly through exaggeration than through reality. It's like a John Woo or a Tarantino scene, where the characters are doing awful things and, simultaneously, talking about everyday things in a really humorous way. There is a humour in there that is straight-ahead funny and uncomfortable. It makes you laugh and think. (quoted in O'Hagan 24)

More than any other contemporary playwright, McDonagh has brought Irish comedy back to the forefront of public attention. His plays—which feature a unique fusion of macabre humor, Tarantino-style violence, and postmodern themes—have garnered a great deal of critical acclaim while at the same time they have bewildered the theater community. Critics differ in their assessment of his work, and scholars are unsure of where to place him in the grand tradition of Irish theater. Most agree that McDonagh is a gifted writer and craftsman whose strength lies in his ability to confound audience expectations and to breathe new life into previously outmoded theatrical conventions.

An English playwright with an Irish heritage, McDonagh is able to work within the genre of rural Irish drama while infusing the form with a new energy and aggression. *The Beauty Queen of Leenane*, his most widely produced play to date, illustrates McDonagh's skill in combining traditional storytelling with the "savage and ironic humor of the modern generation"

(Feeney 30) while employing several distinctive postmodern themes and devices—intertextuality with other Irish plays; the relationship between reality, fiction, and identity; the dehumanization of character; and the instability and ambiguity of language and meaning.

First performed by the Druid Theatre Company at the Town Hall Theatre Galway on February 1, 1996, *The Beauty Queen of Leenane* premiered when McDonagh was only twenty-five years old. The production, directed by Garry Hynes, garnered the playwright three major London Awards— the George Devine Award for Promising Newcomer, the Writer's Guild for Best Fringe Play, and the *Evening Standard* Award for Most Promising Playwright. The play also received several Broadway and off-Broadway awards: an Obie Award for sustained excellence of performance, a Drama League Award for Best Production of a Play, a Lortel Award for Outstanding Play and Direction, an Outer Critics Award for Best Broadway Play, and four Tony Awards for excellence in acting.

McDonagh claims to have written the play in just eight days, an assertion supported by the fast-paced dialogue and simple narrative of the work. Ostensibly, *The Beauty Queen of Leenane* is an old-fashioned melodrama, depicting a classic tumultuous mother/daughter relationship. Mag Folan and her daughter, Maureen, live in a small, dreary village in Connemara, western Ireland. The aging Mag is childishly selfish, demanding, and manipulative. Maureen, a frustrated forty-year-old virgin who cares for her mother, is mentally fragile and emotionally trapped. At a neighbor's party, Maureen renews her acquaintance with Pato, an Irish immigrant her own age who works in England. The meeting leads to a mutual attraction and an unconsummated one-night stand. Mag attempts to destroy the budding relationship. Pato returns to England but writes to Maureen, asking her to go to America with him. Mag intercepts and burns the letter, but when Maureen later taunts her mother with the sexual affair that never happened, Mag inadvertently reveals her knowledge of the truth about Maureen and Pato's relationship. As revenge for her mother's deception, Maureen tortures Mag by scalding her with boiling oil. Mag confesses to burning the letter and reveals its contents, which precipitates Maureen's murder of her mother and her apparent descent into madness.

John Lahr of the *New Yorker* calls *The Beauty Queen of Leenane*, like each of his other Irish plays, "a sort of cautionary fairy tale for our toxic times" (N. pag.) and Rebecca Wilson further suggests that the play is actually "an inversion of a fairy tale trope in classic melodrama":

> In a tower on top of a mountain, incarcerated by an ogress-cum-wicked witch, the virgin heroine, albeit a 40-year-old resentful, frustrated and repressed virgin, waits for a lover-saviour. The lover-saviour, after braving "all that skitter" rather than an enchanted forest, proves impotent to deliver her from the ogress. But then what can the heroine be but an ogress herself, since one ogress can only beget another? (130)

Obviously, Mag's and Maureen's relationship does not represent a typical mother/child relationship. The characters are crudely drawn and they do not seem to live in a realistic emotional landscape that is immediately recognized by an audience. Their emotional interactions are reduced to the lowest common denominator—suffering caused by psychological and physical violence. Mag and Maureen are grotesque figures, bitter and unhappy monsters, who continuously wound each other with vicious hatred and mean-spirited banter. Into this dysfunctional arena comes the stranger, Pato, a normal, ordinary man who catalyzes the tragedy. Wilson notes that McDonagh, in creating his story, employed "an astringent inversion of a formulaic melodramatic structure":

> Instead of the villain despoiling the place of innocence and activating the plot, the potential hero enters a vile place and activates the plot. There is also the reverse, absolute adherence to the moral principles (the moral occult) of melodrama: because she has tortured and killed, Maureen cannot be saved. The ordinary, normal, innocent man offers Maureen escape and a normal, ordinary life which the ethics of the "moral occult" must perforce deny her. (131)

At first sight, McDonagh's story seems far from humorous, but as Charles Spencer points out, the play is "blessed with a mix of wild humour, deep feeling, and macabre cruelty" (N. pag.). Manipulated by McDonagh's brilliant use of language (dialogue that is as Irish, lilting, and artificial as John Millington Synge's) and universal comic devices, the audience cannot help but laugh at some of the most intense moments of the play. However, the play's humor is not designed to provide comic relief; instead, it intensifies the pain of the characters while focusing and clarifying the darker moments of the play.

McDonagh's dramaturgy and comic treatment of matricide recalls Synge's patricide in his controversial play, *The Playboy of the Western World* (1907), about an oppressed son who murders his father (or at least tries to kill him), and which caused a stir reminiscent of recent reactions to McDonagh's work. In *The Beauty Queen of Leenane*, McDonagh gives us a story of an oppressed daughter who succeeds in torturing and killing her mother. Synge played with the idea of attempted patricide in *Playboy*; McDonagh shows us the effects of accomplished matricide in *Beauty Queen*. Of course, as Vivian Mercier explains in his masterful study, *The Irish Comic Tradition*, Irish playwrights have long had an obsession with the macabre and grotesque (47–77). Martin McDonagh, however, explores the comic possibilities of matricide more thoroughly than any writer in the Irish canon.

McDonagh's rural, dispossessed characters and their squalid surroundings also resemble those of Synge. McDonagh sets *The Beauty Queen of Leenane* in rustic Ireland, but the poetic terrain of Synge and the idyllic countryside of Dion Boucicault have been replaced by a bleak "big ould hill" that is steep, muddy, and rocky, which can be reached only by "wading through all that skitter" (*BQLOP* 14). From the Irish peasants so beloved by Yeats to the lyrical poets of Synge to the lonely wayfarers of Beckett, the natives of western Ireland have been portrayed in many ways on stage, but they have never been depicted as scurrilously as they are by McDonagh. While he is certainly not the first writer to explore the crueler side of Ireland, McDonagh's dramatic voice is unquestionably the strongest and freshest of the postmodern era. His characters make up a gallery of rogues and miscreants unrivaled in the Irish canon. His Ireland is populated by evil mothers, bored daughters, warring brothers, and belligerent neighbors. Their antics are often narcissistic, brutal, and yet somehow mercilessly funny. Murder, thievery, and mayhem occur so often in McDonagh's Ireland that such actions appear to be normative. The town of Leenane is a place of gratuitous violence, greed, and amorality where death appears to be nothing more than a meaningless intrusion into the self-absorbed ritual of daily life.

Nicholas Grene has coined the term "black pastoral" to describe plays like *The Beauty Queen of Leenane* that self consciously invert the earlier idealization of life in the west of Ireland by presenting it as violent and unidyllic. In his essay, "Black Pastoral: 1990s Images of Ireland," Grene demonstrates how *The Beauty Queen of Leenane* satirizes and subverts the customary motifs of mother, child, and emigrant, those traditional motifs that connect the space of pastoral with the world the audience inhabits. Grene explains that "Pastoral" concerns an idealized place of origin, while "Black Pastoral" mocks the very desire to go back to that origin:

> "Black Pastoral" as a concept is formed by analogy with black comedy, a genre that self-consciously inverts or flouts the earlier conventions of the form. Comedy normally avoids the more painful dimensions of the human situation; black comedy makes laughter out of unhappiness, suffering, death, all the things traditionally ruled out by the comic mode. Black Pastoral involves a similar kind of travesty of the pastoral mode. (68)

McDonagh certainly makes no pretensions about uncovering the truth behind Ireland's idyllic façade. Rather than being a dramatic elegy to Ireland, *Beauty Queen* is a work of fiction and imagination as much influenced by Quentin Tarentino, Sam Shepard, American soap operas, and British situation comedy as by Irish history. McDonagh is not completely tied to the Irish dramatic tradition. His Ireland is a place where all authority has collapsed—where church, politics, and family no longer hold sway. The town of Leenane is a stereotype built around traditional clichés juxtaposed with postmodern pop culture illustrated on radio and television. The grand narratives of Catholicism and Irish nationalism have lost their hold on characters who are inundated with such media images. Characters are unable to make sense of their experiences without comparing them to the illusory world of the American and Australian television shows that reverberate in the background of their lives.

In *Beauty Queen*, reality and identity are often confused with images of television soap operas and situation comedies. The television set blares constantly, even in the middle of the day, as evidenced in two scenes with Mag and Ray. In the first scene, an old episode of *The Sullivans* is airing, and in the second, an episode of *Sons and Daughters*. Ironically, Mag is not watching either; she is "waiting for the news," for some indication of what is happening in the real world (*BQLOP* 13). Ray is waiting for Maureen, and when she does not appear, he becomes increasingly bored. Frustrated, he switches the television off and admits to Mag, in a moment of comic irony: "A whole afternoon I'm wasting here. (*Pause*) When I could be at home watching telly" (56). For Ray, television is an escape from the boredom of life, and the only shows that really interest him are those in which "Everybody's always killing each other and a lot of the girls do wear swimsuits"(52). In contrast, his perception of his Irish homeland is quite twisted and ridiculous: "Who wants to see Ireland on telly? All you have to do is look out your window to see Ireland. And it's soon bored you'd be. There goes a calf" (76). Within the play's melodramatic structure, Ray serves as both a grotesque clown and an incompetent messenger and symbolizes the play's most pervasive postmodern theme—the dialectic between reality and imagination.

Ray Dooley unknowingly lives in a fictive, soap opera world, and he dreams of living a life based on the ideals presented in situation comedies. He, like Maureen and all of McDonagh's characters, is stuck in the past and unable to move forward. He is tied to his birthplace yet does not feel at home anywhere. The grass seems greener elsewhere and his life always seems harder than the lives of others. Ray's frustrated stasis illustrates the truth of José Lanters's claim that in *The Leenane Trilogy*, "reality always loops back into popular media images; it is merely the reflection of old television reruns, just as art in the postmodern era is no longer a leap into the Future but a replay of quotations from the Past" (210).

In one sense, Martin McDonagh's works are a natural evolution of the Irish canon, a counterpart to a century of mourning for an idyllic homeland and a reminder that people and places can often be exactly what is least expected. Fintan O'Toole suggests that McDonagh's play depicts a "mental universe of people who live on the margins of a globalized culture" ("Shadows over Ireland" 18), a world in which everyone struggles for truth and identity. He points out elsewhere that, as an English-born child of Irish parents, McDonagh was, and is, "a citizen of an indefinite land that is neither Ireland nor England, but shares borders with both":

> Alongside this redefinition of special borders comes a kind of temporal uncertainty, in which motifs redolent of Irish drama from Synge onwards are combined with an utterly 1990s sensibility, in which knowing and

playful pastiche becomes undistinguishable from serious and sober intent, so that the country of the play is pre-modern and postmodern at the same time. The 1950s is laid over the 1990s. ("Introduction" xi)

Lanters agrees with O'Toole and further suggests that in McDonagh's plays "language has lost the ability to capture reality—if there is such a thing—let alone recreate it" (214).

The language of *Beauty Queen* clearly reflects the postmodern crises that O'Toole and Lanters suggest. Language is so destabilized in the play that the possibility of real communication seems on the verge of collapse at any moment. Characters constantly mistake each other's meanings, twist words around to their own ends, or simply cannot distinguish truth from fiction. As Lanters points out, McDonagh's characters "all speak in short, paratactic sentences and are prone to repetition, banal pronouncements, and stating the obvious [...] . The treacherous surface of words keeps drawing attention to itself and hence prevents true depth of feeling" (217). For example, Pato's response to Maureen's intimate description of her horrific stay in the insane asylum at Difford Hall is an insensitive "Put it behind you, you should" (*BQLOP* 44). Unfortunately, this is something Maureen cannot do, what with her mother Mag "eyeing [her] every minute" and using the past as a weapon against her (44).

Like many of McDonagh's characters, Maureen is imprisoned by her past, trapped in a web of horrible memories that she is unable to forget. She dreams of breaking away from the bitter tedium of her daily life and moving to London, but she is emotionally crippled by thoughts of her experiences there. She admits to Mag: "If it wasn't for the English stealing our language, and our land, and our God knows-what, wouldn't it be we wouldn't need to go begging for jobs and handouts" (8). Pato is also unhappy with his life in London and hopes for a new beginning in America. Although emigration is a major theme in most Irish drama, McDonagh's characters tend to reduce their deeper discussions of this subject to small talk or comic banter. O'Toole notes that the value of *The Beauty Queen of Leenane* in regard to emigration is its function as a play "at once local in its setting and dislocated in its content that deals with the way a culture characterized by emigration exists on a continual fault-line between reality and imagination" ("Introduction" xi).

McDonagh's unique writing style, which constantly shifts between reality and imagination, blending melodrama with comedy, becomes more than a stylistic feature in *The Beauty Queen of Leenane*. In fact, it is in the form of storytelling, rather than the content, where the originality of this dark comedy is to be found. McDonagh is a skilled craftsman and he brilliantly employs all the dramatic resources at his command: classic and Gothic melodrama; elements of macabre comedy and Grand Guignol style violence; grotesque humor; moments of lasciviousness; and the blending of the mundane with the shocking. His ability to fuse all the disparate elements of traditional melodrama and comedy into a single dramatic vision recalls the works of the great masters of the Irish comic tradition. However, McDonagh moves beyond the traditional to create a highly personal and unique writing style by combining realism, with the "flashy violence" of contemporary films, and an "unstable postmodernism" (Feeney 29).

In *Beauty Queen*, McDonagh's comic imagination is apparent from the initial description of the setting. The set is a "*living room/kitchen of a rural cottage*" (*BQLOP* 3), reminiscent of the rural kitchens of Synge and much of Irish peasant drama. It features an old range, a table, and a rocking chair, but unlike the imaginary settings of his Irish predecessors, McDonagh's kitchen is no haven of nurture and nourishment. The kitchen of Mag and Maureen is a place of unwholesomeness and disease, used for storing poteen and Complan, pouring urine, burning letters, scalding hands, and torturing mothers. Scattered around the room are several kitschy objects such as a "crucifix," "a framed picture of John and Robert Kennedy," and "a touristy-looking embroidered tea-towel" bearing the macabre, comic inscription "May you be half an hour in Heaven afore the Devil knows you're dead" (3). Once a symbol of family refuge, the foul-smelling kitchen in McDonagh's world is what Rebecca Wilson calls "a disembodied presence of evil—a hell's kitchen" (131). The kitchen stinks of urine that Mag, who suffers from a kidney infection, pours down the sink. As Wilson points out, "this kitchen is as warped as the symbiotically empoisoned, mother and daughter who inhabit it; it signifies evil as a real, irreducible force" (135). The kitchen sink is also a fountain of comedy, a useful dramatic device that elicits some of the funniest verbal and visual moments in the play:

Ray: This house does smell of pee, this house does.
Mag: (*Pause. Embarrassed*) Em, cats do get in.
Ray: Do cats get in?
Mag: They do. (*Pause*) They do go to the sink.
Ray: (*Pause*) What do they go to the sink for?
Mag: To wee.
Ray: To wee? They go to the sink to wee? (*Piss-taking.*) Sure, that's mighty good of them. You do get a very considerate breed of cat up this way so.
Mag: (*Pause*) I don't know what breed they are. (*BQLOP* 57)

The verbal comedy about "cats" and "wee" is punctuated by pauses that accentuate Ray's bewilderment, then teasing, and Mag's sarcastic dissembling. The scene provides actors with numerous opportunities for expressive verbal and visual comedy through the creative use of vocal inflections and facial expressions.

The kitchen sink gives rise to more visual comedy in a scene in which Maureen, after offering Pato a cup of tea, convinces him to "smell the sink," upon which "*PATO leans into the sink, sniffs it, then pulls his head away in disgust*" (41). Pato's facial expressions are bound to inspire laughter in an audience. The entire scene is, in fact, an absurdly hilarious picture of Mag demanding attention for her "scoulded hand" and denying having poured "wee" down the sink; Maureen complaining that she has to wash her "praities in an unhygienic sink" while serving Pato tea; and Pato, too polite to refuse the drink, sipping his tea "*squeamishly*" (41).

This scene reveals McDonagh's skill at juxtaposing the mundane with the shocking. In the world of the play, characters are ignorant of the difference between the mundane and the meaningful, the trivial and the tragic, but the audience recognizes the difference and responds to the appalling nature of their actions. Such a wildly funny and darkly disturbing moment occurs when Maureen berates Mag in front of the unexpecting Pato: "Doesn't she pour a potty of wee away down there every morning, though I tell her seven hundred times the lavvy to use, but oh no. And doesn't even rinse it either. Now is that hygienic? And she does have a urine infection too, even less hygienic. I wash me praities in there. Here's your tea now, Pato" (41). The absurdity of this situation, Maureen's unawareness of the inappropriateness of her language and actions, and the ability of the actors to express the various moods of attempted hospitality and physical revulsion inspire laughter.

Then, just as the audience begins to settle into this ludicrous situation, it is forced to witness a scene of cruel comedy and bitter pathos as the narcissistic Mag tells Pato about Maureen's emotional breakdown and her stay in a mental hospital. Mother and daughter respond to each other with hatred and disgust; Pato steps between them; and Mag exits to get Maureen's hospitalization papers to prove that her daughter is an insane "doolally" (43). Maureen sadly confesses her mental instability and Pato tries to comfort her: "What harm is a breakdown, sure? Lots of people do have breakdowns. In fact, if you're well-educated it's even more likely" (43). Pato's sympathy does little to calm Maureen, and Mag soon returns, triumphantly waving the papers. Pato leaves, promising to write, as Maureen crouches on the floor, hugging her new dress that Mag has thrown in a corner. Maureen is shattered, as broken as if she had been physically beaten. After a medley of frenetic stage business Maureen exits, and we are left with an image of heart-rending despair. Comedy seems impossible at this moment, but then Mag, totally unaware and indifferent to the pain she has caused, sticks her finger in her porridge and comically complains, "Me porridge has gone cold now. (*Loudly*) Me porridge has gone cold now!" (47) The effect of Mag's action occasions laughter from the audience that recalls Mercier's explanation of a Beckettian "'dianoetic' laugh" that is "tinged with terror" in its lack of mirth (*The Irish Comic Tradition* 47).

Mag's obsession with her porridge typifies what José Lanters has articulated in her discussion of McDonagh's characters' need for objective reality in the midst of their postmodern confusion: [They] "invest their emotional capital in consumer items and in the concrete, unchanging reality of in-animate objects" (218). For instance, Mag's world revolves around food—porridge, soup, Complan, cod in butter sauce, shortbread fingers—and she is obsessed with being fed. She is: like a child: her comfort and very survival depend on Maureen's continuous care and she is prepared to betray her daughter to maintain this ruthless routine. Food becomes the focus of several ingenious and comical scenes as McDonagh blends the grotesque with the familiar, visually as well as verbally.

Scene one, for instance, centers on a funny and harrowing fantasy that foreshadows the play's final tragic moment. The dialogue begins with Mag's motherly advice not to speak to strangers and then moves into Maureen's macabre daydream of a man from Dublin clobbering an old woman he did not know.

Mag:	(*Pause*) Sure why would he be coming all this way out from Dublin? He'd just be going out of his way.
Maureen:	For the pleasure of me company he'd come. Killing you, it'd just be a bonus for him.
Mag:	Killing *you* I bet he first would be.
Maureen:	I could live with that so long as I was sure he'd be clobbering you soon after. If he clobbered you with a big axe or some-thing and took your oul head off and spat in your neck, I wouldn't mind at all, going first. Oh no, I'd enjoy it, I would. No more oul Complan to get and no more oul porridge to get, and no more . . .
Mag:	(*interrupting, holding her tea out*) No sugar in this, Maureen, you forgot, go and get me some. (*BQLOP* 10–11, emphasis in original)

The scene, which abounds in pathos and humor, exemplifies the violent way in which Maureen controls her mother and sheds light on Mag's narcissistic obsession with food. Maureen's absurd reply heightens the comedy in this darkly comical scene and establishes the grotesque bitter-ness of the mother/daughter relationship.

Another scene in which the characters focus on their obsession with the surface value of material objects occurs in the middle of a vicious fight between mother and daughter. As Maureen revels in dreams of her moth-er's death and Mag gloats at her daughter's virginity, the two nonetheless argue over the value of Kimberley biscuits:

Maureen:	I suppose now you'll never be dying. You'll be hanging on forever, just to spite me.
Mag:	I *will* be hanging on forever!
Maureen:	I know well you will!
Mag:	Seventy you'll be at my wake, and then how many men'll there be round your waist with their aftershave?

Maureen:	None at all. I suppose.
Mag:	None at all is right!
Maureen:	Oh aye. (*Pause*) Do you want a Kimberley?
Mag:	(*pause*) Have we no shortbread fingers?
Maureen:	No, you've ate all the shortbread fingers. Like a pig.
Mag:	I'll have a Kimberley so, although I don't like Kimberleys. I don't know why you get Kimberleys at all. Kimberleys are horrible.
Maureen:	Me world doesn't revolve around your taste in biscuits. (24–25, emphasis in original)

The emotional distance between Mag's ludicrous discussion about Kimberley biscuits and her daughter's virginity and Maureen's cruel, grotesque discussion about her mother's murder is much too great to be bridged rationally by an audience. Laughter is the only release mechanism from such absurdity and emotional brutality. As McDonagh masterfully alternates laughter and horror in the play he thereby creates an aesthetic distance between the action and the audience.

Another aspect of his comedy, involving his use of licentious humor, which has its roots in Irish myth, introduces comic moments that melt into pain and despair. For example, the morning after Pato has spent the night, Maureen enters from the bedroom in her bra and slip. She flaunts her sexuality, much to Pato's dismay, sits across his lap, kisses him, and taunts Mag with lewd and sexually charged lies: "We was careful, weren't we, Pato? Careful enough, cos we don't need any babies coming, do we? We do have enough babies in this house to be going on with" (39). Maureen's sexual innuendos, designed to torment Mag, eventually evolve into hilarious lasciviousness:

Maureen:	(*To PATO*): You'll have to be putting that thing of yours in me again before too long is past, Pato. I do have a taste for it now, I do . . .
Pato:	Maureen . . .
	She kisses him, gets off, and stares at MAG as she passes into the kitchen.
Maureen:	A mighty oul taste. Uh-huh.
	PATO gets up and idles around in embarrassment. (39–40)

Mercier suggests that licentious comedy is prompted by a penchant for the "excessive and absurd" (49), which certainly seems to define Maureen's behavior. Her actions release her from her sexual repression; however, her narcissistic desire to irritate her mother leaves little room for Pato's affections. Her sexual fantasies simply provoke Mag's vicious retaliation.

As the old woman divulges secrets from Maureen's past, the comic moment is suddenly replaced by a troubling and somber mood. Maureen's state of undress, initially intended to be provocative, now exposes her emotional vulnerability. Her self-esteem is crushed and as she begins to express her feelings of being a victim of her mother, of mental instability, and of prejudice in England, Maureen is unable to move beyond her past and consequently mistakes Pato's suggestion that she "be putting on some clothes" for personal rejection (*BQLOP* 45–6). Shamed by her break-down and by what she believes to be Pato's disapproval, Maureen sinks into hopeless resignation and turns into a sad, broken figure to be pitied by the audience. Here, McDonagh has remarkably transformed licentious com-edy into despair and foreboding tragedy. The comedy of the scene not only focuses the action of the episode but also illuminates the harsher moments of Maureen's suffering and pain.

A similar technique is used in scene seven, which opens with a sexually charged verbal battle between mother and daughter. Maureen brags about her fictitious sexual affair while Mag sneers with her knowledge that Maureen is still a virgin. Maureen's lascivious language and gestures give the argument a comic dimension, especially when Maureen crudely tempts her mother once more with thoughts of food:

Maureen: Do you want a shortbread finger?
Mag: I *do* want a shortbread finger.
Maureen: Please.
Mag: Please.
    MAUREEN *gives* MAG *shortbread finger, after waving it phallically in the air a moment.*
Maureen: Remind me of something, shortbread fingers do.
Mag: I suppose they do, now.
Maureen: I suppose it's so long you've seen what they remind me of, you do forget what they look like. (64, emphasis in original)

Once again, crude language and obscene gestures inspire laughter, but the mood of the scene quickly shifts when Maureen realizes that Mag is with-holding information about Pato. Suddenly, a scene that begins with sexual comedy becomes an episode of horrific torture and violence as Maureen splashes boiling oil on Mag's body. The scene ends in despair as Mag is left tortured and alone and Maureen frantically rushes off to find Pato. As illustrated in this scene, the manipulation of the instability of language and audience expectations is a central tenet of McDonagh's dramaturgy.

The ambiguity of the play's events leaves the audience with many ques-tions. McDonagh uses Pato's letter, a traditional and important ingredient of melodrama, to trigger disaster. The audience is led to believe that had the letter reached Maureen, she could have gone to America with Pato and escaped her lonely existence. However, questions arise that test the boundaries of reality: Will Maureen ever realize her dream? Does Pato really want her to join him in America? Ultimately, the chance is taken from her when Mag maliciously burns the letter. Mag's treacherous act sets in motion a chain of events that entraps Maureen and leaves her broken and alone.

Rebecca Wilson explains that McDonagh employs four elements of traditional melodrama to tell his story: secretive treachery, the letter, the oath, and the thwarted escape (136). McDonagh infuses each of these elements with theatrical suspense and comic vitality. We hold our breath when Ray breaks his word to Pato and leaves the letter with Mag. Ray's stage business with the letter, repeatedly putting it down and picking it up, and Mag's sly attempts to see the contents of the letter are effective bits of comedy that enhance the suspense. Coupled with Mag's childish but all-important oath, "And may God strike me dead if I do open it, only he'll have no need to strike me dead because I won't be opening it" (*BQLOP* 58), is another traditional bit of stage business that never fails to get a huge laugh—the comic exit:

> RAY *grimaces at her again and exits through the front door, but leaves it slightly ajar, as he is still waiting outside. MAG places her hand on the sides of the rocking-chair, about to drag herself up, then warily remembers she hasn't heard RAY's footsteps away. She lets her hands rest back to her lap and sits back serenely. Pause. The front door bursts open and RAY sticks his head around it to look at her. She smiles at him innocently.* (59)

This scene clearly exemplifies McDonagh's ability to weave elements of black comedy into the melodramatic plot of the play. Consider Mag's comic oath and her murderous demise, both of which question the role of morality in a world devoid of God, a place where family and religion have collapsed. Wilson explains how McDonagh, within a melodramatic frame, has interwoven elements of the serious and the merry play:

> Mag has broken a vow, one of melodrama's sacrosanct icons. Not only has she sworn dishonestly, she has dishonestly invoked the Sacred. She does open the letter and she is struck dead, not by God but by Maureen. Thus Mag's retribution is not numinous, it can be rationally explained by Maureen's rage, yet a Gothic reverberation is unmistakable in the manner of her death. However, the instrument of her nemesis is not some metaphysical phenomenon but a corporeal fury. (137)

Wilson's assessment of Mag's plight echoes Peter Brooks's belief that "in the absence of a true sacred, what is most important in man's life is his ethical drama and the ethical implications of his psychic drama" (quoted in Wilson 137). McDonagh's Connemara is not a place of deep faith or moral responsibility, but rather a world where torture and murder define the ethical state of humanity.

Violence always lurks beneath the surface of the play's action. For example, Ray's comic attempts to purchase the "great oul poker," with which he could strike "[...] a half a dozen coppers and then clobber them again just for the fun of seeing the blood running out of them," provides a running gag throughout the play (*BQLOP* 55). Ray's comic fantasy is both sinister and ironic. By refusing to sell Ray the poker, Mag ironically retains the instrument of her own death. McDonagh uses Ray's "*wielding*" of the "*poker*" (55) as a form of mimed violence that foreshadows the final act of murder.

Maureen's torture of Mag is as violent and horrific a scene as has ever been staged and comparable to the blinding of Gloucester episode in Shakespeare's *King Lear*. The scene is steeped in the horror of Grand Guignol. Maureen burns Mag's already scalded hand with boiling oil, an act that seems to be motivated by her desire to obtain information about Pato. However, Maureen's reason for torturing her mother is not so easily explained. The events of the scene leave the audience caught in a state of emotional confusion. Has Maureen tortured her mother before? Why does the mere preparation of the event send Mag screaming in pain and agony? Why does Maureen continue to torture Mag after obtaining the information she seeks?

The premeditated preparation of the event, the use of the radio to drown out Mag's screams, the patient waiting for the oil to boil, and the brutality of the act itself—"*MAUREEN slowly and deliberately takes her mother's shrivelled hand, holds it down on the burning range, and starts slowly pouring some of the hot oil over it, as MAG screams in pain and terror*" (66)—suggest a sadistic ritual that has little if anything to do with Pato's letter. Mag begins to scream in pain even before the oil has heated, suggesting that this is not the first time that Maureen has tortured her in this manner. The preparations alone are enough to make Mag confess to having read the letter, but it is after Mag's confession that Maureen begins to pour the hot oil over her mother's hand. Mag admits to having burnt the letter and reveals its contents, but Maureen nevertheless throws the "remainder of the oil" over her mother's body in a fit of sadistic rage. Mag's torture session ends with a warning: "If you've made me miss Pato before he goes, then you'll *really* be for it, so you will, and no messing this time. Out of me fecking way now . . ." (68, emphasis in original). Maureen believes there is still a chance to escape her nightmarish existence and she frantically races to catch Pato before he leaves for America. She leaves her mother writhing in pain but still alive.

Following this horrific act the audience's sympathy suddenly shifts to Mag, who has undergone horrific suffering, and this pain leads the audience to ponder, Who is the real monster, Mag or Maureen? Given Maureen's sexual repression, which is a central focus of the play, one might assume that Mag's torture session is merely a sadistic act charged with repressed sexuality. Yet McDonagh gives Maureen a kind of pathos that elicits our sympathy. While the brutal act is taking place and the audience is sympathizing with Mag, it is simultaneously being reminded of Mag's previous treachery and cruelty. As the torture subsides, Mag is still oblivious to what her actions have done to her daughter's future. She thinks only of herself: "But who'll look after me, so"? (68). Mag has gone too far this time, and Maureen has finally taken control of her life by asserting her autonomy over her mother. Of course, Maureen does not catch Pato in time, or so we are led to believe. Mag has apparently destroyed her daughter's life, but rather than mourn the loss of Pato and live like a martyr, Maureen ultimately destroys the one thing standing in the way of her independence and happiness. Unlike Christy Mahon in Synge's *The Playboy of the Western World*, Maureen does more than talk; she acts. She does not accept her plight with long-suffering Irish resignation. She takes a fireplace poker, smashes her mother's head, and kills her. Maureen's action has ended her oppression, or has it? As the final scene unfolds we begin to question whether her act may have actually enslaved her in a world of madness.

The concluding scene between mother and daughter is as ambiguous as the previous one. Much like the opening scene of the play, it is full of macabre humor. Mag sits motionless in her rocking-chair, *"which rocks back and forth of its own volition,"* while Maureen, *"still in her black dress, [. . .] idles very slowly around the room"* (70) with the poker in her hand. Maureen delivers a monologue which is apparently a hallucinatory delusion of having seen Pato at the train station and promising him that she would soon join him in America. The monologue ends with the graphic Grand Guignol image of Mag toppling forward from her chair: *"A red chunk of skull hangs from a string of skin at the side of her head"* (72). With the revelation of Mag's death, the audience becomes aware that Maureen's reality cannot live up to the possibilities of her imagination. Several intriguing questions begin to surface. Did Maureen actually speak to Pato before he left for America? Are we to believe that she really had a last-minute reconciliation with him at the train station, where the two kissed and pledged their love to each other? Are we to believe Ray's version that Pato actually left by taxi and has recently announced his engagement to Dolores Healey/Hooley? Perhaps Ray is simply making the whole thing up as revenge for Maureen confiscating his "swing ball" so many years ago! Although these questions are never answered, they do heighten the suspense of an already tension-filled comedy.

Lanters explains that "in an incoherent world, confusion is not an ignoble condition; in the case of McDonagh's characters, it is their only saving grace" (226). This point is brilliantly played out in *Beauty Queen*'s final scene. Maureen appears with a suitcase, and we assume she is preparing to go to America until Ray arrives and questions her with "What station? Be taxicab Pato left," (*BQLOP* 78) and announces Pato's engagement to a girl in America. The comedy, already established earlier by Ray's ridiculous discussion of Kimberley biscuits, Jaffa Cakes, and Wagon Wheels, percolates alongside the seriousness of the situation. Maureen "is dumb-struck" and apparently descends into madness as Ray chatters on about Pato's fiancée's brown eyes, the priorities of European Championship football over weddings, and the problems of name changing:

Ray: It won't be much of a change for her anyways, from Hooley to Dooley. Only one letter. The "h." That'll be a good thing. (*Pause*) Unless it's Healey that she is. I can't remember. (*Pause.*) If it's Healey, it'll be three letters. The "h," the "e" and the "a." (80)

Stunned and confused, Maureen can only mumble the name, "Dolores Hooley . . ." (80). The juxtaposition of the mundane, the sinister, and the serious, which makes for a compelling dramatic moment, is repeated when Ray bargains with Maureen for the fireplace poker: "A fiver I'll give you. [. . .] G'wan. Six!" Maureen, of course, refuses: "No. It does have sentimental value for me" (82). Ray confides to Maureen that he is thinking of moving to London: "To work, y' know. One of these days. Or else Manchester. They have a lot more drugs in Manchester. Supposedly, anyways" (76). Ironically, Maureen asserts that drugs are dangerous and Ray responds, "Maybe they are, maybe they are. But there are plenty of other things just as dangerous, would kill you just as easy. Maybe even easier" (76). The comic irony of the moment is cut short by Maureen's outrage at Ray's accusations that she is a "loon" (81). Suddenly, Maureen advances on Ray with the poker but is distracted by his childish tantrum at finding the "swing ball" she had confiscated years ago. She *lets the poker fall to the floor with a clatter* (82), but the act has signaled to the audience just how emotionally troubled Maureen has become. Finally, Ray exits, taking with him any hope for comedy and leaving Maureen dazed, sitting in Mag's rocking-chair.

In the play's final moment, a mixture of the comical, the sad, and the tragic haunts the audience as does the uncertainty of Maureen's future.

> *"The Spinning Wheel" by Delia Murphy is played. MAUREEN gently rocks in the chair until about the middle of the fourth verse, when she quietly gets up, picks up the dusty suitcase, caresses it slightly, moves slowly to the hall door and looks back at the empty rocking-chair a while. Slight pause, then MAUREEN exits into the hall, closing its door behind her as she goes. We listen to the song on the radio to the end, as the chair gradually stops rocking and the lights, very slowly, fade to black.* (84)

The ending events of the play offer a vivid example of postmodern instability and ambiguity. What will happen to Maureen? Will she use her new-found freedom to build a happier, more fulfilled life, or will she become, as

Ray suggests, "the exact fecking image" of her mother (83), only lonelier and more isolated? How are we to respond to the brutal act of matricide? What meaning does McDonagh intend for us to take from the play?

There have been many critical attempts to answer these questions. For example, Grene believes that "the final twist of the plot [. . .] is that the murder proves futile. Pato, the one suitor who might have given Maureen happiness, is gone to America, is engaged to marry someone else, and Maureen is left as much a prisoner in her loneliness as she was in the hell of her forced companionship with her mother" (69). O'Toole agrees that the work is "essentially pessimistic. Nothing much is going to change. It is impossible that these people will be transformed by their experience into confident agents of change" ("Shadows over Ireland" 18). Michael Billington sees the characters all as victims "of history, of climate, and of rural Ireland's peculiar tension between a suffocating, mythical past and the banalities of the global village where American soaps hold sway" (26). Ann Dillon Farrelly, on the other hand, views McDonagh's works as dramatic parodies. She believes that beneath the excessive violence and black humor of the play, McDonagh offers an empowering message of affirmation to the Irish people:

> McDonagh creates an exaggerated world in which the people defy tradition and invent their own moral codes. These exaggerated communities exist to urge the audience—and, more specifically, the Irish people—that they are no longer required to let the traditional structures control their lives. [. . .] The plays are extremely optimistic, and the violence that occurs is a symbol of the characters' complete control over their own lives. (8)

These are all possible readings, given that McDonagh himself has said: "I'm not into any kind of definition, any kind of -ism, politically, socially, or religiously, all that stuff. Besides, I've come to a place where ambiguities are more interesting than choosing a strict path and following it." "All I want to do," he once said, "is to tell stories" (quoted in Feeney 27). As McDonagh's remarks imply, the answers to the questions he poses depend entirely on the extent to which one is willing to read beyond the surface of the plays and construct a personal meaning for them. For McDonagh, "storytelling is not a means but an end in itself" (Lanters 222). The very act of telling a good story is more important than "saying things in general about human nature which most people can do if they try" (Feeney 27). Storytelling is, in fact, what ties McDonagh to the grand tradition of Irish drama. From Lady Gregory to Synge to McDonagh, each writer has told compelling stories that reflect the concerns and anxieties of his or her own age.

In *The Beauty Queen of Leenane*, McDonagh has clearly demythologized the west of Ireland by creating a fictional world that subverts customary motifs of the Irish dramatic canon. He infuses the traditional melodramatic structure of the play with an array of comic ingredients: macabre humor, crude language, and grotesque characterizations, facets of comedy that illuminate the darker side of life. The play speaks to several aspects of cultural transition in the Ireland of the 1990s, such as the disintegration of the ideal family unit as depicted in traditional Irish melodrama. It shatters the idea of the idyllic home and family and offers a horrific portrait of the dysfunctional and destructive relationship between Mag and Maureen. This aspect of the play points to a wider, more global concern: the break-down of the contemporary family and the physical and psychic violence that often accompanies it. Grene believes there is additional significance in McDonagh's depiction of matricide:

> It acts out a kind of ultimate revenge on all those pieties about Mother Machree—"You'll never miss your mother 'till she's buried beneath the sod.' And that's where you want to put her, says McDonagh. Yet the play enacts this in a form that allows us a good safe distance away from any real complicity with such emotions. This is backward, rural, old Ireland, and not even that, but an imagined grotesque version of the same. We can securely laugh at the idea that this is our place of origin, can mock indeed the cult of the place of origin itself, and in watching the murder of the mother can exorcise any sense that we need to venerate where we come from. (69–70)

While this dramatic distancing, of which Grene speaks, allows us to laugh at the incongruity of Maureen smashing the skull of her mother, we do recognize the horrifically violent and unnatural nature of the deed. As John Peter states, laughter in the face of such acts "is both unsettling and liberating: a combination of terror and the sense of relief that lurks in all comedy that all this is happening to other people" (quoted in Lanters 220).

Another factor that marks this play as belonging to 1990s Ireland is its crude language, blatant sexuality, and excessive violence. The presence of these elements seems to be contingent on a number of factors: the social revolution of the 1960s, the confluence of different cultures capable of increased travel, the weakening of the Catholic Church, the rising popular-ity of American film, and the coming of age of the postmodern generation, to name only a few. Aleks Sierz, who coined the phrase "in-yer-face theatre" to define plays by McDonagh and other Nineties playwrights, characterizes this new trend in British and Irish drama by stressing "its intensity, its deliberate relentlessness, and its ruthless commitment to extremes" (xiii). He also stresses the need for violence and provocative images on stage because they undermine traditional stage constraints, "affronting the ruling ideas of what can or should be shown on stage [and also tapping] into more primitive feelings, smashing taboos, mentioning the forbidden, creating discomfort" (4). Catherine Rees adds that this new breed of Irish and British playwright refuses to ignore the sordid violent aspects of life and is determined to represent them in the theater as realistically as possible:

The justification for the explicit violence in these plays is that in the "jagged and violent decade" of the "nineties," plays sometimes need shocking images which are impossible to ignore. Similarly, comedy is a valid device for tapping into the audience's psyche: Sierz argues that a common reaction to terror is either to ignore it or to laugh at it. We cannot ignore the terror in McDonagh's play because we are laughing at it, but on a deeper level the audience is also implicated in the violence because we are vicariously enjoying it. This is exactly the uncomfortable position McDonagh wishes to put us in. (30)

Like his predecessors, John M. Synge, Sean O'Casey, and Samuel Beckett, Martin McDonagh delights in creating laughter in darkness, finding humor in the pain and torture of living. He is rooted and inspired by the same human landscape as his dramatic ancestors yet he has created a unique writing style. *The Beauty Queen of Leenane* reveals McDonagh's skill in telling an imaginative story that is both distinctive and memorable and points to his remarkable ability to create a dramatic world that resonates with universal significance. As Karen Vandevelde remarks, "The microscopic picture of Leenane becomes the macrocosm of modern life, at once emblematic of modern Irish culture and representative of any unsettled nation torn between dreams and despair" (301). Ultimately, *The Beauty Queen*'s comedic power stems from the directness of its shock tactics, the immediacy of its language, and the relevance of its themes.

References

Billington, Michael. "Excessive Talent for Plundering Irish Past." [*Manchester*] *Guardian Weekly* 10 Aug. 1997: 26.

Farrelly, Ann Dillon. " 'It Depends On The Fella. And The Cat.' Negotiating Humanness through the Myth of Irish Identity in The Plays of Martin McDonagh." Diss. Ohio State University, 2004.

Feeney, Joseph. "Martin McDonagh: Dramatist of the West." *Studies: An Irish Quarterly Review* 87.345 (1998): 24–32.

Grene, Nicholas. "Black Pastoral: 1990s Images of Ireland." *Litteraria Pragensia* 20.10 (2000): 67–75.

Lahr, John. "Blood Simple." *New Yorker* 13 Mar. 2006. N. pag. 25 May 2006 <http://www.newyorker.com/printables/critics/060313crth-theatre>.

Lanters, José. "Playwrights of the Western World: Synge, Murphy, McDonagh." *A Century of Irish Drama: Widening the Stage*. Ed. Stephen Watt, Eileen Morgan, and Shakir Mustafa. Bloomington: Indiana UP, 2000.

McDonagh, Martin. *The Beauty Queen of Leenane and Other Plays* (*A Skull in Connemara* and *The Lonesome West*). New York: Vintage, 1998.

Mercier, Vivian. *The Irish Comic Tradition*. Oxford: Oxford UP, 1962.

O'Hagan, Sean. "The wild west." *Guardian* 24 Mar. 2001. N. pag. 30 May 2005 <http://www.guardian.co.uk/archive/article/0,4273,4158003.00.html>.

O'Toole, Fintan. "Introduction." *Martin McDonagh Plays: 1*. London: Methuen, 1999. ix–xvii.

——. "Shadows over Ireland." *American Theatre* July/Aug. 1998: 16–19.

Rees, Catherine. "The Good, the Bad, and the Ugly: The Politics of Morality in Martin McDonagh's *The Lieutenant of Inishmore*." *New Theatre Quarterly* 21:1 (Feb. 2005): 28–33.

Sierz, Aleks. *In-yer-face Theatre: British Drama Today*. London: Faber, 2001.

Spencer, Charles. "Too Heartless To Be Called Great." 11 Jan. 1997. *Daily Telegraph* 28 June 2002.

Vandevelde, Karen. "The Gothic Soap of Martin McDonagh." *Theatre Stuff: Critical Essays on Contemporary Irish Theatre*. Ed. Eamonn Jordon. Dublin: Carysfort P, 2000. 292–302.

Wilson, Rebecca. "Macabre Merriment in McDonagh's Melodrama: *The Beauty Queen of Leenane*." *The Power of Laughter: Comedy and Contemporary Irish Theatre*. Ed. Eric Weitz. Dublin: Carysfort P, 2004. 129–44.

4 The "ineffectual Father Welsh/Walsh"?: Anti-Catholicism and Catholicism in Martin McDonagh's *The Leenane Trilogy*

Stephanie Pocock

For a dramatist whose unapologetically violent plays have provoked reviews with titles like "Sick-buckets needed in the stalls" and whose *The Leenane Trilogy* impressed reviewer Matt Wolf as "the scattershot vitriol of a dramatist drowning in his own bile," Martin McDonagh has been surprisingly insistent in his claim that each of his plays has a "heart" (quoted in Wolf 49). Despite his description of his "idea of theatre" as "some kind of punk destruction of what's gone on before," he maintains, when confronted with remarks about his plays' darkness, that "what the blackness does is allow the heart to shine through" (quoted in Feeney 28, 29). In an interview with Dominic Cavendish, McDonagh repeated this emphasis: "I always like a dark story that's seemingly heartless, but where there's a heart, tiny and camouflaged as it might be. I care about the characters an awful lot" (26). Such statements may seem, as Joseph Feeney complains, singularly unhelpful in reading or viewing plays that delight in undercutting any positive identification the audience may be tempted to make with the characters (29). An audience searching for a heart in *The Beauty Queen of Leenane* may believe they have found it in Maureen Folan, whose verbal abuse of her manipulative mother seems forgivable at first given her dismal existence and history of mental illness. Such illusions are shattered, however, when Maureen punishes her mother's deceit by calmly pouring a boiling pan of chip fat over her already scalded hand. This pattern, in which characters who initially seem likeable or harmlessly entertaining reveal appalling depths of cruelty, is repeated so often throughout McDonagh's plays that most audiences and critics abandon the search for any sort of protagonist or moral center and simply enjoy the ruthless and hilarious satire at face value.

For some critics, the difficulty of finding an emotional or moral center in McDonagh's plays indicates that they are essentially flawed. Clare Wallace, after examining the plays in the context of various theories of postmodernism, concludes that "authenticity, reality, depth in the McDonagh play-world are never to be found where they ought to be" (33). Kevin Barry claims that the playwright "has no imaginative empathy with the characters or their language. It's a relationship of distance" (quoted in

Wallace 34). Other critics, less willing to dismiss McDonagh's obvious talent, but equally disturbed by the bleakness of his vision, have focused on finding the elusive "heart" of his plays not within the works themselves but in their relationship to the Irish dramatic tradition. Shaun Richards writes that one of the central difficulties of McDonagh's *The Leenane Trilogy* is that the plays' wholesale satire does not offer a moral alternative to the violence and chaos they so bitingly capture:

> The problem, and hence the frequent difficulty of interpreting McDonagh's work, is that while exploring a world that has imploded, in which order has collapsed, he does not stage "some basis for the new morality he seems to be seeking, some ground for reconciliation." (8)

According to Richards, the only way to critically understand this gap, which might render the plays merely entertaining pastiches rather than constructive parodies, is to read them as engaging with John Synge's *The Playboy of the Western World* (1907). Despite the similarities between the two playwrights' dark humor, Synge's plays contained "vital, if marginalized characters whose dynamism was an explicit condemnation of the multiple failures in the community" (8). In the absence of such characters, Richards concludes, the *Trilogy*'s literary value must be found in its interaction with Synge's "original."

While few have gone as far as Richards in asserting the absolute necessity of Synge's plays to a critical appreciation of McDonagh's, much criticism to date has focused on debating the relationship of McDonagh's work to Irishness in general and the work of the Abbey founders in particular. While such efforts have often been compelling and important, they have tended to shift attention away from the plays themselves toward repeated debates about the playwright's national identity and readings of influential predecessors. An understanding and appreciation of the literary traditions in which McDonagh is working can be a rich resource for thinking about his drama, but the tracing-out of allusions and influences has too often been done without serious scrutiny of the world McDonagh has created, preempting any search for the "tiny and camouflaged heart" that the playwright insists is there.[1]

Richards's frustrated dismissal of *The Leenane Trilogy* as lacking "vital, if marginalized characters whose dynamism" serves to condemn "failures in the community" (8) seems to undervalue characters like Father Welsh, whose presence explicitly critiques the materialism, loneliness, and violence of his community. The fact that Father Welsh is deeply flawed and perhaps ultimately ineffectual does not undermine his value as a positive character, but rather reveals that, at the core of McDonagh's vision, hope and despair are ultimately inseparable. Acknowledging the important role that this inadequate yet sympathetic priest plays in the *Trilogy* further suggests McDonagh's place in a slightly different literary tradition than most critics have considered. While *The Leenane Trilogy* has been extensively analyzed for the influence of the Protestant Abbey founders, it may also be fruitfully considered in the context of writers like George Moore and James Joyce, who both, despite rejecting Catholic religious beliefs early in life, were drawn to its narratives, each creating complex and sometimes sympathetic priest characters.

Like both Moore and Joyce, McDonagh was raised Catholic, and attended primary and secondary schools "half run by priests" (quoted in O'Toole, "Martin McDonagh" 66). While he rejected the faith early in life, troubled by "details of the doctrine that didn't seem quite right, as well as not being bothered to leave an hour of every week to go to church," he notes that Catholicism was an integral part of his childhood identity:

> I didn't see it [Catholicism] as important when I was growing up because I didn't think about it, like you don't think about being white when you're growing up, being white is just something that's there. It's only in the process of rejecting something that you think about why you were brought up that way in the first place. (66)

While the playwright has emphasized that he is "definitely not Catholic" now, claiming that he is "not into any kind of definition, any kind of -ism, politically, socially, religiously," the influences of a Catholic heritage and culture permeate the stories he tells (quoted in Feeney 27).

On one level, Catholicism provides an easy target for McDonagh's irreverent sense of humor. Each of the three cottages that provide the settings for the *Trilogy* features a large crucifix hanging from the back wall, a prop which highlights the ironic contrast between the characters' profound cruelty and the often superstitious remnants of their religious beliefs. For instance, in *A Skull in Connemarra*, Mick Dowd, a gravedigger suspected of killing his own wife, will not allow young Mairtin Hanlon to curse God in a graveyard. Earlier in the same play, shortly after bragging that she never curses, Maryjohnny Rafferty hopes that some five-year-old boys she caught "weeing in the churchyard" twenty-seven years ago will burn in hell (*BQLOP* 90). Valene Connor in *The Lonesome West* screams that while "shooting your dad in the head" may be a sin, destroying plastic figurines of the Virgin Mary is "against God outright" (206). This highly entertaining blend of irreverence and superstition forms part of several larger-scale parodies of church rituals and traditions. As Steven Price has noted, Mairtin's surprising return from the dead in *A Skull in Connemara* parodies the resurrection, while the entire action of *The Lonesome West* following Welsh's suicide is a drawn-out parody of the confession ritual (112).

More specifically, the Catholic clergy are a frequently recurring source of jokes throughout *The Leenane Trilogy*. In *Beauty Queen*, Mag Folan and Ray Dooley discuss the clergy's predilection toward various kinds of abuses:

Ray: It's usually only the older priests go punching you in the head. I don't know why. I suppose it's the way they were brought up.

Mag: There was a priest in the news Wednesday had a babby with a Yank!

Ray: That's no news at all. That's everyday. It'd be hard to find a priest who hasn't had a babby with a Yank. If he'd punched that babby in the head, that'd be news. (*BQLOP* 15)

Coleman Connor in *The Lonesome West* tells Father Welsh that he is "a fine priest," since he does not go "abusing poor gasurs" like "half the priests in Ireland" (177). In an interview with Fintan O'Toole, McDonagh said that, while he "never set out to comment on Catholicism or priests," reports of sexual abuse by clergy were clearly on his mind while writing the *Trilogy*: "All the things that have been going on in Ireland in the last few years, the revelations about child abuse by priests, were at the back of my mind while I was writing" (quoted in O'Toole 66–7). Despite the flippant way in which the characters discuss the child abuse scandals, their reality adds a serious note to the plays' persistent mockery and suspicion of clerical authority.[2] Thus the fact that "the majority of the jokes are anti-Catholic" may indicate that beneath the comic irreverence lies a serious critique of religious belief and clerical practice (McDonagh, quoted in O'Toole 67).

Initially, it seems as though Father Welsh will fit comfortably into the anti-Catholic tenor of the *Trilogy* as a priest who is both comic and seriously flawed. The intertextuality of the three Leenane plays ensures that Welsh assumes a presence in the community before he becomes a fully realized character in the last play, *The Lonesome West*. Although Welsh is never accused of sexual abuse, the rumors about him during the first two plays are usually unflattering, much like the discussions of the clergy in general. Besides being so unassuming that one of the running jokes through-out the three plays is the other characters' inability or willful refusal to remember if his name is "Walsh" or "Welsh," the first mention of the young priest in the *Trilogy* refers to his violent behavior:

Ray: Oul Father Welsh—Walsh—has a car he's selling, but I'd look like a poof buying a car off a priest.

Mag: I don't like Father Walsh—Welsh—at all.

Ray: He punched Mairtin Hanlon in the head once, and for no reason.

Mag: God love us! (*BQLOP* 15).

The rumor is at least partly confirmed in *A Skull in Connemara*, when Mairtin, having run to ask Father Welsh to confirm Mick's gruesome stories, returns rubbing his cheek and complaining that the priest has slapped him. Earlier in the same play, Mary says of Welsh that she would not "give a bent ha'penny for that young skitter" (91).

When Father Welsh finally appears on stage in *The Lonesome West*, he lives up to most of the negative expectations created by the earlier two plays. Soon after the young priest enters the Connor brothers' house for a drink after their father's funeral, Coleman tells him, "A bent child with no paint could paint you as an alcoholic" (*BQLOP* 171). The assessment is a fair one; later in the play when one of his parishioners commits suicide, Welsh has to be hauled out of the pub where he is sitting alone drunk to say a prayer over the body. He is also deeply depressive, demanding constant reassurance about his faith and value as a priest. When Girleen finds the priest sitting with his head in his hands, she asks Coleman jokingly, "He's not having another crisis of faith is he? That's twelve this week" (181). Confronted with the violence in his community, Welsh's characteristic response is to blame or even to physically harm himself, a habit which contributes to his ultimate suicide.

Father Welsh's glaring faults have led most critics to dismiss him as an unimportant caricature of the drunken, "maudlin" Irish priest. Price calls him "the comic priest" (112), while to Richards he is the "ineffectual and finally suicidal Father Welsh/Walsh" (8). Peter Lenz objects more strongly to the failed priest, whom he sees as the empty and "depraved" remnant of a once powerful Church:

> Father Welsh is the rusted-up pivot of this dead society and mirrors its rottenness. In this way he is the exact opposite of his clerical brothers in traditional Irish literature. He uses the same abusive language as the others, is deprived of any trace of clerical dignity, treated as scum, an alcoholic with strong depressive tendencies. (30)

While such assessments of Welsh are largely accurate, they fail to take into account the positive elements of his character, which, in McDonagh's world of humorous stereotypes and exaggerated cruelty, demand a closer look. Critical dismissals of the ineffectual Father Welsh/Walsh tend to overlook his importance as the first character in the three plays who is genuinely kind, self-sacrificial, and moved by the spiritual depravity and violence of his community. Welsh's suicide, which fails in its aim of preventing further violence between brothers Valene and Coleman, could be seen as his final failure, a surrender to the mindless violence that surrounds him. Yet it is, in the unremittingly cruel landscape of McDonagh's imagined Leenane, more significant as an act of defiance against materialism, against the town's tendency to privilege possessions over relationships and physical actions over the spoken or written word.

If viewed or read in order, the three plays create a building sense of Father Welsh's significance in the community, which heightens the importance of his surprising appearance in *The Lonesome West* as perhaps the *Trilogy*'s most sympathetic character. *The Beauty Queen of Leenane*, which contains by far the fewest references to religion in the *Trilogy*, only mentions the priest once, and then only in connection with a commercial trans-action: Ray Dooley is considering purchasing Welsh's car. In *A Skull in Connemarra*, Welsh's presence becomes more prominent: he is Mick's and Mairtin's employer; a message from him begins the play's graveyard action; and Mairtin runs offstage to ask him to confirm Mick's stories. As his significance to the plays increases, so does the sense of his existence as a complex, well-rounded character. Although the majority of the rumors about him are, as previously mentioned, negative, he is rarely discussed without someone coming to his defense. After Ray Dooley recalls that Welsh "punched Mairtin Hanlon in the head once, and for no reason," he admits that "that was out of character for Father Welsh. Father Welsh seldom uses violence, same as most young priests" (*BQLOP* 15). Mary's dismissal of Welsh as a worthless "young skitter" in *A Skull in Connemara* earns Mick's quick retort, "Nothing the matter with Father Welsh" (*BQLOP* 91). While this faint praise may initially seem insignificant, no other character in the maliciously gossipy world of Leenane is treated with such loyalty when offstage.

The small but noteworthy amount of respect that Father Welsh has earned stems from the fact that his primary concern, above any sort of traditionally religious defense of God or morality, is fostering community. Though Leenane is a small, insular town in which everyone knows every-one, he is the only character that appears to actively maintain relationships with most of the plays' other characters. He calls bingo in the church hall, leads the choir that both Ray Dooley and Mairtin Hanlon have been involved in, and coaches the girls' under-twelve football team. Mick Dowd, who has the gruesome job of digging up graves to make room in the church graveyard, brags in *A Skull in Connemara*, "Doesn't the priest half the time stand over me and chat to me and bring me cups of tea"? (91). Welsh befriends policeman Thomas Hanlon and employs his brother Mairtin, whose own grandmother calls him "a rotten blackguard with nothing but cheek [. . .]" (108). Perhaps most significantly, he earns the love of Girleen in *The Lonesome West*, one of the few positive characters in the *Trilogy*, who spends four months selling poteen to earn enough money to buy him a "heart on a chain" from her mother's catalogue (*BQLOP* 232).

Welsh's most persistent and challenging effort to create community occurs in his relationship with the Connor brothers and provides the plot of *The Lonesome West*. Significantly, as he and Coleman enter the kitchen, his first words in the play are, "I'll leave the door for Valene" (*BQLOP* 169). This first line establishes his open, inviting character in opposition to the patricidal, bickering brothers who are constantly slamming literal and metaphorical doors on one another. Throughout the play, he provides a consistent, if often disregarded, voice for a communal ethic that contrasts sharply with Valene and Coleman's endlessly materialistic and individualistic debates over poteen, crisps, and Valene's prized stove. Welsh reminds

Coleman, who denies it flatly, that the house is sure to be "awful lonesome" with their father dead, then asks him about the presence of any "lasses on the horizon" (171, 172). Throughout the play, he attempts in vain to make Valene and Coleman act as brothers and to decrease their constant fighting. His frequent bouts of depression are mostly brought on by a sense of his own failure to create a healthy community; despite his best efforts he has two unconfessed murderers in his parish, coaches a girls' football team with the world record in red cards, and cannot convince the Connor brothers to stop fighting. For Welsh, these failures represent his inability to fulfill what he sees as the primary goal of the priest: supporting healthy and constructive relationships. When Coleman makes a rare (and facetious) positive comment about Mick and Maureen, Welsh responds self-deprecatingly, "See? You do see the good in people, Coleman. That's what I'm supposed to do, but I don't. I'm always at the head of the queue to be pegging the first stone" (178).

Father Welsh's emphasis on community offers a religious alternative to Valene's materialistic and individualistic conception of religion. Throughout the play, Valene buys saint figurines and marks them with a "V," commenting at one point, "I'm sure to be getting into heaven with this many figurines in me house" (226). When Coleman melts the figurines in Valene's stove, the opposition between the two understandings of religion is clearly delineated:

Valene: I'll blow the head off him! The fecking head off him I'll blow! I tell him not to touch my figurines and I tell him not to touch my stove and what does he do? He cooks me figurines in me stove! (*Looking into bowl.*) That one was blessed be the Pope! That one was given me mammy be Yanks! And they're all gone! All of them! They're all just the fecking heads and bobbing around!

Welsh: You can't go shooting you brother o'er inanimate objects, Valene! Give me that gun, now.

Valene: Inanimate objects? Me figurines of the saints? And you call yoursel' a priest? No wonder you're the laughing stock of the Catholic Church in Ireland. And that takes some fecking doing, boy. (204–05)

While the argument is farcical and entertaining, it quickly becomes serious as Coleman returns and Valene threatens him with the same gun that Coleman used to murder their father.

In order to stop the brothers from killing each other, Welsh submerges his hands in the molten plastic of the melted saints:

WELSH *stares at the two of them dumbstruck, horrified. He catches sight of the bowl of steaming plastic beside him and, almost blankly, as the grappling continues, clenches his fists and slowly lowers them into the burning liquid, holding them under. Through clenched teeth*

and without breathing, WELSH *manages to withhold his screaming for*
about ten or fifteen seconds until, still holding his fists under, he lets
rip with a horrifying high-pitched wail lasting about ten seconds,
during which VALENE *and* COLEMAN *stop fighting, stand, and try*
to help him . . . (208)

While this self-mutilation may be seen as a manifestation of Welsh's
depressive tendencies, it is also a statement against the purely materialistic
worldview of the other characters. His action parallels the scene in *Beauty*
Queen in which Maureen pours boiling oil over her mother's hands, providing a direct contrast to her appalling cruelty. By deliberately placing his
love for the two brothers over the material comfort of his physical body,
Welsh demonstrates his belief in a reality beyond the violent physicality of
Leenane.

By scalding his hands, Welsh expresses the unique mixture of despair
and hope that is finally realized in his suicide. On the one hand, his suicide
is an escape from a bleak, frustrating existence in a violent and materialistic town. When discussing Thomas Hanlon's suicide, Welsh describes
it as a final decision that recognizes that the loneliness of life outweighs its
positive aspects:

Welsh: To think of poor Tom sitting alone there, alone with his thoughts,
the cold lake in front of him, and him weighing up what's best, a
life full of the loneliness that took him there but a life full of good
points too. Every life has good points, even if it's only . . . seeing
rivers, or going traveling, or watching football on the telly [. . .]
Or the hopes of being loved. And Thomas weighing all that up on
the one hand, then weighing up a death in cold water on the
other, and choosing the water. (200)

Described in this way, suicide is the ultimate act of despair, a complete loss
of faith in the goodness of living. As Father Welsh indicates, this is the
view that the Catholic Church has traditionally taken of suicide; he tells
Valene, "You can kill a dozen fellas, you can kill two dozen fellas. So long
as you're sorry after you can still get into heaven. But if it's yourself you
go murdering, no. Straight to hell" (201–02). Self-murder, in other words,
represents a complete despair which is understood to be irreconcilable
with faith in God.

Father Welsh's suicide clearly stems at least partly from an overwhelm-
ing sense of despair. Sitting by the lake with Girleen on the night of his
suicide, Welsh tells her that he is leaving Leenane, "the murder capital of
fecking Europe," because "Nobody ever listens to my advice. Nobody ever
listens to me at all" (212, 213). His failures as a priest cause him to doubt
the value of his own life even in the face of Girleen's obvious affection for
him and her delivery of a powerfully life-affirming speech. When Welsh
asks why she is not afraid of cemeteries at night, she responds:

Girleen: It's because ... even if you're sad or something, or lonely or
something, you're still better off than them lost in the ground or
in the lake, because ... at least you've got the chance of being
happy and even if it's a real little chance, it's more than them
dead ones have. And it's not that you're saying "Hah, I'm better
than ye," no, because in the long run it might end up that you
have a worse life than ever they had and you'd've been better off
as dead as them, there and then. But at least when you're still here
there's the *possibility* of happiness. (218, emphasis in original)

Welsh's decision to kill himself even after this speech seems a powerful
argument for despair, a surrender to a belief that no individual life can
alleviate the meaningless cruelty of the world. Vic Merriman reads the
play's ending this way, arguing that

> the entirety of the *Leenane Trilogy* stages not one moral voice, save
> that of the ludicrous Father "Walsh" ... "Welsh" [...] His contribu-
> tion ends in a suicidal walk into the fjord at Leenane, leaving the
> fictional world of the West of Ireland with nothing to counter the
> craven barbarity of its inhabitants, except the strong possibility that
> they will one day wipe each other out. (60)

Viewed in this light, Welsh's despair is an act of desertion, one which
leaves the murderous and hateful town devoid of any possibility of hope.

While Merriman's is a common and utterly understandable reaction to
Welsh's suicide as a final act of violence in a series of violent plays, it fails
to fully account for the young priest's desperate attempt to reinscribe
suicide as an act of hope: of faith in human nature and in the written
word. Before he walks into the lake, Welsh writes a letter begging Valene
and Coleman to forgive each other for years of bitter arguments and
become "true brothers again" (*BQLOP* 223). He ends the letter with a
powerful expression of his faith in the brothers, placing the responsibility
for his soul on their ability to reconcile: "Valene and Coleman. I'm betting
everything on ye. I know for sure there's love there somewheres, it's just a
case of ye stepping back and looking for it. I'd be willing to bet me own
soul that love is there [...]" (223). The letter precipitates what begins as
the brothers' earnest attempts to apologize but which quickly becomes "a
great oul game," a contest to outdo each other in the number and atrocity
of the crimes confessed (239). Father Welsh's sacrifice does not result in
the reconciliation he hopes for between the brothers and indeed escalates
the tensions between them as they reveal long-buried crimes against one
another.

Yet Welsh's continued presence after death in the form of his letter
indicates that although his efforts to create a peaceful community have
failed, he has demonstrated the existence of realities beyond the dreary

materialism of daily life. Before Coleman realizes that Welsh's letter is a suicide note, he complains, "I've no time for letters. I've never seen the sense in them. They're just writing" (233). Welsh's desperate act, however, convinces the brothers to reevaluate the importance of writing, to read the letter carefully and at least attempt to fulfill its requests. While the letter cannot undo a lifetime of "daily grudges and faults and moans and baby-crimes," neither can it be forgotten or destroyed (223). In the final scene of the play, furious with Coleman and with their failure to forgive each other, Valene begins to burn Father Welsh's letter:

Valene: *He strikes a match and lights the letter, which he glances over as he holds [it] [sic] up. After a couple of seconds, the letter barely singed,* VALENE *blows the flames out and looks at it on the table, sighing. (Quietly.)* I'm too fecking kind-hearted is my fecking trouble.
         He returns to the cross and pins the chain and letter back onto it, smoothing the letter out. He puts on his jacket, checks it for loose change and goes to the front door.
         Well I won't be buying the fecker a pint anyways. I'll tell you that for nothing. Father Welsh Walsh Welsh.
         VALENE *glances back at the letter a second, sadly, looks down at the floor, then exits. Lights fade, with one light lingering on the crucifix and letter a half second longer than the others.* (258–59)[3]

Little has changed, and it seems likely that little will change in Leenane. Yet Father Welsh has left behind a moving, deeply human story in which profound despair mingles with desperate hope. McDonagh has said of his plays, "All I want to do [. . .] is to tell stories [. . .] We're all here and we have our time on the earth. [. . .] Leaving little things behind that nobody else could is much more interesting than saying things in general about human nature which most people can do if they try" (quoted in Feeney 27). If the *Trilogy* is taken as a general statement about human nature, its message is both bleak and unforgiving. With his suicide, however, Father Welsh leaves behind a story that no one else in Leenane could have told, and, in this at least, his death is more than a meaningless "suicidal walk into the fjord" (Merriman 60).

Following Welsh's death, the Connor brothers reminisce about him, and come to a conclusion that both sums up his importance to the *Trilogy* and indicates his significance in the tradition of literary representations of the Irish Catholic priest:

Valene: He wasn't a great fella, but he wasn't a bad fella.
Coleman: Aye. (*Pause.*) He was a *middling* fella. (*BQLOP* 257, emphasis in original)

Welsh is neither a saint nor a corrupt representative of a powerful Church, but simply a "middling fella," a human being struggling to overcome his own flaws and those of his society. O'Toole asked McDonagh about why, in light of the playwright's rejection of Catholicism, Father Welsh was such a sympathetic character. In response, McDonagh calls Welsh both an ordinary man and the savior figure of the *Trilogy*:

> He is actually seen as an ordinary man. I guess maybe I don't see him as a priest. I see him as a bloke, a decent man. He's probably more a representation of my idea, or my faith in the Christ I was taught about as a kid. I guess it's a suicidal Christ figure, which is a figure I've always been interested in. Somebody who kills himself for the sake of others. I think the general tone of the voice is—maybe, I don't think about it in these terms, but the majority of the jokes are anti-Catholic. And the portrayal of the priest is pro. He's the savior figure of the *Trilogy*. More because he's a decent man than anything. (quoted in O'Toole 67)

In a world of poverty, violence and materialism, McDonagh suggests that sometimes a "decent man" provides the only hint of transcendence.

The fact that the *Trilogy*'s most decent man is also a priest has troubled some critics, who see the combination as a nod to the vanity of the powerful, an easy reinforcement of a bourgeois *status quo*. Welsh's humanity, oddly enough, troubles Peter Lenz, who seems frustrated by the fact that he fits neither of the common stereotypes of the Irish priest:

> The priest, the most prominent character in traditional Irish literature, has always embodied essential traits of Irish society, representing either stern, restrictive moral and social principles or, rarely, faint traces of liberalism. Father Welsh, however, embodies neither of them. (29)

Lenz goes on to decry McDonagh's failure to portray the Catholic Church as a powerful, oppressive force: "In traditional Irish realist literature [. . .] it was the Catholic Church and its restrictive moral code that was at the bottom of young people's suicides or suicide attempts. In McDonagh this, like everything, is the other way round" (31). Rather than seeing this difference as evidence of McDonagh's ability to create complex, unexpected characters, he concludes that the playwright is "merely using the emptied shell of peasant life for smug dismissal by a metropolitan audience, and [. . .] neglecting to take an analytical look at the conditions in which such images are produced" (34). Such objections reveal a critical oversimplification, an attempt to reduce history to the product of supposedly monolithic institutions, rather than recognizing history as the cumulative product of the beliefs and decisions of millions of human beings: some corrupt, some well-meaning, all complex. McDonagh's decision to portray Father Welsh as both a priest and a "decent man" indicates his awareness of this fact, and places him in a tradition of Irish writers who, despite their disapproval of the Catholic Church and its power in Ireland, have been able to separate the individual practice of religion from its institutionalized form and thus to create complex and sympathetic priest characters. Briefly examining a few of these Irish literary priests reveals the ways in which McDonagh is both working within and adding to this tradition through his portrayal of Father Welsh.

An outspoken anti-Catholic who claimed that one of the "dominant notes" in his character was "a brutal loathing of the religion," George Moore nonetheless filled his stories and novels with priest characters (quoted in Frazier 162). Some of these characters were clearly designed to reveal the deficiencies of a religion that Moore saw as a powerful hierarchy interested only in maintaining an ignorant, superstitious, and repressed peasant class. For example, Father Maguire in the short story collection *The Untilled Field* thinks of little beyond squeezing enough money out of his impoverished parishioners to build a new church. In the course of several short stories he chases people out of his parish by denouncing their sexuality; forces a young, flirtatious girl to commit herself to a marriage she dreads and eventually flee the country; and refuses to marry a couple who lack the resources to pay for the ceremony. In "The Window," he attempts to manipulate an old woman into paying for the walls of the new church rather than the stained glass window she wishes to donate. When she finally gets her window and stands in front of it, claiming to hear music and see visions, he doubts her sanity and resents her disruption of the Mass. Maguire is Moore's embodiment of the worst elements of institutionalized religion; his greed and thirst for power combine with a mistrust, not just of physical experience, but of all spiritual experience outside of his direct control.

Yet even the deeply anti-clerical Moore was unwilling to reduce all priests to this one stereotype; he writes in his Preface to *The Untilled Field* that "the somewhat harsh rule of Father Maguire set me thinking of a gentler type of priest, and the pathetic figure of Father MacTurnan tempted me" (xxix). MacTurnan, unlike Maguire, values the needs of his parishioners above the precepts of the Church and even above his own desires. In "A Letter to Rome," MacTurnan becomes obsessed with a plan to write a letter to Rome suggesting that allowing clergy to marry would revive the waning numbers of Catholics in Ireland. Yet at the end of the story, when MacTurnan's superior gives him the monetary gift that will allow two of his poor parishioners to marry, "the priest forgot his letter to Rome in the thought of the happiness he was bringing to two poor people" (*The Untilled Field* 96). The other stories involving MacTurnan reveal that this is not an isolated instance of charity, but rather that he has been actively, if not always successfully, pleading the cause of his parish before the government and the Church, devising schemes to help his starving parishioners earn enough to feed their families. The contrast between the two priest characters reveals that, while Moore believed firmly that the Catholic Church was a corrupt and destructive influence on Ireland, he saw and was able to portray its individual priests in a more subtle and varying light.

While McDonagh's decision to combine anti-Catholic humor with a positive priest character demonstrates his participation in a tradition of writers that includes Moore, perhaps the most interesting parallel between the two writers is one that reveals their essential differences. Both *The Lonesome West* and Moore's novel *The Lake* end with a priest who walks alone at night into a lake in order to escape his parish.[4] Yet comparing the two priests and their respective escapes reveals a fundamental disparity between the two authors' attitudes toward Catholicism. While Welsh's walk is a suicide, Father Oliver Gogarty's only looks like one. In reality, it is an elaborately planned escape; he intends to disappear from his parish and start a new life as a journalist in America. Though, like Father MacTurnan in *The Untilled Field*, Gogarty is a complex and basically well-meaning human being, *The Lake* is fundamentally an anti-Catholic novel, one which reveals that Gogarty's humanness is at odds with his religious function. Gogarty falls in love with a young woman he has driven from the parish for an illegitimate pregnancy, and in the process of their epistolary relationship, begins to discover himself and to lose his faith. His walk into the lake is a renunciation of Catholicism in favor of "the personal life—the intimate exaltation that comes to him who has striven to be himself, and nothing but himself" (*The Lake* 266). Moore makes the moral of the story abundantly clear; as Gogarty swims across the lake, the narrator informs us:

> In losing interest in religion he had lost the intimate life which the priesthood had once given him. The Mass was a mere Latin formula, and the vestments and the chalice, the Host itself, a sort of fetishism —that is to say, a symbolism from which life had departed, shells retaining hardly a murmur of the ancient ecstasy. [...] The life he was going to might lead him even to a new faith. Religious forms arise and die. The Catholic Church had come to the end of its thread. (266)

For Gogarty, the Church is a distant institution whose prescriptions limit his ability to love other people and so keep him from a full knowledge of himself. By swimming across the lake, he baptizes himself into a "new faith" in which Catholicism will have no part, embodying Moore's hopes for Ireland as a whole.

Interestingly, although Father Welsh's suicide is a more direct defiance of the Church's teachings than Gogarty's potentially reversible defection, the ending of *The Lonesome West* bears a far more ambiguous relationship to Catholicism than the ending of Moore's novel. On the one hand, partly due to the difference in genre and style, Welsh is far less identifiably "Catholic" than Gogarty. Since the Church hierarchy is rarely mentioned in the *Trilogy*, Welsh appears less like the representative of a larger religious body than an isolated humanitarian. While he does say Mass and hear confessions, he appears far more concerned with community-building activities on the level of bingo and team sports than with more traditional priestly functions. Thus Father Welsh is mostly just "a decent man," moved to despair by his love for a town full of human beings who insist on destroying themselves and each other. Yet in his very ordinariness, Welsh reenacts the central story of the Catholic faith, becoming, according to McDonagh, "a suicidal Christ figure [...] somebody who kills himself for the sake of others" (quoted in O'Toole 67). His death is less renunciation than reform, a revival of a story that has long ago lost its power in Leenane. The final image of the *Trilogy* is of Valene pinning Welsh's letter and Girleen's necklace back onto the brothers' crucifix, adding a new, personal story of sacrificial love to the ancient image (*BQLOP* 258). This ending is at once more traditional and more surprising than that of Moore's novel, demonstrating the failure of Catholic belief to alter human behavior while acknowledging the enduring power of its central narrative.

Like Moore, James Joyce denounced Irish Catholicism, once terming it "black magic," and claiming in a letter to Nora Barnacle, "I make open war upon it by what I write and say and do" (quoted in Ellmann 731, 169). Yet, also like Moore, Joyce could write about priests who were complex and sympathetic. In *A Portrait of the Artist as a Young Man*, the sadistic cruelty of Father Dolan is balanced by the gentle understanding of the rector of Clongowes, Father Conmee.[5] The Father Conmee character in *Ulysses* is more ambivalent, obsessed with appearances and often condescending. Yet despite his introduction as "the superior, the very reverend John Conmee S.J.," who displays his pride in his teeth cleaned with "arecanut paste," and by his tendency to genuflect before the socially powerful, Father Conmee, like Welsh, ties the community together; he knows almost everyone he passes or learns their names (*Ulysses* 180). Stephen Schuler has described Father Conmee as a likeable, if flawed, character:

> There is some disagreement on whether Father Conmee is a genuinely sympathetic character. He does, after all, represent the church, an institution of which Joyce and his works are constantly suspicious. But Father Conmee is on a mission of charity to help the late Paddy Dignam's son Patrick, and while he is sometimes nauseatingly patronizing, he is sincere in his care for others. Despite his foibles, Father Conmee is a genuine human being who insists on doing as much good as he can. (5–6)

While Joyce delighted in exposing the "foibles" of the Catholic Church, particularly in denouncing what he saw as its repression of natural human sexuality, his works are continually drawn to its characters and invariably acknowledge the presence within the institution of a variety of deeply humane individuals.

Upon reading *A Portrait of the Artist*, Paidraic Colum, while noting the book's attacks on Catholicism, wrote that it was deeply and irreversibly shaped by the Catholic tradition:

> James Joyce's book is profoundly Catholic. I do not mean that it carries any doctrine or thesis: I mean that, more than any other modern book written in English, it comes out of Catholic culture and tradition—even that culture and that tradition may turn against itself. (quoted in Potts 4)

Despite his intellectual and artistic rejection of Catholicism, Joyce's work is marked by his childhood experiences of its doctrines, its narratives, and its characters. A similar claim could be made for McDonagh's *The Leenane Trilogy*, although it would most likely meet with objections from both the playwright and the Church. Alongside the influence of Quentin Tarantino films, television sitcoms, and the plays of John Synge, McDonagh's world bears the unmistakable marks of the Catholic tradition. In the *Trilogy*, as in Catholic teaching, human beings are seriously and dangerously flawed, capable of appalling levels of cruelty and indifference.

When asked in an interview why he consistently creates such extreme, violent characters, McDonagh replied that in his understanding, all human beings are cruel in some way, yet all are occasionally capable of transcendence:

> Well, we're all cruel, aren't we? We're all extreme in one way or another at times, and that's what drama, since the Greeks, has dealt with. I hope the overall view isn't just that, though, or I've failed in my writing. There have to be moments when you glimpse something life-affirming even in the most twisted character. That's where the real art lies. See, I always suspect characters who are painted as lovely, decent human beings. I would always question where the darkness lies. (quoted in O'Hagan 24)

There is little question "where the darkness lies" in McDonagh's plays. His characters display the human tendency toward cruelty so frequently and with such relish that his vision can seem heartless, bereft of those "life-affirming" glimpses. Yet a search for the elusive "heart" of *The Leenane Trilogy* leads to Father Welsh, whose alcoholism, depression, and self-loathing cannot entirely disguise his love for the equally broken people who surround him. John Waters accurately describes Welsh as "a brooding, self-accusing, incompetent priest who acquires the qualities of a creeping redeemer" and calls his "melodramatic self-sacrifice [...] a strange and beautiful achievement in what is without doubt McDonagh's best play to date" (51). Welsh's sacrifice, motivated by equal amounts of hope and despair, is hilariously unsuited to its goal of reconciling the Connor brothers. Yet it leaves Leenane with an enduring and personal story of self-sacrifice to counter the seemingly endless tales of homicide. This story reveals McDonagh's signal contribution to a tradition of Irish writers who, despite rejecting Catholicism, have found themselves repeatedly drawn to its narratives and characters as rich sources for their art.

Notes

1 A notable exception is Patrick Lonergan's reading of *The Lieutenant of Inishmore*, which argues persuasively that McDonagh's work "trusts audiences and producers to interpret the action intelligently themselves" (76). The emptiness at the heart of the plays is, Lonergan claims, a deliberate attempt to force audiences to fill the space with their own moral responses: "McDonagh's work is often described as 'empty,' but *The Lieutenant* illustrates that a better word might be 'vacuous'; the play leaves spaces that demand to be filled. Faced with the amorality onstage, the only response is to react *morally*; faced with representations that attempt to manipulate, the only response is to mistrust *all* representation" (76). This is a powerful and persuasive reading, but one that deserves to be considered along-side readings that attempt to isolate the moral voices within the plays themselves.
2 This tragic note is captured most poignantly in *The Cripple of Inishmaan*. When Helen boasts to her brother Bartley, "I'm pretty enough to get clergymen grop-ing me arse," Bartley retorts, "Sure, getting clergymen groping your arse doesn't take much skill. It isn't being pretty they go for. It's more being on your own and small" (*TC* 22).
3 This final scene foreshadows a similar one in McDonagh's 2003 play *The Pillowman*, in which Katurian Katurian, a writer of grotesquely violent short stories in an unnamed totalitarian state, is interrogated and finally shot. Katurian's one request is that his stories be allowed to survive. In the last scene, Katurian's ghost narrates as the policeman begins to burn the stories, then reconsiders: "For reasons known only to himself, the bulldog of a policeman chose not to put the stories in the burning trash, but placed them carefully with Katurian's case file, which he then sealed away [...] A fact which would have ruined the writer's fashionably downbeat ending, but was somehow ... somehow ... more in keep-ing with the spirit of the thing" (*TP* 103–4). Both plays maintain an unquenchable faith in the inherent value of stories while doubting their ability to change human behavior for the better. *The Pillowman*, in fact, maintains this faith even in the face of the appallingly destructive results of Katurian's stories.
4 Since McDonagh has never mentioned reading any of Moore's work, I will not assume that the ending of *The Lonesome West* was influenced by that of *The Lake*. It remains, however, a distinct and intriguing possibility.
5 Father Conmee was the real-life rector of Clongowes, of whom Richard Ellmann writes: "Joyce did not forget Conmee's encouragement, and when, long after-wards, his biographer Herbert Gorman described Conmee as 'a very decent sort of chap,' Joyce struck out the words and wrote 'a very bland and courtly humanist'" (29).

References

Cavendish, Dominic. "He's back, and only half as arrogant." *Daily Telegraph* 6 April 2001: 26.

Druids, Dudes and Beauty Queens: The Changing Face of Irish Theatre. Ed. Dermot Bolger. Dublin: New Island, 2001.

Ellmann, Richard. *James Joyce.* Oxford: Oxford UP, 1982.

Feeney, Joseph. "Martin McDonagh: Dramatist of the West." *Studies* 87.345 (1998): 24–32.

Frazier, Adrian. *George Moore, 1852–1933.* New Haven: Yale UP, 2000.

Joyce, James. *A Portrait of the Artist as a Young Man. The Portable James Joyce.* Ed. Harry Levin. New York: Penguin, 1976.

——. *Ulysses.* New York: Vintage, 1986.

Lenz, Peter. "'Anything new in the feckin' west?': Martin McDonagh's *Leenane Trilogy* and Juggling with Irish Literary Stereotypes." *(Dis)Continuities: Trends and Traditions in Contemporary Theatre and Drama in English.* Ed. Margarete Rubik and Elke Mettinger-Schartmann. Trier: Wissenschaftlicher Verlag Trier, 2002. 25–38.

Lonergan, Patrick. "'Too Dangerous To be Done?': Martin McDonagh's *Lieutenant of Inishmore.*" *Irish Studies Review* 13.1 (2005): 65–78.

McDonagh, Martin. *The Beauty Queen of Leenane and Other Plays.* New York: Vintage, 1998.

——. *The Cripple of Inishmaan.* New York: Vintage, 1998.

——. *The Pillowman.* New York: Faber and Faber, 2003.

Merriman, Vic. "Settling for More: Excess and Success in Contemporary Irish Drama." *Druids, Dudes and Beauty Queens: The Changing Face of Irish Theatre* 55–71.

Moore, George. *The Lake.* London: William Heinemann, 1921.

——. "Preface." *The Untilled Field.* Gerrards Cross, UK: Colin Smythe, 2000. xxix–xxxiii.

——. *The Untilled Field.* Gerrards Cross, UK: Colin Smythe, 2000.

O'Hagan, Sean. "The wild west." *Guardian* 24 Mar. 2001: 24.

O'Toole, Fintan. "Martin McDonagh." *BOMB* 63 (1998): 62–68.

Potts, Willard. *Joyce and the Two Irelands.* Austin: U of Texas P, 2000.

Price, Steven. "Martin McDonagh: A Staged Irishman." *Cycnos* 18.1 (2001): 109–17.

Richards, Shaun. "'The Outpouring of a morbid, unhealthy mind': The Critical Condition of Synge and McDonagh." *Irish University Review* 33.1–2 Spring/Summer (2003): 201–14.

Schuler, Stephen. "Trams and Style in the 'Aeolus' and 'Wandering Rocks' Episodes of Joyce's *Ulysses.*" Paper delivered to the 2006 Southern Regional Meeting of the American Conference for Irish Studies. University of South Carolina, Columbia, 23 February 2006. Unpublished essay.

Wallace, Clare. "'Pastiche Soup,' Bad Taste, Biting Irony and Martin McDonagh." *Litteraria Pragensia* 15.29 (2005): 3–38.

Waters, John. "The Irish Mummy: The Plays and Purpose of Martin McDonagh." *Druids, Dudes and Beauty Queens: The Changing Face of Irish Theatre* 30–54.

Wolf, Matt. "Martin McDonagh on a Tear." *American Theatre* 15.1 (1998): 48–50.

5 Postmodern theatricality in the Dutch/Flemish adaptation of Martin McDonagh's *The Leenane Trilogy*

Karen Vandevelde

In the theater season of 2000–2001, a Dutch and Flemish theater company collaboratively staged Martin McDonagh's *The Leenane Trilogy* in The Netherlands and Flanders. This production was part of a worldwide response to McDonagh's rising reputation as a playwright, but the way in which the companies decided to stage his first trilogy elicits an unusual analysis and interpretation of it. One of the interesting features of this adaptation is the weaving of the three original parts—*The Beauty Queen of Leenane*, *A Skull in Connemara*, and *The Lonesome West*—into one four-hour-long production. A comparative structural analysis of this adaptation can be found in my essay "Martin McDonagh's Irishness: Icing on the Cake"? (2006). In that article, I also discuss the way in which the Dutch director, his two dramaturges, and a cast of Dutch and Flemish actors translated Irish topicality into a more universal context without doing any injustice to the play's Irishness.

The adaptation remains interesting for other reasons as well, not least because it provides a refreshing view of the often uneasy relationship between *The Leenane Trilogy*'s realistic setting and its portrayal of the grotesque. This area of tension has prompted many critics dealing with these plays to focus on issues of mimesis and representation. Mimesis in particular is often—although not always correctly—linked to the aesthetics of realism (Diamond vi). Modern life in the West of Ireland and McDonagh's microscopic portrayal of this life are not the same, but the mimetic relationship between the two has fed the arguments of McDonagh's supporters and detractors alike.

The debate over whether McDonagh's trilogy is "representative" of Irish society has not been easy. Information regarding the trilogy's genesis is scarce and often misleading or contradictory. Very little is known about the format of McDonagh's *The Beauty Queen of Leenane* before it was submitted to Druid Theatre, nor about the way in which the script was transformed before audiences witnessed the play on stage, nor about the "great creative relationship" between author and director (Hynes 203). We do know, though, that *The Leenane Trilogy* is as much Garry Hynes's achievement as it is McDonagh's. Throughout her work as a director for

Druid Theatre (from 1975 to 1991 and again since 1995), she has developed a reputation for a realistic production style (Dromgoogle 212) and from the start, helped to shape the Druid style as one of "exploding naturalism from within" (O'Toole, "Murderous Laughter" 12). While Hynes received plenty of credit from drama critics for her contribution to the Leenane productions and a Tony Award for Best Director in 1998, her work on *The Leenane Trilogy* has received remarkably little analytical attention from the academic world.

The little we know about *The Leenane Trilogy*'s genesis is based on the author's and director's interviews and myths. We are told that *A Skull in Connemara* was McDonagh's first completed play (O'Toole, "Nowhere Man" 1), although it comes second in the published trilogy. In *A Skull in Connemara* a gravedigger, Mick Dowd, tries to dig up the body of his late wife, but instead of her body he metaphorically unearths Leenane's secrets, prejudices, gossip, and violence. The first play in the published trilogy, *The Beauty Queen of Leenane,* presents a dysfunctional mother–daughter relationship. Maureen's repeated threat of killing her mother is carried out but fails to provide any sense of accomplishment. McDonagh claims to have written it in eight days (O'Toole, "Nowhere Man" 1). The trilogy closes with *The Lonesome West*, where the theme of violence culminates in the antagonistic relationship between two brothers, Coleman and Valene, after the "sudden" death of their father. At the start of rehearsals, this play supposedly had only three characters, so either the character of Girleen or that of Father Welsh was added during rehearsals (Ross). The characters in each of the plays reappear by means of cross-referencing in the dialogues in the other parts of the trilogy.

Separating the author's contribution from the director's contribution to the final version of each of these plays is a nearly impossible task, in particular when the plays in question are debut productions. The myth of McDonagh as having "sprung from the womb a fully-fledged playwright" (Richard Eyre, quoted by Coveney 13), magnified by the author's own stories, persists, while other pieces of information suggesting the opposite are far less quoted. Few academic critics take note of Garry Hynes's particular method of working with new writing, which apparently "involves a good deal of chopping and changing of untried texts, more than most directors at her level of experience" (Ross 10). Patrick Lonergan is an exception, drawing attention to the fact that Hynes "[worked] with him to cut scenes and lines from his original scripts, and [suggested] additions— many of them significant" ("Druid Theatre's *Leenane Trilogy on Tour*" 151). However, without further information about either the author's or the director's contribution, a fitting reconstruction of *The Leenane Trilogy*'s genesis is impossible.

Contrasting the original staging of *The Leenane Trilogy* with a production in a different country, however, suggests how the Druid Theatre production and Garry Hynes's work as a director helped shape the trilogy. Acknowledging the fact that even the text of the trilogy was "authored" by McDonagh as well as Garry Hynes, the published text is still a useful point of departure in an analysis which tries to distinguish between text and production. This essay argues that the realistic style of production, rooted in Garry Hynes's personal stylistic preference as well as in the realistic theater tradition in mainstream English-speaking theaters, has contributed to the mixed reception of McDonagh's first trilogy far more than has been acknowledged. Contrasting the Druid/Royal Court version with a radically different—and successful—Dutch/Flemish production of the same trilogy demonstrates how different emphases in production can bring to the fore certain aspects of a dramatic script which are latent, if not obscured, in another production.

This analysis will not discuss what is "lost" or "gained" in the process of translation or adaptation, but instead aims to reveal the potential of a play beyond the choices made by its first director. Choices are by their very nature limitations, which is why a good play will always prompt re-interpretations. The moment of production mediates between a play's script and an audience's interpretation of it, and as such has the potential to stimulate very different readings. It is not until a play has been staged by different directors, in a range of contexts, or read outside of a context of production, that its multi-layeredness can be uncovered. Different readings and interpretations have begun to emerge (Pilný, Wallace, Lonergan, to name but a few), and examples from productions worldwide are now available (See *The Theater of Martin McDonagh*). This article takes as its focal point the Dutch/Flemish adaptation of *The Leenane Trilogy* and deals with the trilogy's potential to address the pressing ontological concerns of a postmodern society. By reflecting upon its own nature as drama, as artifice, the Dutch/Flemish production poses questions about the nature of life and existence and the difficulty in defining truth and knowledge. Some of these concerns are latent in McDonagh's dialogue, some are more obvious, but in the hands of the Dutch and Flemish dramaturges and director they receive a prominence that changes the overall impression of the trilogy from a depressing slice of life to a celebration of the artistic imagination.

The Dutch/Flemish production of *The Leenane Trilogy*, first staged in May 2001, originated through a meeting of two dramaturges, Kurt Melens of the Flemish company *Het Toneelhuis*, and Paul Slangen of the Dutch company *Zuidelijk Toneel Hollandia*. Melens had been involved in the previous Flemish production of *The Beauty Queen of Leenane*, which Het Toneelhuis had staged in 1999. The Flemish company steered clear of the play's realistic setting and its shape as a "well-made-play," two traditions which have become anachronisms in the professional theaters in Flanders, the Netherlands, and many other parts of the European continent. Nevertheless, their attempt to break the play's realistic setting by casting a 76-year old male actor in the role of Mag Folan failed to offer an adequate alternative to a realistic production style, despite the aged actor's excellent performance (Anthonissen N. pag.).

A new opportunity to explore McDonagh's potential on the Dutch-speaking stage arose when Melens and Slangen discussed their plans for an adaptation of the trilogy with director Johan Simons. First, they commissioned a well-known Flemish author, Peter Verhelst, to provide a new translation for the three plays. They wanted the adaptation to overcome the slight linguistic differences between the Dutch spoken in The Netherlands and the Dutch spoken in Flanders and to sound natural to a mixed cast of Flemish and Dutch actors. Next, the translator, director and two dramaturges re-structured the three texts in order to create one overarching narrative in which the scenes of the three plays, *The Beauty Queen of Leenane*, *A Skull in Connemara*, and *The Lonesome West*, were interwoven. A brief overview of the trilogy's new structure will be helpful in this discussion:

The Leenane Trilogy, adapted for Toneelhuis/Zuidelijk Toneel Hollandia:

Part 1:   *A Skull in Connemara* / Scene 2
Part 2:   *The Lonesome West* / Scene 1
Part 3:   *The Beauty Queen of Leenane* / Scenes 1 and 2
Part 4:   *A Skull in Connemara* / Scenes 3 and 4
Part 5:   *The Lonesome West* / Scene 2
Part 6:   *The Beauty Queen of Leenane* / Scenes 3 and 4
Part 7:   *The Lonesome West* / Scenes 3 and 4
Part 8:   *The Beauty Queen of Leenane* / Scenes 6 and 5
Part 9:   Father Welsh's suicide letter (*The Lonesome West* / Scene 5)
Part 10: *The Beauty Queen of Leenane* / Scenes 7 and 8
Part 11: *The Lonesome West* / Scene 6
Part 12: *The Beauty Queen* / Scene 9
Part 13: *The Lonesome West* / Scene 7

In the Dutch/Flemish production, no major cuts were made in the first and third plays of the trilogy. *A Skull in Connemara*, however, was significantly reduced in contents, but its graveyard setting became the framework for the entire adaptation. As such, what was cut from the text was incorporated into the mood and the setting of this production. For the first ten minutes of the adapted trilogy, a man—Mick Dowd—heaves large refuse bags down from the flat roof of a building. The suspense develops slowly and gives the audience plenty of time to take in the various features of the set. The black building resembles Pandora's box, while the floor is covered in soil and littered with full plastic bags. To the left, spectators recognize a dozen or so old stoves and plaster figurines, and in the background two characters appear, Mairtin and Thomas Hanlon. At the end of this opening scene, Mick Dowd is frustrated by not finding what he is looking for in the rubbish bags. Whatever makes him scream when he rips open the fourth bag remains a mystery to the audience. The stage lighting then changes and Mairtin Hanlon appears front-stage and speaks this adaptation's

Figure 5.1 Mag burns Pato's letter in the stove

powerful opening lines—"When will we start on your wife's grave"?—the Dutch translation of McDonagh's phrase "When will we be starting on your missus's patch anyways"? (*Plays 1* 82).

This introduction to *The Leenane Trilogy* is far more "open" than Garry Hynes's. From the very beginning of the production, Dutch and Flemish audiences are challenged to make sense of the scene and the characters because their meaning is not fixed or coherent. In contrast, McDonagh's text as well as Hynes's style of production channel the audience's process of interpretation by providing a detailed introduction to the lead characters of *The Beauty Queen* and to a set which is all too familiar—the rural cottage kitchen (*Plays 1* 1–7). Mick Dowd's opening action and Mairtin Hanlon's opening line point to the first significant element foregrounded in the Dutch/Flemish adaptation: the elusive status of truth and knowledge. The graveyard setting of this adaptation, which remains the same for the duration of the play, confirms this elusiveness. Props such as a make-shift table or various coal stoves (Figure 5.1) indicate scene switches, but the life-size rubbish bags and soil continue to dominate the stage. On the one hand, director Johan Simons suggests that there is little difference between the living and the dead in Leenane and that neither seems to know the answers to life's questions, a point to which I will return later in this essay. On the other hand, the set indicates that while McDonagh's *Trilogy* may not have been designed to be surreal-istic, it certainly contains the potential for surrealism. The villagers of Leenane have equal disrespect for the living as for the dead, but in the Dutch/Flemish production they are also victims of existential fear and fear of the unknown.

The staging of scene three from *A Skull in Connemara*, in which Mick Dowd and Mairtin Hanlon batter the skulls and bones of the unearthed bodies to pieces, illustrates this two-fold fear of the villagers. In Hynes's production for Druid Theatre and the Royal Court, the loss of values and of moral judgment in Leenane becomes a source for comedy, providing welcome relief from the village's bleakness. With comic timing and a scatter-ing of bone shards, Hynes and the cast exploit the skull-battering scene's comic potential to the maximum. Interestingly, this is also the scene Druid selected for the play's advance publicity on the *Late Late Show* in September 1997. Whatever serious questions arise for the spectators, they are con-stantly negated by laughter. Laughter itself does have the potential to open one's mind, but when spectators at the end of the play become painfully aware that there was not much reason to laugh, this sense of discomfort limits rather than develops a person's ability to make coherent reflections.

The Dutch/Flemish production does not present something familiar to the audience in order to, as Fintan O'Toole has argued about the Hynes production, "explode" it "from within" ("Murderous Laughter" 12); it takes as a point of departure the sense of strangeness and distrust McDonagh aims to achieve at the end of each play. Mick Dowd and Mairtin Hanlon's skull battering game occurs off-stage with perverse gravity, and the script's comic topical references to television-series, films, and singers are cut. Scene three switches to scene four, as Mick Dowd reappears on stage and speaks to himself instead of to Maryjohnny Rafferty as in McDonagh's original text. With serious concentration Dowd washes his face and hands in a bucket full of blood. In this version of the *The Leenane Trilogy*, the village's loss of morality is translated into a surreal territory of uncertainty and fear. No one finds out whether Mick killed his wife or not, but the staging gives visible shape to the rumor that Mick Dowd has blood on his hands. The contours of knowledge are thus elusive in the Dutch/Flemish adaptation. Suspense becomes suspension, a deferral of revelation, because there is no such thing as "truth." The Dutch/Flemish production does not set out to provide answers, nor does it create suspense by means of raising expectations and supplying revelations. As such, the feature of ambiguity is raised to a status of its own.

In her productions for Druid Theatre, however, Garry Hynes exploits the potential of suspense in line with the expectations of tragicomedy. Tragicomedy depends to a large extent on the transition from ignorance to knowledge and creates suspense in order to reveal the truth. Between the opening and closing of the curtain, characters and audience move scene by scene toward a dénouement. In Hynes's hands, *The Beauty Queen of*

Leenane develops skilfully toward a single climax: the realization of Mag Folan's murder. In a more complex development, *A Skull in Connemara* toys with audience expectation and doubt, but turns this process into a comic feature when Mick Dowd first confesses, then denies the murder of Mairtin Hanlon. The unmistakeable intertextual parallel with the faked murder in Synge's *The Playboy of the Western World* adds to the script's humorous potential. The confessions in *The Lonesome West*'s final scene at once parody and endorse the process of suspense and revelation. When Coleman and Valene discover that disclosing information can generate more power than keeping it secret, neither of the two brothers reveals the truth to put matters straight but instead raises the stakes to redefine their relationship.

In the Dutch/Flemish *De Leenane Trilogie*, Coleman and Valene's confession scene becomes a competitive truth-or-dare game which culminates in the effacement of the boundaries between "truth" and "dare." As the confessional box changes from the locus of humbleness to a minimalist pedestal for performance (see Figure 5.2), the contents of their revelations become far less important than the performance of confession, the "play" element itself. This final scene of the trilogy, then, turns the problems of truth and fiction into a metatheatrical commentary—a point to which I will return later in this essay.

The elusive status of knowledge is not something the Dutch and Flemish dramaturges and directors merely injected into the play. McDonagh, too, plays with the characters' and audience's uncertainty in the final pages of his trilogy script. After Coleman destroys Valene's stove, the dramatic tension in the final moments of *The Lonesome West* depends entirely on the mystery of whether Coleman's gun is loaded:

> COLEMAN *opens the barrel of the gun, tosses away the spent car-tridges, fishes in his pocket, comes out with a clenched fist that may or may not contain another cartridge, and loads, or pretends to load, the bullet into the gun, without* VALENE *or the audience at any time knowing if there is a bullet or not.* (Plays 1 193)

The truth is revealed in the very last minute of the play, but this revelation is wholly ineffectual: Valene simply follows Coleman to the pub, deter-mined not to grant his brother anything: "Well I won't be buying the fecker a pint anyways. I'll tell you that for nothing, Father Welsh Walsh Welsh" (196). From a dramatic point of view, but also within the siblings' relationship, uncertainty is more powerful than the truth.

This different status of knowledge creates a new hierarchy between the scenes of the play. Scenes that depend heavily upon the shock of informa-tion are less important in the Dutch/Flemish adaptation than in the original production. In the Druid/Royal Court version, for example, the dramatic effect of *The Beauty Queen of Leenane*'s scene eight, in which a dead Mag

Figure 5.2 Coleman and Valene on the "confession pedestal"

is rocking in her chair during Maureen's monologue, depends entirely on the audience's belief that Mag is still alive (*Plays 1* 49–51). In the Dutch/Flemish adaptation, however, Mag crawls on the floor in agony during Maureen's monologue, which foregrounds Maureen's accountability and mental instability. In this staging, Maureen's imagined future with Pato in scene nine is not interrupted by the shock of Mag's death at the end of scene eight, which allows for a stronger connection between Maureen's cruelty, her mental instability, and her failure to take control of her own life. Through the voice of Pato, McDonagh's text promotes the "normality" of mental distress earlier in the play (30–32), but *The Leenane Trilogy's* traditional structure is too reliant on the opposition between the two to really support Pato's view.

The letter-revelation scenes are dealt with in similar fashion in the Dutch/Flemish adaptation. Parts eight and nine include the two letter-reading moments of the *Trilogy*: Pato's letter to Maureen from London (scene eight in *Beauty Queen*), and Father Welsh's letter to the brothers Coleman and Valene (scene five of *The Lonesome West*). Exhibiting the typical features of melodrama and the well-made play, these letter-reading scenes were entirely unsuitable for the non-traditional Dutch/Flemish production. Although the information conveyed through the letters constitutes a signal moment in McDonagh's original plot, the letters are dealt with quickly in the Dutch/Flemish adaptation. The essentially undramatic act of reading is "theatricalized" by presenting them in tandem (in parts eight and nine) and making the unauthorised receivers of the letters, Mag and Girleen, respectively, read them out, instead of Pato and Father Welsh. As such, the adaptation focuses not on the contents of the letters but on the effect they have when read by an unintended recipient. Mag's sense of threat is emphasized rather than her discovery of the contents of the letter, while Girleen, reading out the letter of her much-adored Father Welsh in scene five of *The Lonesome West*, is obviously frustrated at not being mentioned in his farewell message.

This is not the only moment where Girleen's hopes and frustrations are highlighted in the Dutch/Flemish trilogy. In McDonagh's script and in the British/Irish staging, Girleen is a minor character, who was possibly added to the text at the suggestion of Garry Hynes (Lonergan, "Druid Theatre's *Leenane Trilogy* on Tour" 151). In the Dutch/Flemish adaptation she becomes a far more interesting, multi-dimensional character. Girleen first appears on stage in part one, observing Mick Dowd's and Thomas Hanlon's bullying of Mairtin Hanlon from the background, as well as overhearing allegations regarding the death of Dowd's wife (*Plays 1* 93–94). She is carrying a suitcase, as if about to leave, or having just arrived. She re-appears backstage in part seven to witness Father Welsh scalding his hands in Valene's melting plastic figurines (159). In addition to her limited role as "character" in *The Lonesome West*, Girleen also becomes a prominent witness of Leenane's violence in the entire trilogy. Despite her teenage flirtations and vulgar language, Girleen possesses a disarming sense of naïveté which makes her rise above the misery, gloom, and malice that typifies her neighbors.

As Girleen's character is made more prominent in the Dutch/Flemish production, her lines and actions weigh more heavily than perhaps original-ly intended in McDonagh's script. Her lake-side dialogue with Father Welsh hardly features in analyses of *The Leenane Trilogy*, but in fact provides a key to the vision of the Dutch and Flemish adaptators. In this scene from *The Lonesome West*, Father Welsh and Girleen comment on the number of men who have drowned themselves in the lake at Leenane. Father Welsh, distraught and inebriate, is no longer the authority on matters of life and death, but Girleen gives evidence of her life-instinct:

Welsh: We should be scared of their ghosts so but we're not scared. Why's that?
Girleen: You're not scared because you're pissed to the gills. I'm not scared because . . . I don't know why. One, because you're here, and two, because . . . I don't know. I don't be scared of cemeteries at night either. The opposite of that, I do *like* cemeteries at night.
Welsh: Why, now? Because you're a morbid oul tough?
Girleen: (*embarrassed throughout*): Not at all. I'm not a tough. It's because . . . even if you're sad or something, or lonely or something, you're still better off than them lost in the ground or in the lake, because . . . at least you've got the *chance* of being happy, and even if it's a real little chance, it's more than them dead ones have. And it's not that you're saying "Hah, I'm better than ye," no, because in the long run it might end up that you have a worse life than ever they had and you'd've been better off as dead as them, there and then. But at least when you're still here there's the *possibility* of happiness, and it's like them dead ones know that, and they're happy for you to have it. They say "Good luck to ya." (*Quietly.*) Is the way I see it anyways. (*Plays 1* 176–77, emphasis in original)

In the Dutch/Flemish production, the entire trilogy, including this lake-side scene, is performed in a minimalist graveyard setting, which amplifies the significance of Girleen's words. If the dead are so oppressively present in Leenane, if the violence leads to nothing except more deaths, what purpose is there in life for the living? Thomas Hanlon and Father Welsh have no answer to this question and choose to die, but Girleen embraces life because of "the *chance* of being happy . . . even if it's a real little chance." There may not be much to hope for in Leenane, but at least for the living there is that little chance of happiness.

Girleen's lines give evidence of a sparkling innocence that mitigates the bleakness of Leenane. Her views on life and death grant her presence on stage a different meaning: while her fellow characters literally "walk over" dead bodies on the cemetery-stage, Girleen "rises above" the dead. She is the only one of the characters in *The Leenane Trilogy* who can transcend the village's oppression. Even her anger over not being mentioned in Father Welsh's goodbye letter is swept away by her belief that his death will provide salvation for Coleman's and Valene's frighting. Girleen witnesses the events in Leenane; she is rude and violent; but she is also a teenager with naïve but powerful hopes and dreams.

In the Dutch/Flemish adaptation, Girleen's innocence develops into a more powerful dramatic tool than it does in the British/Irish production. Her unique status is reinforced by other aspects of the dramaturgy. For example, the suitcase in her first appearance on stage suggests mobility, an opportunity for mutability, and serves as a mirror image to Maureen's escape with her suitcase at the end of *The Beauty Queen of Leenane*. Maureen's teenage illusions are illustrated by the song which appears on the radio, "J'aime la vie" ("I love life"), the only song with which Belgium ever won the Eurovision song contest, and which was performed by a then fourteen-year-old girl (throughout the adaptation, Eurovision songs serve as alternatives to the Irish music selected by McDonagh and/or Garry Hynes). For Maureen, having just killed her mother, the "I love life" lyrics are painfully ironic, whereas for Girleen, the "real little chance" of being happy contains significant elements of hope.

Girleen's neighbors minimize the distance and difference between the living and the dead because of their morbid and cruel outlook on life exemplified by their battering of skulls, bones, family, and friends with equal fervor. In McDonagh's text, and even more so in the Dutch/Flemish adaptation, time is the villagers' enemy: nothing is going to change because the future will be cruel just as the present and the past are gruesome. For Girleen, the distance between the living and the dead is minimal for a very different reason. The dead and the living understand and do not envy each other. According to Girleen, the dead are merely separated from the living by time, but it is exactly the time left for the living, the time before death, which might make a difference between gloom and hope.

Girleen's speech about the living and the dead also gives substance to the level of theatricality and self-reflexivity in the Dutch/Flemish adaptation. The level of realism in McDonagh's *Trilogy* helps to illustrate this point. Neither Garry Hynes nor the team of director and dramaturges in the Dutch/Flemish adaptation chose to present these three plays as fully realistic drama. There is too much comedy and exaggeration in the script to fully maintain the fourth-wall illusion of typically realist drama. Nevertheless, the ways in which Irish director Garry Hynes and Dutch director Johan Simons compromise this fourth-wall illusion differ greatly.

Hynes, for instance, never intended to stage an authentic picture of Leenane. She explained in an interview with Cathy Leeney: "It's an artifice. It's not authentic. It's not meant to be. It's a complete creation, and in that sense it's fascinating." Nevertheless, Hynes asked her spectators "to believe in it for the moment they're watching it" (Hynes 204). Even at its most comic, Hynes's style of production does not undermine the conventions of realism. Her staging compels the audience to suspend its disbelief about the trilogy's subject matter. These contents, however, are a blend of the familiar and the grotesque and must be disorienting to the spectator. This sense of "confusion and ambiguity" (Lanters 220) invites a post-modernist reading of the trilogy, but the aesthetics of realism, so dominant in *The Leenane Trilogy*'s stage descriptions and in Druid's style of production, do not allow spectators or critics to make their imaginative engagement with the trilogy a constructive one. McDonagh poses a number of ontological questions about the world we live in, but as each play of the trilogy returns to the same point from which it departed, none of these investigations leads to any sense of hope, escape, or change. The message the audience receives is essentially a pessimistic one, a point articulated by Fintan O'Toole in his essay, "Shadows over Ireland."

The Dutch/Flemish production does not set out to answer any of these weighty questions but simply presents ontological uncertainty as part of the human condition. We cannot know the truth in this life nor in the next, but this is not necessarily a depressing thought. After all, as Girleen argues, the living still have hopes and dreams. The comic dimension in this adaptation, then, is of a more surrealist kind as it constantly mediates notions of real versus unreal, rehearsed versus improvised. An example of how the comic element lifts the play from the real up to the surreal and on to the level of metatheater is the way in which the tragedy of Coleman's and Valene's relationship is counteracted by postmodern theatricality. The two brothers from *The Lonesome West* are acted by two actors wearing similar, but otherwise inconspicuous, red-haired wigs. During one of their scuffles, their wigs fall off, but the two actors "save" this comic breach of illusion by returning the wig to its owner in a graceful throw. The audience does not know whether this is a deliberate exposition of dramatic convention or purely accidental, until it happens a second time, whereupon the mixed-up wigs are thrown back to each other in the same graceful gesture. This time, the incident not only exposes but also celebrates theatricality as a creative force within, across, and outside the boundaries of theater.

Throughout the trilogy, similar incidents emphasize the actors' double presence on stage as characters and as actors: when they change the props and set for their fellow-actors/characters; when they appear in the background during a scene from another play; or at times when they speak dialogues facing the audience instead of addressing one another. As the distinction between the actors' roles as characters and their roles as actors is deliberately blurred, the lines they speak develop into metatheatrical commentaries on the nature of drama. As such, the actors' double roles on the graveyard stage, as well as the deliberately theatrical playfulness, illustrate the many dimensions of Girleen's ruminations on life and death. Just as Girleen rises above the dead in the graveyard, so do the actors transcend the limitations of the stage. Life provides few answers to the villagers of Leenane and Leenane provides no answers to the audience, but art has the potential to rise above issues of life and death. Theater as mimesis exposes the cruelty, violence, and darkness of the human condition, but at the same time, the adaptation's self-reflexive theatricality suspends this condition to provide momentary escape. The remarkable vitality with which the Dutch and Flemish actors (en)act their roles in the Dutch/

Flemish production is possible only because Girleen's vision of the meaning of life permeates the complete actor/character relationship.

The final scene of the adapted trilogy, corresponding with the final scene in *The Lonesome West*, epitomizes this celebration of theatricality in a partly rehearsed, partly improvised moment. Coleman is about to reveal to Valene his torture of Valene's cherished dog, but intensifies the mental torture by holding back the dramatic pace of his revelation:

Coleman: (*pause*) Is it evidence, so, you're after?
Valene: It *is* evidence I'm after, aye. Go bring me evidence you did cut the ears off me dog. And be quick with that evidence.
Coleman: I won't be quick at all. I will take me time.
He slowly gets up and ambles to his room, closing its door behind him. (*Plays 1* 190, emphasis in original)

In the Dutch/Flemish on-stage adaptation, Coleman plays with the words "I will take me time," and repeats them to the audience in the same wicked tone while he procrastinates on stage—"We have all the time in the world." When speaking such words to spectators who have concentrated on a marathon session of three and three-quarter hours of drama, who are looking forward to the play's completion as much as to fresh air and leg room, the actor's improvisation from the script encapsulates the height of postmodern theatricality. The siblings' mental abuse is at one of its most intense moments of the play, and this moment doubles as a commentary on the state of play without negating the cruelty or torture in the playscript, deferring and at once corroborating the trilogy's dramatic tension, its questions about the nature and meaning of life, and its celebration of theater's life-giving force.

The metatheatrical puns, as well as the rejection of a traditional introduction–development–dénouement structure in the Dutch/Flemish adaptation of *The Leenane Trilogy*, set this production apart from tragedy and tragicomedy, because "catharsis," the purging of emotions by the audience, is not its main purpose. Instead, this kind of theater returns to the original meaning of "play-acting," emphasizing the spontaneous play-for-pleasure. This type of play, similar to children's play, is not without depth or meaning. It redefines theater itself as the space of the archetypical "fool," operating outside the rules of society, resisting the usual laws of interpretation, and embodying the human urge to laugh in the most desperate of situations. There is no character of the "fool" in the trilogy, but the Dutch/Flemish adaptation transfers the features of the fool to theater as a medium. As such, drama becomes a powerful tool for subversion as well as a way to provide comic relief and life wisdom.

Contrasting two very different productions of the same trilogy illustrates the extent to which theatrical traditions influence a director's choices of how to stage a play, as well as on spectators' interpretations. Staging *The*

Leenane Trilogy as it was produced by Druid and Royal Court for an English-speaking audience would have been far less successful on the Dutch and Flemish stage than this adaptation, not only because the socio-historical context is different, but also because realism is a far less practiced style on the contemporary stage in these countries. Paradoxically, it takes a company with two dramaturges—the "watchdogs" of faithfulness to the original script—to take a much more liberal approach to a dramatic text than that of Druid or Royal Court. The adaptation was surprisingly faithful to Martin McDonagh's written text, but it sent radically different messages to the audience from the stage. The theatricalized style of production in the Dutch/Flemish adaptation was thus a seemingly minor operation with far-reaching consequences: it entirely rearranged the trilogy's multi-layeredness. The realistic production style emphasized *The Leenane Trilogy*'s pessimism, now and again lifted by witty humor, while the more "theatrical" staging brought to the fore those elements of the text that celebrate life, without negating any of the trilogy's darkness. Garry Hynes has expressed an interest in working with a dramaturge, someone who "has to do with the examination of the text in a wider context" (Hynes 207). Perhaps the custom of working with dramaturges, which has led to a much more experimental treatment of the dramatic text in Germany, the Netherlands, and Flanders, would have a similar impact on McDonagh productions on the English-speaking stage.

References

Anthonissen, Peter. "Moeder beu, vent nodig." Dutch-language rev. of *The Beauty Queen of Leenane*. *De Morgen* 15 Feb. 1999. N. pag. 19 Apr. 2006 <http://www.mediargus.be>.

Coveney, Michael. "He compares himself with the young Orson Welles. Oh Dear." *The Observer* 1 Dec. 1996: 13.

Diamond, Elin. *Unmaking Mimesis*. London: Routledge, 1997.

(Dis)Continuities: Trends and Traditions in Contemporary Theatre and Drama in English. Ed. M. Rubik and E. Mettinger-Schartmann. Trier, Germany: Wissenschaftlicher Verlag, 2002.

Dromgoole, Dominic. *The Full Room, An A-Z of Contemporary Playwriting*. London: Methuen, 2000.

Hynes, Garry. "Garry Hynes in Conversation with Cathy Leeney." *Theatre Talk: Voices of Irish Theatre Practitioners*. Ed. Lilian Chambers, Ger Fitzgibbon, Eamonn Jordan. Dublin: Carysfort P, 2001. 195–212.

Kroll, Jack. "The McDonagh Effect." *Newsweek* 16 Mar. 1998. N. pag. 15 May 2006 <http://www.lexisnexis.com>.

Lanters, José. "Playwrights of the Western World: Synge, Murphy, McDonagh." *A Century of Irish Drama: Widening the Stage*. Ed. Stephen Watt, Eileen Morgan, and Shakir Mustafa. Bloomington: Indiana UP, 2000. 204–20.

Leenane Trilogie (De), staged by Toneelhuis/Zuidelijk Toneel Hollandia. Premiere 3 May 2001 and Touring Flanders and The Netherlands. Revival 2001–2002 and 2003–2004.

Leenane Trilogy (The), staged by Druid Theatre/Royal Court. Premiere 21 June 1997 and Touring 1997–1998.

Lenz, Peter. "'Anything new in the feckin' west?': Martin McDonagh's *Leenane Trilogy* and the Juggling with Irish Literary Stereotypes." *(Dis)Continuities* 25–38.

Lonergan, Patrick. "'The Laughter Will Come of Itself. The Tears Are Inevitable': Martin McDonagh, Globalization and Irish Theatre Criticism." *Modern Drama* 47.4 (Winter 2004): 636–58.

——. "Druid Theatre's *Leenane Trilogy* on Tour: 1996–2001." *Irish Theatre on Tour.* Ed. Nicholas Grene and Christopher Morash. Dublin: Carysfort P, 2005. 146–68.

Luckhurst, Mary. "Contemporary English Theatre: Why Realism"? *(Dis)Continuities* 73–84.

McDonagh, Martin. *Plays 1 (The Beauty Queen of Leenane, A Skull in Conne-mara, The Lonesome West)*. London: Methuen, 1999.

——. *De Leenane Trilogie.* Trans. Peter Verhelst. Unpublished script, 2000. (Courtesy of Paul Slangen and Sarah Claeys).

Melens, Kurt. Interview with Sarah Claeys. "*The Leenane Trilogy*: An Ethnographic Study of Flemish Translation Practise." M.A. Thesis. Ghent U (Belgium), 2006.

O'Toole, Fintan. "Murderous Laughter." *Irish Times* 24 June 1997, Arts Section: 12.

——. "Nowhere Man." *Irish Times* 26 Apr. 1997, Supplement: 1. 15 May 2006.

——. "Shadows over Ireland." *American Theatre* 7 Jan. 1998. N. pag. 19 Apr. 1998.

Pilný, Ondřej. "Martin McDonagh: Parody? Satire? Complacency"? *Irish Studies Review* 12.2 (2004): 225–32.

Richards, Shaun. "'The outpouring of a morbid, unhealthy mind': The Critical Condition of Synge and McDonagh." *Irish University Review* 33.1–2 (Spring/Summer, 2003): 201–14.

Ross, Michael. "Hynes means business." *Sunday Times* 18 May 2003, Features: 10.

The Theatre of Martin McDonagh: A World of Savage Stories. Lilian Chambers and Eamonn Jordan, Ed. Dublin: Carysfort P, 2006.

Vandevelde, Karen. "Martin McDonagh's Irishness: Merely Icing on the Cake"? *The Theatre of Martin McDonagh: A World of Savage Stories* 349–62.

Wallace, Clare. "'Pastiche Soup,' Bad Taste, Biting Irony and Martin McDonagh." *Litteraria Pragensia: Studies in Literature and Culture* 15.29 (2005): 3–38.

6 Breaking bodies: The presence of violence on Martin McDonagh's stage

Maria Doyle

I do like finding out where the line is drawn, deliberately crossing it, bringing some of them with me across the line, and having them be happy that I did.

(George Carlin, *The Aristocrats*, 2005)

At the end of a performance of Martin McDonagh's *The Lieutenant of Inishmore* at the Atlantic Theater in New York City, the woman next to me turned from a stage bathed in blood and littered with rubber (yet realistic enough) body parts and commented, "They looked like they were having fun." It was an accurate assessment of the experience, from the first dribble of cat brains to the last blood-spattering execution; McDonagh has an odd way of using destruction to generate glee.[1] In McDonagh's repertoire *The Lieutenant* stands as the most unrelentingly violent and the most unrelentingly comic play, a piece that in fact turns the violence into play. Certainly McDonagh is not the only Irish dramatist to mix comedy and violence, which is a tactic popular from J. M. Synge to Marina Carr. Yet rather than alternating verbal comedy with unexpected moments of serious violence, McDonagh's story of a mad gunman returned home to seek vengeance for the death of his beloved cat employs the violence *as* comedy; the rising body count and the gallons of stage blood (five a night in the New York production)[2] become the literal substance of the escalating farce. Richard Hand and Michael Wilson's study of the Grand Guignol Theatre in France argues that those famed horror productions purposely restrained their use of stage blood because too much gushing liquid would generate laughter rather than fear (60). When the lights went up on the final scene of *The Lieutenant* that evening, revealing a stage doused in red—not only the windows and door that were spattered in the previous scene but also the floor was now pooled in sticky liquid that dripped over the edge of the playing area—that dictum proved true: the audience responded with the loudest laughter of the evening.

Martin McDonagh's approach to theater hinges on violence—violence recalled, violence threatened, violence narrated, and violence enacted. Yet what does violence mean in McDonagh's theater, and particularly, what does it mean when it is funny? And what is the value of having such comic violence take place on the stage in the continual present of the theater, performed by live actors? Comedy itself lives in the present much more fully than does tragedy. Fiona McIntosh argues that in tragedy, "the past is never, strictly speaking, past" while the future is similarly "made palpably real" in a way that freights the present moment with obligations to what was and is to come (56–57). Yet comedy derives its force from the imaginative play of the moment, the ability of characters to remake their circumstances as the situation demands—what Wylie Sypher calls "the agility of the clown" who is more flexible than the tragic hero who "dare[s] not *play* with life as the comic hero does" (239, emphasis in original). This genre is inherently creative and simultaneously subversive, because that remaking of worlds can threaten the established foundations on which the characters play.

McDonagh, dubbed by one critic "the bastard offspring of J. M. Synge and Quentin Tarantino" (Spencer 18), has argued that he takes his inspiration from film, a medium in which his Oscar-winning short film *Six Shooter* (2005) suggests he may find future success, and *The Lieutenant* exemplifies his claim that he wanted to "get as much John Woo and Sam Peckinpah into the theatre as possible" (quoted in Rosenthal 10). Audiences attuned to the sensibilities of *Pulp Fiction* and *The Sopranos* are used to characters who view violence as all in a day's work; thus "mad" Padraic's slightly peevish response when his father's phone call interrupts his torture session with a drug dealer—"I'm at work at the moment, Dad, was it important now"? (*TL* 13)—is not an altogether unfamiliar maneuver, even as it plays with the boundaries of law in lawlessness, normalcy in deviance. What intensifies the comedy, however, is not so much our particular awareness of the danger of this subject matter, as it is the shift to murderous buffoons with a political agenda instead of the generic gangsters McDonagh originally imagined for the piece (Dening 12), who place the play's play within a specific and active rhetorical debate.

We are also, however, particularly aware of the novelty of this kind of violence as stage material: director Wilson Milam has noted that unlike the many "great reloading moments in film," audiences "never see plays in which the characters have to reload their guns" (Segal C01), a disparity *The Lieutenant* seems determined to remedy. Some critics consider McDonagh's tactic unoriginal, a rehashing of the tropes of another genre (Pilný 230). Yet the translation of film conventions to the stage world reshapes our relationship to the material because we are conscious of these characters as present stage figures. When Padraic, for instance, reaches for the interrupting cell phone, he leaves a half-naked drug dealer swinging by his ankles only a few feet from the front row of the audience, instituting an immediacy that forces the audience into an intimate relationship with the actors that film cannot achieve.

Thus, while film may be McDonagh's model, his chosen medium of theater shapes both how violent actions must be framed and how audiences position themselves emotionally and intellectually in relation to the present moment. First performed in 2001 but composed in 1994, two years before his theatrical debut with *The Beauty Queen of Leenane*, *The Lieutenant of Inishmore* represents something of an experiment in how far a writer can push these boundaries. One reviewer has described the play as "a comedy so dark you practically need a torch" (Tweedie 10), and McDonagh admits that "this is the furthest I'm going to push this whole violence, black-comedy thing, because I don't think it can get much blacker or more violent" (quoted in Rosenthal 10). If McDonagh sees this play as the limit of comic violence, it is important to examine where that boundary lies, as well as how it is alternately threatened and maintained, both to understand the significance of constructing comedy out of violence and to reveal what this boundary suggests about how McDonagh employs violence in his wider work.

As Stanton Garner argues in *Bodied Spaces: Phenomenology and Performance in Contemporary Drama*, theater plays with the idea of presence: "the theatrical field offers itself in terms of an irreducible oscillation between perceptual levels" (42), a displacement of "presentness" that derives from perceiving objects and individuals that are not what they claim to be and an assertion of presence that stems from the tangible physical reality of light, of bodies, of objects. While an audience may thus be able to step back from danger and violence, asserting, "My fear at a play is not a real fear; I know this danger is not real" (40) because stage death is not, after all, real death, that disconnection is not total: "my fear" still exists as a response to the present reality of the stage world that emotionally involves audiences in its fictional constructs. Staging can deliberately blur these levels. The audience's fear for the safety of a character is an emotional response that can be rationalized away by the awareness of presentness disrupted, but the stage can simultaneously engage our anxiety for the actor performing the suffering: the actor's body brings the "play of actuality [. . .] to a point of illusionistic crisis" (43), heightening our response by overlaying the fictional and real worlds of the performance. Audiences are familiar with the mechanisms of certain kinds of violence, such as when trick knives or guns come into play, or when stage fights are badly choreographed, which mitigate this second level of fear. But when the illusion is not recognizable as an illusion, the more likely it is to produce that undercurrent of anxiety.

The Lieutenant throws this dynamic into powerful relief in its second scene when the lights come up on James, the marijuana dealer, who appears "*bare-chested, bloody and bruised* [. . .], *hang[ing] upside down from the ceiling, his feet bare and bloody*" while "**Padraic** *idles near him, wielding a cut-throat razor, his hands bloody*" (TL 10). While the opening moment of the play has offered us the spectacle of a dead cat, but one that is obviously an object, a stuffed facsimile of Padraic's beloved Wee Thomas, the spectacle of James functions very differently because the theatrical display has shifted from bloody object to bleeding subject. Clearly, the character has suffered, as the makeup bruises and fake blood on his foot signify Padraic's forceful assertion of disciplinary authority, and the nearly acted-on assertion that he will suffer further in front of us threatens to implicate the audience in violence performed at least in part for our benefit. In remarks with profound implications for this scene, Keir Elam argues that "it is the spectator who *initiates* the theatrical communication process. [. . .] In sponsoring the performance, the audience issues, as it were, a collective 'directive' to the performers" (95–96, emphasis in original), while Garner argues that the audience is at least partly conscious of "the fact that this spectacle is set in motion by our gaze" (49), going on to suggest that the audience "sanctions" the events of the stage world. Catherine Rees directly relates such perceived culpability to *The Lieutenant*, arguing that "the audience is also implicated in the violence because we are vicariously enjoying it" (30), while Charles Spencer suggests that the most violent scenes in the play "create [. . .] a conspiracy of guilty hilarity," a trio of quite telling terms. Thus, the audience's perception of the actor himself and the literal, very present discomfort of his having to play the scene while suspended by the ankles from the ceiling generates greater awareness of the actor and his "impressive display of physical stamina" (James E1) than we would display while watching a film. That awareness, however, far from decreasing our investment in the scene, augments it by disturbing the boundaries of the theatrical fiction.

McDonagh wastes no time in offering this striking visual moment, telegraphing the play's desire to manipulate the audience into accepting a rising level of violent spectacle. While all of his other plays present scenes of disturbing violence against both people and objects, most save the particularly jarring visual images for later in the play, such as Cripple Billy's beating in *The Cripple of Inishmaan* (1996), Maureen Folan's torture of her mother in *The Beauty Queen of Leenane* (1996), and Coleman Conner's destruction of his brother's stove and his ceramic figurines in *The Lonesome West* (1997). Those plays prepare us for these assaults in the opening scenes by throwing the audience into a verbally violent world that simultaneously sets the tone for the possibility of physical violence and manipulates us into believing that people will not actually do such things, at least not in front of us. Horrific threats are often perceived as part of the creative one-upmanship that enlivens the characters' verbal sparring, or, as William Boles puts it, "as the violent and rather shocking exchanges take place, spectators, engrossed in laughter, miss the sinister overtones of these conversations" (129). Thus, when Maureen pours boiling oil over her mother's hand, for instance, in *The Beauty Queen*, the shock comes not just from the fact that we are witnessing this act but that we have disbelieved Mag when she levels the charge that Maureen burns her hand.[3]

Made thus present, the torture of Mag now forces us to see that we have stepped beyond the safe boundaries of a form that has taught us to read spinster daughters as victims of nagging mothers and to take "creative" retorts as mere intellectual exercises for our amusement, a situation that in turn generates a reassessment of our own powers of perception.

The Lieutenant likewise opens with McDonagh's characteristically biting dialogue, liberally sprinkled with iterations of the euphemism "feck," threats, and descriptions of past violence, but it quickly launches into the realm of physical violence earlier than in his other works. Thus, the very first stage image features Padraic's father Donny holding the dripping, dead cat up by the tail and then kicking the teenaged neighbor Davey for bringing the dead cat back to the house. This violent scene indicates an immediate desire to experiment with the literal presence of violent action and violent after-effect. The action that follows continues McDonagh's pattern of escalating violence, as the play moves on to a triple murder committed onstage and a protracted scene of mass dismemberment, a movement that allows the play to reconstruct our preconceived notions of bodies.

Therefore, the character James has the potential to become a prop before us, a figure whom Padraic has contained as a vessel upon which to demonstrate his authority. Ultimately James does succeed in fighting back, taking advantage of Padraic's "slow [. . .] fecking train [of thought]" (*TL* 12) to win his freedom by ingratiating himself as a fellow cat lover. Yet the presence of James's vulnerable body here signals the potential for bodies in the play to be stripped of their humanness, and we are forced to confront from the very beginning the fact that people in this play will actually do very bad things to one another. If the delay of visualizing the violence augments our terror at Mag's suffering in *The Beauty Queen*, *The Lieutenant*'s series of escalating visual shocks seems calculated to lead us by degrees into a very different relationship to the disturbing events that follow. In *The Beauty Queen* we have had to reassess the alignment of our sympathies; in the later play, the continual presence of violence makes it difficult to establish any allegiance at all, leaving us on shifting, unstable ground.

McDonagh's particular success in this maneuver comes partly through an astute manipulation of basic tenets of old-fashioned forms like melodrama and farce—Ben Brantley calls him "one of the few contemporary playwrights [. . .] who never leaves loopholes in his plot" ("Terrorism" E1)—and partly through a narrative sleight of hand that keeps the audience uncertain about how far the playwright will go to disrupt the safety zone implied by the familiarity of these structures. Eric Bentley argues that "in all comedy, there remains something of destructive orgy, farce being the kind of comedy which disguises this fact least thoroughly" (xiii), and asserts further that farce employs violence in an abstracted way by unrealistically escalating its assaults, rendering the action a psychological "safety valve" (xii–xiii). While McDonagh's farce does employ multiplication—

two dead cats, four dead terrorists shot with two guns each, sixteen eyes shot out before and during the action—what seems on one level to be fantastical is actually less a distorted exaggeration than a representation of violence that is too disturbingly real. After all, Irish nationalist paramilitaries did target petty criminals, bombs did go off in shops, and bodies of victims did often end up in pieces. The farcical mold creates safety using material that is inherently unsafe, and McDonagh alternately mitigates and exacerbates the emotional danger for the audience through the way that he manipulates our perception of the mangled bodies we encounter in this play world.

McDonagh has been categorized as one of Britain's "New Brutalists," a group of young playwrights devoted to generating a "visceral response" in the audience (Boles 126) through a new level of "verbal and physical atrocities" (Broich 210). When *The Lieutenant* opened at the Royal Shakespeare Company in 2001, critics frequently compared it to Sarah Kane's *Blasted* (1995), which many have identified as the starting point of the New Brutalist movement. One commentator went so far as to assert that McDonagh's play "makes *Blasted* look like the *Teletubbies*" (Lawson 20) and another raised the specter of Kane's intensely graphic play only to assert that nevertheless "*The Lieutenant of Inishmore* is certainly the most gruesome play [she had] ever seen" (Clapp 10). The comparison, however, seems oddly incongruous; if *The Lieutenant* resembles *Blasted* in the level of violence in the play, the nature of that violence differs drastically. In *Blasted* a soldier eats another man's eyes out of his head after raping him, the culmination of a series of enacted, described, and implied acts of sexual aggression and torture, some of them previously perpetrated by Ian, the now blinded victim. Mary Luckhurst claims that

> *The Lieutenant* does seem a rather obvious attempt to outdo [Kane] for blood and guts. But whereas Kane's aesthetic agenda was serious and uncompromising in terms of her refusal to accept limits on naturalistic representation, McDonagh has responded with comic strip violence. (38)[4]

The difference Luckhurst defines, however, can alternately be described as one of intimacy: in Kane's play, violence as an assertion of power is never far removed from violence as an expression of need, and this distorted need manifests itself as an assault of one body on another, sometimes with the aid of a gun, but never with a gun by itself. *The Lieutenant*'s characters, however, adore guns. Nearly everyone but the cat tries to shoot someone, and this excessive violence is significantly framed as an activity that preserves distance: even Padraic, whose signature shot is two guns at point-blank range, still keeps his victims at arm's length, the goal being eradication, or perhaps reconstruction, rather than enforced connection. While Kane's characters seem to seek a reflection and validation of the self through violence, McDonagh's perpetrators, when they are not shooting one another, literally seek to reshape their victims to assert their own sense of the proper order of things. Thus Mairead renders cows one-eyed (a protest against the meat trade that she justifies with the claim that "there's no profit at all in taking ten blind cows to market [. . .] . For who would want to buy a blind cow"?) to Padraic's effort to enforce gender norms by chopping off Davey's "girl's minge" (*TL* 19, 42) of hair. James serves as a body template for this kind of activity. The threat of "nipples off" (12) becomes the play's way of signaling its desire to evoke the taboo boundary of intimate violence, and significantly, it never approaches any closer to sexual violence against James or anyone else; to do so would disrupt the comedic distance McDonagh's balancing act requires. In the end, however, "toenails off" (11), an act detached from the audience's perception, suf- fices for the construction of a visual rhetoric that uses violence to strip away details and differences, the particulars of identity.

As the play progresses to bigger acts of mutilation than those perpe- trated or threatened against James, it keeps them offstage, like the toenail removal. Showing only the aftermath of particular and particularly dis- turbing acts thus eliminates half of the audience's investment in them because we are not drawn into the mechanism of the violent act in the same way that we are led to ponder the stamina of the actor playing James and further prevents us from observing the bond created between charac- ters in the moment of violent contact. Perhaps one of the most telling examples of how McDonagh's play uses this distance to its comedic advantage is in sixteen-year-old paramilitary wannabe Mairead's blinding of the three INLA men who have set out to entrap Padraic. Blinding is an "archetypal act of cruelty" (Peter 16), and its performance onstage is particularly unsettling since it serves as a physical and irrevocable stripping of the victim's external perception. A. C. Bradley has argued that the scene of Gloucester's blinding in *King Lear* is essential to evoking the imagina- tive, readerly world of the drama but constitutes "a blot upon *King Lear* as a stage play" because in performance "the mere physical horror of such a spectacle would [. . .] be a sensation so violent as to [. . .] seem revolt- ing or shocking" (251). This sentiment is certainly echoed in audiences' responses to Ian's blinding in Kane's *Blasted*, the scene that John Peter notes "most upset people" (16). Yet in both cases, part of the horror of the scene derives from the physical proximity of attacker and victim, the intimate disruption of bodily boundaries, which in *Blasted* becomes a disturbingly cannibalistic communion. Moreover, witnessing an act of tor- ture this gruesome requires that the audience consider the victim's pain, and our awareness of pain leads to an awareness of human suffering: the character Ian is far from ideal as a human being, but his anguish is palp- able both in the moment of his loss and in its aftermath.

Not only are we moved by the vulnerability of the victim and the irrevo- cability of the action, but also by our perception of the precariousness of the actor's position, partaking as he is in what appears to us to be a dangerous, or at least unfamiliar, bit of stagecraft. While McDonagh's play engages that actorly anxiety in the cause of the trussed-up James, it follows Bradley's logic regarding the Gloucester scene in shifting the site of the blinding to the imagined rather than the enacted world of the play. Thus, while McDonagh's play may be "a horrible comedy version" (Peter 16) of what happens in *Blasted,* this horror is significantly out of our range of vision: what enables the comedy is, in this case, the fact that the blinding has been accomplished offstage, at a distance and quickly, as the stage directions indicate that the shooting is *"rapid fire"* (*TL* 50). This is not to say that the audience has not anticipated this possibility. If the act is out of our field of vision, it is certainly not out of the realm of expectation: when Padraic is dragged offstage to be shot by his former INLA comrades who are responsible for Wee Thomas's demise, there is one gun unaccounted for whose owner has a penchant for aiming at eyes, and if we have temporarily forgotten Mairead, the audible click that Donny and Davey respond to reminds us of her signature action, telegraphing the attack to follow. Mairead's efforts in this arena have thus far been less than totally effective: she misses her brother's eye when she attempts to shoot him in the third scene, and although she has shot out the eyes of numerous cows, she has not wholly blinded them, merely eliminated their depth perception, which is in itself an interesting metaphor for the play's use of violence.

When Mairead succeeds with human targets, however, the play takes pains to frame the act as "fair," competing as she is with three gun-toting members of the INLA rather than cows or a boy with a pink bicycle; other characters later describe her method of attack as sporting (56). Cast in a farcical frame that generates a type of suspense that "springs from the recognition of the familiar, the fulfillment of an expectation" (Esslin 121), the plot leads us to anticipate the act with a pleasure that derives at least in part from the momentary anxiety over whether the play will actually obey the rules of the comic frame and step across the boundary to complete the projected action. This suspense, combined with the speed of assault and the fact that it takes place offstage, eliminates the audience's moral depth perception, cutting it off from contemplation of the victims' pain, a situation compounded by the fact that at least two of the three INLA men do not suffer long before Padraic "ends their pain" with two gunshots to the head.

This scene in which Mairead and Padraic jointly execute the INLA men manipulates our perceptions of the meaning of stage space in order to reconfigure our sense of the meaning of violent action. Gay McAuley's *Space in Performance: Making Meaning in the Theatre* asserts that "it is movement rather than mimesis that is the characteristic of theatre" and that all stage interactions are "necessarily spatialized" (92, 94). In the climactic scene of *The Lieutenant* the stage directions suggest that the scene creates two kinds of space existing simultaneously: the blinded gunmen, shooting in a frenzy from the various apertures of the house seem to inhabit a different plane altogether from Mairead and Padraig, who *"seem to almost glide across the room, their eyes locked on each other"* (TL 52). While literally inhabiting what is a single theatrical space, Donny's Inishmore cottage, the characters' movements suggest two very different ways that violence shapes the meaning of the space. For the blinded INLA men, the house is a "safe" base from which to attack an exterior menace, and their literally blind shooting suggests a violence that is a haphazard defense against an ambiguous threat—was the shooter "a boy with lipstick" or "a girl with no boobs" (51) and where exactly has that hermaphroditic culprit gone? Significantly, having been deprived of one sense, the men's response deprives them of the use of another mode of perception, their hearing, as the noise of the gunshots prevents them from noticing Mairead and Padraic's entrance.[5] The blind, deaf, reactive reprisal leads directly to Brendan, Joey, and Christy's deaths, creating a space in which to maneuver for a different kind of violence. Thus, while the play highlights violence as reaction, it also offers a critique of the failure of that approach.

Mairead and Padraic's more decisive, gliding motion through this space, their clearly directed gaze, and their silence, allows them to inhabit what seems to the audience to be an almost separate sphere in which the INLA men become props in a wordless seduction. Guns have served as a mediating factor in the initiation of this romance. Significantly, the only violence Mairead is directly menaced with in the play is Padraic's threat to shoot her point blank when she refuses to give him news about the health of his cat. When she responds by *"point[ing her air] rifle towards one of his eyes, so that the barrel is almost resting against it"* (35), Mairead effectively counters Padraic's threat by defining the intimate potential of the exchange on her own terms, which he understands. If Padraic's "proper guns" (53) are more powerful, Mairead's is physically larger, producing a stage picture in which she is at least as potent as he is.

Moreover, her stance in this first encounter encroaches on his bodily space, thus threatening intimacy more clearly, as her gun nearly touches him. Now these guns work in tandem, Mairead's offstage and Padraic's onstage, and once inside the house Padraic shoots decisively, two guns at close range, while Mairead encourages him physically, *"caressing the muscles in his back and shoulders"* (52). When the pair concludes the killing spree with a passionate kiss, the performance of violence becomes layered with an erotic charge, a choice that further reveals that it is not the violent act itself, the negotiation of power between aggressor and victim, which creates intimacy, but the physicality of the conspiracy between aggressors. While Patrick Lonergan argues that this scene demonstrates that "terrorist violence is shown not to impede sexual expression but to facilitate it" (75), it is not the sex as sex that is significant but rather the means by which destruction seems to breed conspiratorial intimacy. The joint participation in the killing thus solidifies the romantic bond between Padraic and Mairead by enabling a communal defense against an outside threat. Moreover, the

silent presence of violence within the house visually suggests the insidiousness of violence lurking beyond the understanding of the men who think
their enemy is still shooting at them from outside. The play, for all its
blood-spattering gore, is, McDonagh claims, "wholeheartedly anti-violence"
(quoted in O'Hagan 33), and the dual-layered assault of this scene uses the
confluence of comedic subversiveness and eroticized destructiveness to suggest both the seductiveness of violence and the insidiousness of its ability
to destroy from within.

McDonagh keeps the most disturbing acts of violence against the living
offstage so as to maintain the sometimes precarious balance of the comedy. Yet the play revels in the display of disturbing acts committed against
the dead. From the opening scene, in which the *"bits of brain* [*that*] *plop
out"* (*TL* 3) of the cat's mangled head serve as answer to the question,
"Do you think he's dead"?, the play's pointed destruction of bodies serves
as its most obvious transgression of taboo spaces, both culturally and
theatrically. If violence ravages bodies throughout the play—a toenail,
hair, (almost) a nipple, an eye—it is in "stage" death that the body becomes
completely a prop, entirely malleable and subject to the whims of the
survivors. This pacifying of the body can be read politically. On one level,
all the dead are members of the INLA and the play's comic claim to have
eradicated this particular terrorist offshoot—Donny, surveying the carnage
in his living room, exclaims, "Sure there's no fecker left in the INLA now"
(66)—suggests that all the violence of the play has actually destroyed those
who seem to be the most obvious perpetrators of violence. This point is
reinforced when Donny and Davey, the least politically aligned of the
characters, decide to shoot the miraculously returned Wee Thomas and
find that they cannot do it, opting instead to coo over him and offer him
Frosties.

While *The Lieutenant* may in part be an effort to cathartically purge
Irish society of the ranks of Irish paramilitaries,[6] it also bears a disquieting
resemblance to a number of other scenes in McDonagh's repertoire involving the wanton destruction of objects. For example, in *The Cripple of
Inishmaan,* broken eggs become a running joke, culminating in Slippy
Helen's mashing of four eggs on her brother Bartley's head and Bartley's
subsequent smashing of the rest of the eggs on the store counter. Likewise,
The Lonesome West contains repeated acts of object mutilation, as Coleman
first boils his brother's holy figurines, shoots up his prized stove, and then
smashes the replacement ceramic figurines with the butt of a rifle. McAuley
argues that "the crucial factor in defining a stage object is [. . .] human
intervention" (176), the ability of the actor to make an audience aware
of a prop in a particular way so as to generate meaning. She suggests
that "a thing onstage becomes an object if it is touched, manipulated or
simply looked at or spoken about by an actor" (176); how much more
forcefully such things come to our attention when they are smashed to
smithereens.

Such shows of force in both cases are displaced assaults—attacks against Helen's possessions instead of Helen and against Valene's authority rather than Valene himself. Breaking Helen's eggs, for instance, not only threatens her income but also destroys her characteristic method of physical assault on those around her, notorious as she is for "pegging eggs" (*TC* 72) at nearly everyone within striking distance. Similarly, Valene's figurines both occupy the space and mark it as particularly his, evidenced by the "V" he inscribes on each new addition to the collection. His inscriptions thus seem to represent a claim that is both orderly and visible, and the boiling of one set followed by the smashing of its replacement is not just an assault on an object but a deliberate erasure of the boundaries the objects purport to set up: the boiled figures melt into one indistinguishable mass, while the smashed ceramic fragments are scattered around the room, making highly doubtful Coleman's assertion that perhaps they can be repaired with superglue (*BQLOP* 257).

Moreover, the figurines not only represent Valene's authority but also one of the traditional external forces of authority in rural, Catholic Ireland: since they are miniatures of the saints, their destruction, twice, reinforces the play's rejection of church authorities and provides a graphic indication of the failure that Father Welsh-Walsh-Welsh's suicide/sacrifice will become. As such, the now destroyed objects bear the brunt of their destroyers' sense of subordinate rage: Bartley and Coleman fight back, decisively if indirectly, against those who have held power over them.

This pattern of object destruction as an outraged effort to claim dominance reappears in *A Skull in Connemara* (1997), which transfers these assaults to a more taboo space, the body itself, a circumstance that invites closer comparison to the closing bloodbath of *The Lieutenant*. Of course, *Connemara*'s bodies are seven years dead, bones Mick O'Dowd has been hired by the priest to remove from the churchyard so new bodies can be put in the recently vacated graves. The third scene opens with skulls and bones laid out on a table as Mick hands his co-digger Mairtin a mallet. Earlier in the play, Mick has joked that he disposes of the bodies by smashing them to bits but then retracts the statement, distancing himself from the image by saying, "Sure what do you take me for"? (*BQLOP* 100), and providing a plausible counter-story of the bones sunk in the lake with "a string of prayers" (100) said over them. Yet in this later scene he and Mairtin hammer bones with great relish, using the occasion to take out their frustrations on the memory of the deceased.

Both scenes have the potential to involve the audience in quite immediate ways beyond the shock of the desecration of the body. For instance, all that bone smashing creates the potential for debris. As Brantley cautioned in his review of the 2001 New York production:

> When you give a couple of strong, drunken Irishmen a pair of mallets and a set of skeletons to demolish, as only Mr. McDonagh would, it's only natural that some of those soiled white fragments would fly

beyond the proscenium arch. Audience members should be prepared to duck. ("Leenane III" E1).

Similarly, the London production of *The Lieutenant* included concealed squibs in the rubber dummies being dismembered, in order to create "spontaneous" splatter as Donny and Davey hack away (White 7), a messiness also not necessarily contained by the edge of the playing area. Such debris encroaches on the space of the audience—an intrusion McDonagh says he "love[s]" creating[7]—and intensifies the discomfort of those wishing to maintain their separation from the stage world by physically including some of the observers in the moment of performance. Because that inclusion involves dusting the audience in fictional blood and bone, "bodily" remnants, the discomfort is intensified. Like the unavoidable presence of the upside-down James in *The Lieutenant,* these scenes play with the presentness of the theatrical action, feeding our anxiety over the inability of the playing area to contain the fiction it enacts into our anxiety at what is being depicted in the fiction.

Both the bone-bashing in *Connemara* and the body-chopping in *The Lieutenant* extend their carnage over a long verbal exchange; sometimes the physical activity is the primary focus of our attention and sometimes it is background to conversation on other topics, an extension of the quotidian attitude to violence demonstrated in Padraig's cell phone conversation with his father. Thus, unlike the previous examples—*Inishmaan*'s eggs, *Lonesome West*'s figurines—these assaults on the human body draw us into the action more intently by overlaying a seemingly trivial spoken dialogue with a performed action calculated to disturb us. While Mick and Mairtin discuss the shortcomings of the newly pulverized deceased and debate whether it is worse to drown in urine or vomit (*BQLOP* 141), Mick nonetheless feels the need to set rules for the skull battering. "Don't be cursing now," Mick instructs Mairtin, "Not while you're handling the departed" (139)—as if to impose a level of decorum on the otherwise indecorous proceedings. Further incongruity is provided by the syrupy folkiness of Dana's "All Kinds of Everything" as a soundtrack. Similarly, Donny and Davey in *The Lieutenant* pass the time while chopping up the INLA men by comparing Mairead's and Padraic's shooting styles, pondering the relative merits of joining the IRA instead of the INLA and witnessing Padraic and Mairead's engagement (*TL* 55). Unlike the rapid fire that allows us to stand at a remove from the INLA men's blinding, the slow pace of these scenes, in which characters' destructive activities form the extended backdrop to lengthy and sometimes equally macabre conversations, forces us into an increasingly unsettling relationship to the actions depicted onstage. This sustained discomfort adds a peculiar edge to the laughter that accompanies the scenes' verbal and visual absurdities.

In *Connemara* the climactic scene becomes both a taboo wish fulfillment and a means of revelation: inviting the drunken Mairtin to join in the proceedings eventually leads to Mick's discovery that Mairtin and his friends are responsible for digging up the bones of Mick's possibly beloved, possibly murdered wife Oona. Significantly, it is the conversation that proves more dangerous than the bone-bashing as the information it shakes loose leads to the assault offstage on a living human head. Mick's and Mairtin's bone-crushing, however, proves a cathartic release in a way that the limb severing Donny and Davey are compelled to partake in during *The Lieutenant* cannot. While violating proscriptions against the desecration of the dead, Mick's and Mairtin's action can ultimately be viewed as a "safe" mode of violence against those who will feel no pain from the encounter. The very fact that the bones have been dug up in the first place at the request of the local priest suggests that the bones have become insignificant because the priest has offered no advice on how they are to be disposed of properly. Moreover, the audience has no human frame of reference in viewing the bones, which limits the residual humanity contained in them, allowing it more easily to perceive them as objects. While Mick and Mairtin identify them as specific individuals and mix particular insults with their hammer swings, the audience's inability to connect the bones to a body makes this an allowable release. Ben Brantley terms this scene "an oddly ecstatic spectacle" ("Leenane III" E1)—rather like a grotesque version of the Mundy sisters' frenzied dance that lets inner demons out to play for a bit in Brian Friel's *Dancing at Lughnasa* (1990). Only at the end of *Connemara*, when Mick gently kisses Oona's (mostly) preserved skull, does the audience have the opportunity to see the bones as actual human remains rather than objectified playthings.

In *The Lieutenant*, Donny and Davey engage, however, in a very different kind of task, one that they complete by compulsion, an important caveat given that these bodies still look like bodies, not bones, as the rubber dummies have been made up to resemble closely their human counterparts. Here we have an inversion of that first striking scene with James: there, we imagine suffering we do not see and respond to the discomfort of the actor, while here we see quite graphically but respond to what the actors are doing and how their method forces us to reencounter the action. Thus, the dummies that are being destroyed in the final scene of the play are doubly charged—realistically done but obviously fake. They are activated both by their relationship to the characters they represent and to the actors who dismantle them and thus contain a residual humanity, attested to by the "blood" that has poured out of them onto the playing area. Circumventing the question of whether the play will engage in this level of gruesomeness by bringing the lights up on a scene already littered with body parts, *The Lieutenant*'s dialogue intensifies the audience's response to the scene. Characters not only pause to saw at an arm or a neck but also comment on the technical difficulties of the task—"Boy, spines are awful hard sawing, I'll tell ya" and "Be aiming for the vertebree is easiest" (*TL* 64). This tactic makes it impossible for the audience to escape—we have already been plunged into the premise—or to ignore what is happening in front of us. Such attention to technical detail contributes both to the scene's horror and its squeamish humor.

The acts of object destruction in McDonagh's earlier plays are often linked to an effort to claim authority by rewriting, however indirectly, the identity of a human victim, and *The Lieutenant* uses the destruction in a similar way. Yet here the frame destabilizes the concept of identity itself more fully. Donny and Davey gain no authority from this activity: instead it is the self-proclaimed lieutenants, Padraic and later Mairead, who assert the necessity of the chopping, having provided the raw material for it, and who indicate how it is to be done. They demonstrate a practical concern with rendering the bodies unidentifiable, as Mairead instructs Donny and Davey to "[b]e knocking them teeth out them mouths, now. It does hamper the identification process" (57). This maneuver suggests a perceived control that is connected to their earlier efforts to remake the world on their own terms. Padraic, for instance, believes that he can command his destiny, rewriting his identity as it suits him, as he contemplates splintering from his splinter group, ultimately "award[ing] himself a full-blown lieutenant-ship" (57) in an army of two.

It is in part the INLA's desire to reassert their control over his identity that brings them to Inishmore in the first place, making their ultimate erasure—and Padraic's as well—on Donny's cottage floor more ironic. In a play where one dead black cat looks very much like another, to everyone, that is, except Mairead who recognizes her Sir Roger even without the collar Davey anxiously tosses out the window, the scene suggests the similar instability of human identity, the ability of death to reduce bodies to uniformly unidentifiable component parts. Hardly a cathartic purging, then, this activity suggests the profound instability of the chaos generated by the play's escalating cycle of violence, particularly when Padraic is eventually added to the pile for dismantling. As Lonergan asserts, the play "leaves spaces that demand to be filled" (76), and in the absences that the play pointedly generates, the audience must grope its way towards filling that void.

This uncertainty extends in the end even to the play's title, as Padraic's death allows Mairead to "inherit" his lieutenantship. In what army she holds this rank is, however, unclear, particularly given that the gun-slinging Mairead ultimately accedes to McDonagh's "anti-violence" agenda. The change in Mairead comes about not because she has been victimized by violence—as when in Kane's *Blasted* Cate offers the potential for redemption by feeding her now mutilated rapist, a qualified gesture of compassion spawned, presumably, by shared victimization—or because she has a moral revulsion against it. Rather, she has experienced the power of violence and found it wanting: when asked if she is going to go off and join the paramilitaries after Padraic's death, she ponders, "I thought shooting fellas would be fun, but it's not. It's dull" (66). While discovering that killing is not "fun" hardly seems a moral revelation, Mairead's last moments onstage suggest a more thorough reorientation of perspective. Cradling the dead

Sir Roger as she leaves, Mairead has not completely abandoned her republican ideals, but the awareness that the practitioners of that philosophy are hardly themselves ideal generates a degree of distance between Mairead, who must think things over for "a biteen," and militant nationalism (66). Her singing now suggests this shift: if her earlier verse about "O'Hanlon [. . .] [who's] just gone sixteen" (32) suggests that she is reading her similarly aged self into the republican tradition that "The Patriot Game" represents, she has now become instead executioner to a "dying rebel" (65). This circumstance skews the clarity of the ideological frame the songs seek to impose, a fact echoed in her cat Sir Roger (Casement)'s "murder," which is doubly problematic because it has been perpetrated by a professed lover of cats and a supposed patriot. Not only has the image of militant republicanism proven to be a troubled basis for belief, but also, Mairead's own position within that system is likewise unstable: by the end of the play the ideological system sustained by violence has imploded.

The play ends with the entrance of a body that is seemingly uncontrollable. A real cat, well-trained or not, has the potential to disrupt the theatrical boundary by not "acting" as he ought. McDonagh says he "always wanted to involve something live, for the thrill of seeing what the actors would do" (quoted in Dening 12), and he has even written the cat's ambiguous response into the play: there is different dialogue if the cat eats or refuses the proffered Frosties. The live cat does, in fact, "exercise [. . .] a power of fascination by the very fact that it is animate, that it possesses a will and desires of its own" (McAuley 176), and the most genuine note of apprehension in the audience at the performances I attended came from Donny and Davey's threat to harm the real cat. After all, the cat appears to be an innocent both in real and in theatrical terms: the audience perceives it as oblivious to any perceived wrong-doing within the world of the play's fiction and as unaware of the purpose or mechanics of the performance endeavor itself. Yet these gasps of fear, as Rees argues, also force the audience into an uneasy identification with Padraic whose own privileging of feline over human life has helped spill most of the blood on the stage (30). The reappearance of this animal thus further destabilizes the audience's own sense of moral clarity, an uncertainty they "won't be able to *intellectualize.* [. . .] until the curtain falls" (Lonergan 76, emphasis in original), but that nonetheless percolates after the audience disperses.

Yet in a theatrical repertoire that includes numerous dead cats, microwaved hamsters, and severed dog ears, the appearance of the live cat is a genuine comic departure, a comic resurrection that the characters who are left breathing at first fear but ultimately embrace. While this plot twist has been read by some as revealing that "all the violence has been for nothing" (Billington 23), given the nature of the players, it is not that mistaken identity has caused violence. For instance, James, without Wee Thomas's apparent death, would be nipple-less, and Padraic would have further opportunity to put bombs in chip shops, suggesting that the violence has been channeled through a form and a space that we have been forced to witness. Wee Thomas's return reverses the trajectory of the play itself, its progressive destruction of bodies, to make a body whole. And not only is Wee Thomas whole: he is wholly Wee Thomas. If violence allows for the dismantling of identity, Wee Thomas's return also reconstructs an identity, concomitantly allowing Donny and Davey to return to their more human selves as they welcome the cat to his "Home sweet home" (*TL* 69).

If *The Lieutenant* consciously experiments with the visibility of violence, McDonagh's most recent play, *The Pillowman* (2003), complicates that vision by multiplying the frames through which the audience is forced to experience violence. Described by one critic as a "claustrophobic horror show" (Rooney 27), *The Pillowman* presents two deaths that take place on stage as well as various scenes of mutilation and torture heard from offstage, narrated and enacted in front of us. In fact, in multiple instances, the audience is forced to confront particular violent acts in multiple frames simultaneously: Katurian, the imprisoned writer at the center of the play, narrates two of his stories, "The Writer and the Writer's Brother" and "The Little Jesus," while the horrific details of the plots are acted out on a second stage level. The doubling of audible and visible images means that the audience has no escape from the traumatic elements of the scene; if we recoil from the visual, the narration remains. Thus, the stories gain greater intensity, as the visual images create a tangible stage reality for Katurian's fiction that remains concrete for the audience even after we learn the truth of the little girl's fate. Rather than having been subjected to the tortures Katurian describes, she arrives, like Wee Thomas, resurrected—happy and green, not dead—but the audience has still experienced (and retains the experience of) the more gruesome version of the tale, whatever the "real" ending of the story.

This more complex staging creates a darkness that resonates at the end of the play, one that is manipulative and disturbing but ultimately less subversive than the present violence of *The Lieutenant*. The difference lies in the laughter generated by the more recent play. *The Pillowman* employs alternating bursts of what Grand Guignol practitioners termed the "hot and cold shower" (Hand and Wilson 6), a technique of alternating comic with more macabre scenes. At the Grand Guignol, these were separate comic and horror plays performed in a single evening so as to intensify the impact of the darker material. McDonagh's "showers" in *The Pillowman* remain relatively distinct and audiences do not catch themselves laughing at the onstage mutilation of children. Audiences at *The Lieutenant*, however, which liberally mixes the hot "water" with the cold, find themselves laughing at all manner of very bad things.

The success of *The Lieutenant* in London and on Broadway can be linked to the very violence that seems to make it off-putting. James Callahan describes the attraction of performances of violence, arguing, "Most people are vicarious lovers of violence and danger, and the majority of people find the theatrical depiction of violence to be cathartic" (quoted in Hand and Wilson 68). Yet in the end *The Lieutenant* may tempt with violence but it denies the expected release. Cozy as the final embrace of Wee Thomas may be, it nonetheless happens on a stage so slick with fake blood that "the cast has to be careful not to slip [...] when it takes its curtain calls" (Nightingale 5). Catharsis comes from pity and fear, which are arguably emotions that we experience relatively privately since we may cry, but we may do so quietly, and we may also be deeply touched in less physically demonstrative ways. These emotions leave us, at least theoretically, cleansed.

Laughter, however, is an audible and thus inherently public response: those next to us may not know if we were moved by a tragedy, but they can hear us laughing at a comedy. In light of the often raucous laughter that critics report at performances of *The Lieutenant*, Spencer's description of the "conspiracy of guilty hilarity" (18) that the play generates suggests that it draws audiences into a public admission of sentiments that some would perhaps prefer to keep private. A friend who attended one of the New York performances with me offered that the play was "subtle," a comment that seemed odd at first given how unsubtly the play employs gunshots and blood squibs. And yet the subtlety of the play comes precisely from the audience's own simultaneous pleasure and disgust at the carnage and from the playwright's ability to draw us out onto the ledge and leave us there shocked not only at what we have witnessed but also at our own giggling response to that present destruction. If, as Nightingale puts it, "to laugh is not necessarily to laugh something off," (2) the comic playfulness in McDonagh's play actually provides a disquieting enlightenment as we are forced to contend with how susceptible to the playwright's manipulation we are.

Notes

1 Numerous critics and theatergoers have echoed the response of a woman who came up to Garry Hynes, who directed *The Beauty Queen of Leenane*'s Druid Theatre premiere, and exclaimed, while "wiping the tears from her eyes, [...] 'I have a funny feeling I shouldn't be laughing so hard.'" Hynes went on to comment, "That, for me, is a pure Martin McDonagh moment" (quoted in O'Hagan 33).

2 The Atlantic Theater production averaged five gallons of blood a night, including nine different blends, each tailored to produce a specific effect (Segal C01).

3 The play, as Heather Diehl argues, has led us to sympathize with Maureen, which places us in an uncomfortable position when we realize the truth (102).

4 While Luckhurst suggests that the level of blood in the play resulted from McDonagh's having "recognized the flavor of the theatrical times after Sarah Kane's *Blasted*," it is important to note that the earliest version of *Lieutenant* was completed before *Blasted* appeared in 1995 (38).

5 Productions in both London and New York prepared audiences for the noise level with disclaimers in subscriber mailings and the theater lobby. The RSC actually sent warnings to patrons indicating that "the sound generated is within

the legal limit for noise exposure. However, if you or anyone in your party is very young, elderly, pregnant or visually or hearing impaired, you should be aware of the significant noise" (quoted in Ward 8).

6 McDonagh describes the play as coming "from a position of what you might call pacifist rage" (quoted in O'Hagan 33). He has elsewhere commented that the play was written as a response to the 1993 Warrington bombing, an attack by republican paramilitaries that left two children dead, arguing, "I thought, hang on, this is being done in my name [and] I just felt like exploding in rage" (quoted in Spencer 18). The playwright has also criticized the play's initial rejection by the Royal Court and the Royal National Theater as "gutless" and politically motivated; for a fuller discussion of this issue, see Lonergan (65–71).

7 In an interview with Rick Lyman, McDonagh elaborates on the audience response: "I am interested in the whole kind of danger aspect to it [...] . There are times when people in the audiences are hit with bits of stuff flying off the stage [...] . I love to be in the theater and watch that. The people in the audience jump out of their skins" (19).

References

The Aristocrats. Dir. Paul Provenza. Thinkfilm/Velocity, 2005.

Bentley, Eric. "The Psychology of Farce." *Let's Get a Divorce! and Other Plays.* Ed. Eric Bentley. New York: Hill and Wang, 1958. vii–xx.

Billington, Michael. Rev. of *The Lieutenant of Inishmore.* The [Manchester] *Guardian* 12 May 2001: 23.

Boles, William C. "Violence at the Royal Court: Martin McDonagh's *The Beauty Queen of Leenane* and Mark Ravenhill's *Shopping and Fucking.*" *Theatre Symposium* 7 (1999): 125–35.

Bradley, A. C. *Shakespearean Tragedy.* London: Macmillan, 1937.

Brantley, Ben. "Leenane III: Bones Flying." *The New York Times* 23 Feb. 2001: E1.

——. "Terrorism Meets Absurdism in a Rural Village in Ireland." *The New York Times* 28 Feb. 2006: E1.

Broich, Ulrich. "A Theatre of Blood and Sperm: New Trends in British Theatre." *European Studies* 16 (2001): 207–26.

Clapp, Susannah. "Please sir, I want some gore." *The Observer* 20 May 2001: 10.

Dening, Penelope. "The scribe of Kilburn." *The Irish Times* 18 Apr. 2001: 12.

Diehl, Heather. "Classic Realism, Irish Nationalism, and a New Breed of Angry Young Man in Martin McDonagh's *The Beauty Queen of Leenane.*" *Journal of the Midwest Modern Language Association* 34.2 (2001): 98–117.

Elam, Keir. *The Semiotics of Theatre and Drama.* London: Methuen, 1980.

Esslin, Martin. *The Field of Drama.* London and New York: Methuen, 1987.

Friel, Brian. *Dancing at Lughnasa.* London: Faber, 1990.

Garner, Stanton. *Bodied Spaces: Phenomenology and Performance in Contemporary Drama.* Ithaca and London: Cornell UP, 1994.

Hand, Richard J. and Michael Wilson. *Grand-Guignol: The French Theatre of Horror.* Devon, UK: U of Exeter P, 2002.

James, Caryn. "The Trigger Happy Thug in Martin McDonagh." *The New York Times* 4 Apr. 2006: E1.

Kane, Sarah. *Blasted. Sarah Kane: Complete Plays.* London: Methuen, 2001.

Lawson, Mark. "Sick-buckets needed in the stalls." The [Manchester] *Guardian* 28 Apr. 2001: 20.

Lonergan, Patrick. "Too Dangerous to be Done? Martin McDonagh's *Lieutenant of Inishmore.*" *Irish Studies Review* 13.1 (2005): 65–78.

Luckhurst, Mary. "Martin McDonagh's *Lieutenant of Inishmore*: Selling (-Out) to the English." *Contemporary Theatre Review* 14.4 (Nov. 2004): 34–41.

Lyman, Rick. "Most Promising (and Grating) Playwright." *New York Times Magazine* 25 Jan. 1998: 16–19.

McAuley, Gay. *Space in Performance: Making Meaning in the Theatre.* Ann Arbor: U of Michigan P, 2000.

McIntosh, Fiona. *Dying Acts: Death in Ancient Greek and Modern Irish Tragic Drama.* Cork: Cork UP, 1994.

McDonagh, Martin. *The Beauty Queen of Leenane and Other Plays* (*A Skull in Connemara* and *The Lonesome West*). New York: Vintage, 1998.

——. *The Cripple of Inishmaan.* New York: Vintage, 1998.

——. *The Lieutenant of Inishmore.* London: Methuen, 2001.

Nightingale, Benedict. "What does realistic mean on the stage, anyway"? *The New York Times* 13 Jan. 2002, section 2: 5.

O'Hagan, Sean. "The wild west." *The* [*Manchester*] *Guardian* 24 Mar. 2001, Weekend: 33.

Peter, John. "Bloody but unbowed." *Sunday Times* (London) 20 May 2001: 16.

Pilný, Ondřej. "Martin McDonagh: Parody? Satire? Complacency"? *Irish Studies Review* 12.2 (2004): 225–32.

Rees, Catherine. "The Good, the Bad, and the Ugly: The Politics of Morality in Martin McDonagh's *The Lieutenant of Inishmore.*" *New Theatre Quarterly* 21.1 (Feb. 2005): 28–33.

Rooney, David. "Scares are not child's play in this 'Pillow' talk." *Variety* 18–24 Apr. 2005: 27, 39.

Rosenthal, Daniel. "How to Slay, Em in the Isles." *The Independent* (London) 11 Apr. 2001, Features: 10.

Segal, David. "Buckets of Blood Means It's Curtains." *The Washington Post* 13 Apr. 2006: C01.

Spencer, Charles. "Devastating masterpiece of black comedy." *Daily Telegraph* (London) 28 June 2002: 18.

Sypher, Wylie. "The Meanings of Comedy." *Comedy.* Ed. Sypher. Baltimore: Johns Hopkins UP, 1956, 1986. 191–255.

Tweedie, Jenny. Rev. of *The Lieutenant of Inishmore. The Stage* 4 Dec. 2003: 10.

Ward, David. "RSC fires off warning shot to patrons." *The* [*Manchester*] *Guardian* 7 Apr. 2001: 8.

White, Jim. "Box office gross." *The* [*Manchester*] *Guardian* 16 May 2001: 7.

7   Martin McDonagh and the contemporary gothic

Laura Eldred

The only light in the room emanates from the orange coals through the grill of the range, just illuminating the dark shapes of MAG, sitting in her rocking-chair, which rocks back and forth of its own volition, her body unmoving and Maureen, still in her black dress [. . .].
(Martin McDonagh, *Plays 1*: 70)

When readers reach this moment in Martin McDonagh's *The Beauty Queen of Leenane* (1996), they experience a sense of *déjà vu*. The mother in a rocking chair, the strange movement of that rocking chair, the horrifying moment of revelation that the woman is *dead*—all these elements appear in Alfred Hitchcock's masterpiece *Psycho* (1960). More than these similarities, however, *Psycho* offers one further parallel with *Beauty Queen*: half of Hitchcock's film seems to be a suspense movie—definitely not a horror film—as Marion Crane, played by Janet Leigh, steals her boss's money and attempts to avoid capture. The audience's interest and expectations are settled on Marion as the central character; however, audience expectations meet a grisly end during the infamous shower scene, when *Psycho* reveals itself to be something entirely different from the kind of film the audience was led to expect. As Harvey Greenberg states in *Movies on Your Mind*, "With Leigh gone, the comfortable conventions of the Hollywood suspense vehicle have been totally violated" (quoted in Clover 203). When Marion Crane's blood begins swirling down the drain, we know we are in another genre. And when, in *The Beauty Queen of Leenane*, Mag Folan tips forward, dead, in her slowly rocking chair, this allusion to *Psycho* alerts McDonagh's audience that he has played a similar trick—the genre has changed. Indeed, Ondřej Pilný describes this manipulation of genre as a key aspect of McDonagh's work; while he "instigates in his audiences particular genre expectations," he then "proceeds to thoroughly subvert [them]" (228). The intertextual use of *Psycho* in *Beauty Queen* provides audiences with a transition that signals we are no longer in the realm of comedy and have moved into the blood-soaked realm of horror and the gothic.

Figure 7.1 A production poster for *The Beauty Queen of Leenane*, which assumes that a rocking chair, with all its *Psycho* connotations, is sufficiently ominous to symbolize the play. Poster courtesy of TheatreWorks New Milford (2004).

Certainly, there are more parallels between these two films—parallels that make it impossible to call these similarities a coincidence. McDonagh explicitly draws on the traditions and touchstones of the horror genre in its borrowings from *Psycho*. The plots of *Psycho* and *Beauty Queen* are remarkably similar: both Norman Bates and Maureen Folan murder out of sexual repression. For both murderers, the mothers are the source of that repression, as neither Mrs. Bates nor Mag allows her children to develop and act on normal sexual urges; both mothers are later murdered because of this failure.[1] Both children subsequently become the mother that they murdered. Norman internalizes his mother so fully that when he murders, he believes he is Mrs. Bates; the close of *Psycho* shows a Norman who apparently no longer exists, having been entirely taken over by his mother. As *The Beauty Queen of Leenane* concludes, Maureen begins to demonstrate the same verbal and mental ticks that had characterized Mag, so much so that Ray remarks, "The exact fecking image of your mother you are, sitting there pegging orders and forgetting me name! Goodbye!" (*Plays 1* 83).

Beauty Queen can thus be seen as a rewriting of *Psycho* from a female perspective, in which the mother becomes a repressive curmudgeon standing in the way of sexual fulfillment instead of the desirable sexual object that no subsequent woman can approach, as she is for Norman Bates. While extensive plot parallels exist between *Beauty Queen* and *Psycho*, this play exemplifies, perhaps, the least of McDonagh's borrowings from the horror genre.

McDonagh's plays are riddled with similar references to classic and contemporary horror films. These references signal to readers the generic constructs within which the author is operating—encouraging us to consider these texts as examples of a contemporary literature that may operate within the tradition of the gothic horror genre. Indeed, the invocation of these films often serves to destabilize the audience, to force readers or viewers to acknowledge that they are no longer in the realm of drama or simple comedy and that other generic conventions are at work. McDonagh's use of *Psycho* in *Beauty Queen* serves this function, moving the audience from comedy into horror. This chapter will briefly define the contemporary gothic, outline some of the ways McDonagh uses the gothic genre, and then suggest why McDonagh integrates it into his work. The answers to these questions are related, because the gothic enables meaningful discussions of themes that crop up repeatedly in McDonagh's oeuvre and are linked to monstrosity and to the audience's role within violent, horrific entertainment. McDonagh uses the genres of horror and the gothic in order to force his audience into positions that may be uncomfortable—into sympathy with monstrous characters and into recognition of its own atavistic love of aestheticized violence.

Indeed, these are goals for which the horror and gothic genres are well equipped. "Horror" is a term more generally used in reference to twentieth-century literature and film, and it includes a wide variety of subgenres, including the alien invasion film, the slasher, and the religious terror flick. Horror, in both literature and film, is the primary contemporary descendant of the gothic—a genre popularized in the eighteenth and nineteenth centuries in works like Horace Walpole's *Castle of Otranto* (1764) and Anne Radcliffe's *The Mysteries of Udolpho* (1794). Gothic works generally include a rather Byronic hero; dark, atmospheric locales; and a suspicion of the foreigner, especially of the Catholic faith's rites and excesses. They also tend to focus anxiously upon boundaries and taboos, thereby demonstrating, according to many critics, a concern with the fragmentation of the modern subject.[2] Such works thus strive to inspire discomfort and fear, and to center anxiety upon a monstrous other, which is generally expelled or killed by the end of the tale. These mechanics are still in place in the twentieth-century horror movie. Differences between what is called "horror" and what "gothic" are generally not significant, at least for our purposes; the main difference lies in the academy terming "gothic" those works to which critics attribute literary value because of horror's lowbrow connotations.[3] The terms in this essay will be used interchangeably.

The first answer to why McDonagh uses gothic material is that he is a fan of horrific and violent entertainment, especially films. Joseph Feeney notes that McDonagh, when young, was "affected by such violent films as *Taxi Driver* and *Night of the Hunter*" and spent most of his free time "watching films and television" (29, 25). McDonagh has also admitted that "I'm coming to theatre with a disrespect for it. I'm coming from a film fan's perspective on theatre" (quoted in Feeney 28). Despite McDonagh's insistence on a background that owes a great deal to contemporary popular culture, much discussion of him either focuses on his relationship with Synge or merely dubs him "the Quentin Tarantino of the Emerald Isle" (quoted in Feeney 24). By his own admission—though we should take McDonagh's proclamations on his influences with several grains of salt—his roots lie more explicitly in the tradition of violent film than in the Irish dramatic lineage of Synge and O'Casey.[4]

Audiences can note these influences throughout McDonagh's canon; one example is his tendency to adopt and reinvent classic horror film plots by adding his own extra-gory, postmodern twists. As noted above, *The Beauty Queen of Leenane* can be read as a rewriting of *Psycho* from a female perspective since both works present sexual repression as the motive for murder. McDonagh's use of historic horror films goes far beyond this example, however, as most of his plays take a horror film, or a whole

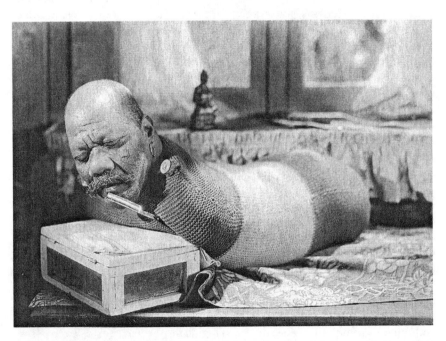

Figure 7.2 Prince Randian (left), aka "the Human Torso," in a still from Tod Browning's film *Freaks* (1932).

horror subgenre, as their foundation. One notable example is in *The Cripple of Inishmaan* (1997), in which Bobby claims to have seen a film that could only be Tod Browning's masterpiece *Freaks* (1932): "I did see a film there one time with a fella who not only had he no arms and no legs but he was a coloured fella too" (*TC* 36),[5] though Bobby is supposedly living on the very isolated Aran Islands in 1934 and this film was widely banned on its release in America two years earlier. It thus seems highly unlikely that Bobby could have viewed this film.

This odd reference really seems placed in order to alert viewers to extensive thematic parallels between *Freaks* and *The Cripple of Inishmaan*: in both films, the plot revolves around the quest of a physically impaired man—with whom the audience is encouraged to identify—for the love of a "normal" girl. Describing *Freaks*, Ian Butler writes, "It is the ordinary, the apparently normal, the beautiful which horrify—the monstrous and distorted which compel our respect, our sympathy, ultimately our affection. The visible beauty conceals the unseen evil, the visible horror is the real goodness" (quoted in Hawkins 152). Certainly this is equally true of *The Cripple of Inishmaan*, in which our sympathies settle on Cripple Billy against the cruelty of murderous parents and heartless young girls.

The Cripple is not the only play in McDonagh's canon to base its plot on the classics of gothic filmmaking; almost all of his plays display similar borrowings. *The Lonesome West* (1997) has extensive parallels with *Whatever Happened to Baby Jane?* (1962), starring Bette Davis and Joan Crawford, a classic horror film similarly concerned with sibling rivalry that also exploits the murder of a cherished pet (in that case, a parakeet). Furthermore, *The Lieutenant of Inishmore* (2001) follows all the plot requirements of a slasher film, especially the pairing of the morally conservative serial killer Padraic with the boyish central female character Mairead—a type of character generally called the "final girl" in horror film criticism.[6] Mairead's eventual murder of Padraic using his own weapons is just what any fan of slasher fare expects.[7]

Furthermore, *A Skull in Connemara* (1997) makes reference to the film *Se7en* (1995)—which features, among other murders, the strange death of a sedentary, hugely overweight man—in Thomas's obsession with the mysterious death of "The fattest bastard you've ever seen in your life. Tits like this. Sitting, no clothes, in his armchair" (*Plays 1* 120). For both works, the detached head of the main character's wife provides a central prop. In *Se7en*, Detective David Mills's wife Tracy is decapitated, and Mills's grief over her murder—which he discovers when her severed head is delivered to him—fuels the film's climax. In *A Skull*, the disappearance and retrieval of Mick's wife Oona's head provides the impetus for the plot. Just as *Se7en* focuses on a series of murders designed to represent the seven deadly sins, McDonagh critiques Leenane as a place where greed, envy, pride, wrath, and sloth have found cozy homes.[8] Most Martin McDonagh plays are thus based on horror films, with only *The Pillowman* (2003) resisting such easy classification. And certainly that play still relies heavily on the genre, as *The Pillowman*'s periodic depictions of torture bear marked similarities to the generic slasher film, which also offers episodic scenes of violence and murder.

McDonagh's work clearly owes much to the horror genre. The question of why the genre is particularly useful to his work is less obvious. Most compellingly, his emphasis on monstrous characters that are often presented within a horror film context forces his audiences into the uncomfortable position of sympathizing with monstrosity. For the monsters of classic and contemporary horror film provide one paradigm through which to consider the possibilities for society's outcasts—those inscribed as its monsters—whether the deformed Cripple Billy in *The Cripple of Inishmaan* or the troubled, murderous Michal in *The Pillowman*. Characters in these works are constantly paralleled with horror film characters, as Maureen in *The Beauty Queen of Leenane* becomes Norman Bates and Billy in *Cripple of Inishmaan* becomes one of Browning's circus freaks. Almost always, however, these contexts are invoked through characters with whom the audience has already been encouraged to identify. In some ways, this is a re-education process. If people generally react to monstrosity with disgust and revulsion, McDonagh complicates that reaction by forcing the reading or viewing audience into sympathy with his "monsters," an uncomfortable position, especially since characters like these are monstrous not only because of the invocation of horrific contexts, but also because of their often amoral behavior and attitudes.

Furthermore, these characters could be read as monstrous because they challenge traditional, de Valerian definitions of a nationalist, Catholic, Gaelic-speaking, rural Irishness. McDonagh loves to parody the Gaelic Romantic vision of Ireland. If Maureen in *Beauty Queen* ostensibly resembles the virginal Irish Catholic girl, she is finally revealed to be an insane, sexually ravenous murderer, as seen in *Psycho*. If Padraic is the macho Republican fighter, he is also a deranged, bloodthirsty killer, as seen in any slasher flick. McDonagh's monsters, then, show the ultimate failure of the de Valerian, Gaelic Romantic paradigm to produce well-adjusted, happy citizens. The characters with whom we are encouraged to identify generally fall well outside of the archetypes produced by this particular nationalist myth. The horrific images and monstrous characters of McDonagh's texts often subvert romantic, nationalist images and histories, as he forces his audience into identification with, and often qualified sympathy for, characters who destabilize traditional ideals of Irish national character.

Most critics of the gothic and horror genres see explicit ties between conceptions of monstrosity and national identity: a culture's monsters tend to reflect those identities rejected as unacceptable by the majority culture. Robert Miles, for example, argues that the gothic emerges alongside nationalism as one way to express the nation's boundaries: monsters are what the nation is not. He suggests that the gothic monsters of Britain's eighteenth and nineteenth centuries are often associated with the Catholic faith or French heritage (61–62). Luke Gibbons argues that this hostility toward Catholicism often merged with specific hostility toward the Irish in the English gothic, as the Irish become associated with monstrous degeneracy, contagion, and disease (43–50). The gothic provides a way to organize national identity: that which must be expelled, which cannot be admitted, is made into a monster and exterminated. As Victor Sage and Allan Lloyd Smith explain in their introduction to *Modern Gothic*, authors in the late eighteenth and early nineteenth centuries used the gothic as a way to contain "the social, economic, and political instabilities of a new order, and the mayhem of a revolutionary period" (5).

According to Judith Halberstam, the gothic novel "produces an easy answer to the question of what threatens national security and prosperity," namely, "the monster" (3). Gothic monstrosity becomes a sort of national scapegoat. Halberstam argues that the Gothic helps to produce the imagined community of the nation by providing a boundary between the nation and all those people (or monsters) outside it:

> If the nation, therefore, is a textual production which creates national community in terms of an inside and an outside and then makes those categories indispensable, Gothic becomes one place to look for a fiction of the foreign, a narrative of who and what is not-English and not-native. The racism that becomes a mark of nineteenth-century Gothic arises out of the attempt within horror fiction to give form to what terrifies the national community. Gothic monsters are defined both as other than the imagined community and as the being that cannot be imagined as community. (15)

Gothic monstrosity is the attempt to cordon off that which is not the nation into the category of the monstrous where it can be easily labeled and killed.

This urge to identify and punish "monsters" is just as much a part of the twentieth-century horror film as the gothic novel. David Skal takes this concept of the monstrous as scapegoat as his starting point for an analysis of the twentieth-century's favorite monsters. While the eighteenth and nineteenth centuries find their monsters in the French, in Jews, or in the Irish, Skal shows that films like *Invasion of the Body Snatchers* (1956) conceptualize communists as alien monsters that can then be destroyed (247–50). Skal also suggests that the monster baby films of the 1970s provide a way to cope with the deformed children that resulted from women's use of thalidomide to cure morning sickness (290–91), and he demonstrates that Freddy Krueger, the child killer, emerges in the 1980s alongside growing public awareness of child abuse, and a slew of scandals involving child care workers (362).

The horror genre, as a rule, is thus deeply embroiled in a nation's cultural imagination, and it provides one way in which people can imagine themselves to be a nation—by locating those things that are not British, American, or Irish in a monstrous form that a film or novel can destroy. Halberstam goes so far as to suggest that "Gothic actually participates in the production of something like a psychology of self" (8). This interesting assertion rests on the fact that the gothic patrols the borders of identity, allowing the individual or the nation to identify and expel that which threatens it. Critics of horror and the gothic often use Julia Kristeva's concept of abjection in order to explain this process; undesirable elements are abjected—labeled as dirty, loathsome, monstrous—and expelled from the community. Because of the monster's abject beginnings, the gothic and horror genre often function as a tool with which to prop up identity—precisely because the genre does away with whatever abject monster threatens a secure national character.

To call such a genre a "tool," however, suggests that it could be used for a variety of goals. If it is often used by those in power to discredit undesirable groups, it can also be used by writers and artists to empower and champion those same groups, which is how McDonagh uses the genre. As Gibbons points out in his discussion of Irish Catholic constructions of a monstrous Protestant ascendancy, "the Gothic as a literary and cultural form could be turned, through acts of semiotic and narrative appropriation, against itself, thereby becoming a weapon of the weak" (15). Who or what constitutes a monster is indeed in the eye of the beholder. One nation's monster may be another's citizen. This potential ambivalence between monstrosity and nationhood perhaps finds its most famous expression in James Joyce's Citizen in the "Cyclops" episode of *Ulysses*; overeager to expel others from his imagined nation as undesirable, the Citizen himself becomes unattractive and monstrous. This possibility of horror offering a counter-narrative—of turning horror against just those constructions of nationality that expel some groups of people—is one on which contemporary authors, including McDonagh, certainly capitalize.

McDonagh's invocations of the horror genre force the audience into sympathy with monstrous characters who fall outside the purview of traditional nationalist identities. In doing so, he conforms to what Halberstam calls the "postmodern gothic:"

> Within postmodern Gothic we no longer attempt to identify the monster and fix the terms of his/her deformity, rather postmodern Gothic warns us to be suspicious of monster hunters, monster makers, and above all, discourses invested in purity and innocence. (27)

Halberstam argues that "the disruption of categories, the destruction of boundaries" inherent in the monstrous is liberating, and that we "need to recognize and celebrate our own monstrosities" (27). McDonagh's interest in forcing audiences into identification with monstrous characters is then part of a larger trope in contemporary literature, which also includes writers like Eoin McNamee, Patrick McCabe, and Bret Easton Ellis. While McDonagh's work stops short of celebrating monstrosity in the way Halberstam suggests, he is explicitly interested in exposing the mechanics of monster formation and in exposing his audiences' tendencies to manufacture monsters, as will be discussed below with *A Skull in Connemara*. McDonagh uses these genres—with their emphases on shock, discomfort, unsavory characters, and violence—to force the audience into uncomfortable positions, from which it is encouraged both to recognize sympathies not before recognized and to come face to face with its own blood thirst. Both of these moves involve a strident critique of abjection, the process of monster-making, as monstrous characters receive sympathy and the monstrous capacity of the audience itself is revealed and indicted.

Indeed, this process of abjection, through which people or communities create monstrous enemies against which to define themselves, is rife throughout McDonagh's world. The making of enemies, generally out of very little cause, and even the murdering of those enemies, is commonplace. As Ray says in *Beauty Queen*, "You can't kick a cow in Leenane without some bastard holding a grudge twenty year" (*Plays 1* 31). The world of McDonagh's works is universally brutal, largely because of his communities' lack of any value system, whether based on the Church, the family, nationalism, or the social ties of a functioning community. His drama suggests that in a world emptied of those forces that might create charitable relationships, what emerges in their place is an unstoppable cycle of abjection. Blaming others for a person's own failures and seeking to "take them out"—making them into monstrous scapegoats that could be fought and killed—may be the only kind of identity possible. This process of abjection forms the basis of most of his plays, as his characters search for a scapegoat who can then be murdered.[9] McDonagh thus uses the horror and gothic genres in a critical investigation of the technologies behind nationalism—technologies which render some people full citizens and others monsters. Without any of the traditional supports for viable, non-atavistic identities—like the Church or the family—the townspeople of his fictional Leenane and Aran Islands turn to murderous violence, to defining themselves negatively by who they are not rather than who they might be.

The most vivid display of this logic within McDonagh's work occurs in *The Lieutenant of Inishmore*, which severely satirizes the need to have enemies—any enemy—in order to feel powerful. Certainly, Padraic gives plenty of lip-service to his distrust and hatred of England's "jackboot hirelings" in Northern Ireland (*TL* 33); as a member of the INLA, he is required to embrace such attitudes. Irish nationalists are not members of the security forces and this distinction provides one clear basis for identity. For Padraic, the English are the monstrous, abjected group. This construction becomes rather ridiculous in the play, however, as he seems unable to find any actual "monsters" to fight; as a result, he tortures and kills people who have nothing to do with colonial oppression, including people supposedly on his own side, such as other members of the INLA. Padraic's need to fight, to have enemies, thus finds more and more ridiculous outlets including a small-time local marijuana dealer and cat killers. Finally he proposes to Mairead that they "leave the INLA altogether" and start their "own splinter group, just me and you" (59). The first act of this splinter group will be to pursue someone Padraic thinks is the "validest of targets": a man who "spun me a yarn about ringworm proved completely untrue too. 'Wrapping pellets up in cheese.' I bet he doesn't even have a cat" (59). Bad cat advice becomes justification for murder, as Padraic's need for an enemy to abject spirals totally out of control. *The Lieutenant of Inishmore* thus offers a sort of parodic excess of abjection, in which Padraic's desperate need for enemies leads him to more and more ridiculous targets; as such, it offers (however comedically) a critique of abjection as a basis for identity consolidation.

Though McDonagh never offers any positive tactics for defining an Irish nation outside of stereotyped identities or abjecting others, he at least does demonstrate that those two options are highly problematic. At the close of the play, Mairead seems ready to take up largely where Padraic left off: her decision to launch an "investigation" into the death of her own cat carries the threat of new violence (67). Once she leaves, Davey cries out: "Oh, will it never end? Will it never fecking end"? to which Donny replies, "It fecking won't, d'you know!" which certainly would be the response that McDonagh's work as a whole suggests (67). Abjection produces its own momentum, especially in a world emptied of those supports that might have allowed for the creation of more humane and well-adjusted identities. All that is left is identity by negation, which is crafted by labeling others as enemies.

If *The Lieutenant* directly critiques abjection through Padraic's excesses, *A Skull in Connemara* does something rather different. Recognizing, and laughing at, Padraic's desperate need for enemies is far from the same as recognizing one's own tendencies toward abjection, toward creating one's own monsters. Ultimately, *A Skull* asks its audience to recognize just this dynamic within itself. Through displaying all the characters' uses of abjection as a basis for identity, and through alternatively pandering to and incriminating the audience's own bloodthirsty tendency toward monster making, *A Skull* encourages audience members to recognize and hopefully reject their more atavistic desires to find, label, and kill the monstrous. While the community remains universally brutal, as in McDonagh's other works, in this play, McDonagh involves his audience in an investigation of Mick Dowd's varied crimes; as the audience attempts to uncover Mick's history, McDonagh toys with their desire for the usual payoff in a McDonagh play—a murder and a murderer—neither of which the play ultimately provides.

As in the other plays of McDonagh's canon, the community in *A Skull* is universally brutal. This drama centers on the manipulation of dead bodies, which are subjected to disrespectful and perhaps blasphemous uses.

It becomes apparent that torturing animals as a pastime in Leenane does not occasion any condemnatory or even surprised response, and the only thing worth discussing is various methods of death. Mairtin cooks a hamster alive, and only laments that he did not have a clear view of its death throes: "If the oven had had a see-through door it would've been more fun, but it didn't, it had an ordinary door. My mistake was not planning ahead" (*Plays 1* 140). Thomas, Mick, and Mairtin have various conversations on possible methods of death, and are especially interested in how likely or unlikely some accidents are. They compare being hit by a tractor to drowning in slurry or meeting one's end in a combine harvester, and later discuss the relative merits of drowning in urine or vomit: "Drowned on wee I'm talking about. Drowned on wee you have to go out of your way. Drowned on sick you don't" (141). The townspeople are thus given to morbid fascinations, and Mairtin's choice to find fulfillment by killing hamsters occasions little response because a fascination with violence and death runs rampant throughout Leenane.

Such attitudes reflect a sadistic morbidity operating within the town and implicitly within the audience, who paid to see this fare. This sadism is not just about discussing varied methods of death or even killing hamsters, since directing violence against other human beings is, to a large degree, an accepted part of town life. Enemies are too easily made and violence against those enemies easily justified. Mairtin defends cutting up two girls' faces with bottles when they refused him as a dancing partner: "Stitches aren't good enough for them sorts of bitches, and well they know. As ugly as them two started out, sure stiches'd be nothing but an improvement, oh aye" (97). It thus takes very little instigation for Mairtin to justify responding with vicious violence. Even Mary, who might be expected to reject this cruelty as the only woman in the play (and an ostensibly religious one), demonstrates similar viciousness when she condemns a couple of five-year-olds who urinated in the churchyard and called her a "fat oul biddy" twenty-seven years ago: "When I see them burned in hell I'll let bygones be bygones, and not before!" (90). When mocked—even by five-year-olds—she responds with murderous rage.[10]

Part of this tendency to abject others seems born of excessive boredom and is a way to cope with a town in which nothing ever seems to happen. As Thomas Hanlon says, longing for the excitement of a more violent world, "I would *like* there to be bodies flying about everywhere, but there never is" (120). Mairtin professes the same belief—that violence provides an escape from small-town monotony—when he expresses his hope that the bloody gossip about Mick is true: "There you got me hoping I was working with a fella up and slaughtered his wife with an axe or something, when all it was was an oul cheap-ass drink-driving. Aren't they ten-a-penny"? (129). Violence emerges as a possible method of breaking the routine and thus functions as a desired kind of entertainment. And again, this desire implicitly condemns the play's audience, who has chosen to pay for entrance into the world of a brutal, violent play. A bit of blood sexes up the story, in Hollywood, Leenane, or the local theater.

The central problem of *A Skull in Connemara* thus concerns how a real act of violence could possibly be detected within this depraved culture. When people talk about little besides violence, and lie as often as they tell the truth, how are guilt and innocence to be determined? McDonagh uses this play to lead his audience through a rather tricky maze of culture, violence, and responsibility. Mick Dowd has been accused of murdering his wife Oona. Though the inquests proved nothing, and Mick himself denies the murder, claiming it was a drunk-driving car accident, no one in the town can let it rest. Everyone seems to want Mick to be a murderer because, as Mairtin suggests, it is sufficiently scandalous. And everyone lies constantly, from Mairtin's obvious lie stating that he did not bottle the two young girls at the disco to Mick's lie that he doesn't batter the skulls and bones into dust and drop them in the slurry. When pressed by Mary, Mick says, "I hit [the bones] with a hammer until they were dust and I pegged them be the bucketload into the slurry." But he shortly changes his tune: "I neither hammer the bones nor throw them in the slurry, Mary. Sure what do you take me for"? (99, 100). Of course, during scene three, the audience watches Mick hammer away at the bones of the community's dead. Though Mick later claims that this was the first time he had done so, and thus that he did not lie to Mary, the claim seems suspect. Mick is not trustworthy, so his constant denials of murdering Oona are similarly un-reliable. The audience is asked to figure out a very difficult problem with-out reliable testimony: is Mick guilty or innocent? Audience members may suspect that he is guilty—this is a Martin McDonagh play, after all—but the evidence that McDonagh presents on this point is vague at best.

Given the centrality of this question, the presence of a detective in the play certainly seems significant. Thomas may be rather incompetent, as he cannot tell the difference between circumstantial evidence and hearsay—"Feck I'm always getting them two beggars mixed up"—but he tries to use the tools of his trade (155). Specifically, he articulates the necessity of paying attention to details. When Mick makes the mistake of asserting that cooking cats or cooking hamsters is "the same difference, sure," Thomas corrects him:

Thomas: A fact is a fact, like. It's the same in detective work. No matter how small a detail may appear to be, you can't go lumping it with a bunch of other details like it's all the same thing. So you can't go lumping cats and hamsters together either. Things like that are the difference between solving and not solving an entire case, sure. (122)

Thomas thus advocates a close attention to detail and a precise method of description. He reacts similarly when Mick draws no distinction between insults and "vague insinuations": "It's not the self-same thing at all, and if you knew anything about the law then you'd know it's not the self-same thing" (127). If audience members, like Thomas, can be assumed to be on Mick's trail, attempting to figure out his status as guilty or innocent, then these instructions apply to the audience as well—viewers must pay careful attention to detail as they attempt to convict or exonerate Mick Dowd.

The play, however, does not ultimately present a clear case either way. Certainly, there is evidence against Mick. As Thomas says, "your wife's head injuries all those years ago weren't especially conducive to only having been in a car crash at all [. . .]" (128). Furthermore, Mary claims to have seen something on the night of Oona's death, something that leads her to believe in Mick's guilt:

Mary: Oh no? I must've been mistaken what I saw that night so, as along the two of ye drove [. . .] . All I'm saying is you'll be meeting up with Oona again someday, Mick Dowd, and not just the bare skull but the spirit of her, and when you meet may down to the stinking fires of hell she drag the rotten murdering bones of you, and may downhill from there for you it go. (164, 165)

Mary certainly seems to believe in Mick's guilt in this passage and, more important, also appears to be a witness to the crime. Furthermore, the audience is likely to latch onto this statement as evidence of Mick's guilt; all of McDonagh's other plays offer a murder and a murderer, so audiences are likely to believe Mary's accusation. However, McDonagh does not allow his audience this easy a solution. The evidence for Mick's guilt and Mick's innocence is finely balanced, and this balance enables McDonagh to use *A Skull* as an investigation of audience expectations and desires—an investigation that ultimately finds the audience guilty as a monstrous and bloodthirsty crowd of voyeurs.

For, while Mary's claim to be an eyewitness may seem damning, Mary herself is inconsistent. Not much earlier than this in the play, she seems genuinely surprised that Mick could be guilty of killing Oona. When he supposedly fills out a confession, she murmurs: "It's true? (*Pause.*) I had always prayed only fool gossiping is all it ever was" (153). This comment seems totally indefensible if Mary, indeed, saw Mick commit the murder. Her evidence is thus compromised. Thomas's claim that Oona's head injuries necessitated something more than a car accident also appears unreliable, as Mick notes that those accusations came out at the inquest and were defeated.

On the other hand, the evidence for Mick's innocence may be more compelling, though it rests on nothing but his own word. He consistently denies any role in Oona's death beyond irresponsibly driving a car while drunk. After Mick believes that he has killed Mairtin, he says to Mary:

"do you want to hear something funny? I *didn't* butcher my wife. Just like for seven long years I've been saying I didn't butcher my wife. I never butchered anybody 'til tonight" (156). The final words of the play are his repeated oaths that he "didn't touch her": "I swear it. [. . .] I swear it" (166). While this claim is certainly not hard evidence, it may be more compelling than Mary's inconsistent testimony and Thomas's vague aspersions. If McDonagh creates a maze of culture, guilt, and responsibility in this play, he finally leaves his audience lost in that maze, as he resists providing exactly those elements that audiences have come to associate with his work—especially a murder and a murderer. In leaving the audience pondering these questions, McDonagh asks his viewers and readers to consider their own bloodthirsty, atavistic tendencies, as we expect, even long for, the payoff of blood and guts. For in A *Skull*, as far as we can know, no one dies as the result of someone else's conscious action.

This overt manipulation of audience expectations is one key feature of McDonagh's work, according to Ondřej Pilný, who suggests that these plays "satirically explore the expectations of particular audiences" by "reflect[ing] and manipulat[ing] the preferences and concerns of their audiences rather than delivering an easily legible image of reality" (228). Patrick Lonergan has similarly noted that these plays "exploit and draw attention to his audience's willingness to receive information passively" ("'Too Dangerous to be Done?'" 71). Certainly, A *Skull* attempts to draw attention to the audience's murderous expectations and to force that audience to an uncomfortable recognition that it has been manipulated into expecting and desiring a murder. This play manipulates its audience with significant skill in inverting the equation offered by The *Beauty Queen of Leenane*; if, in *Beauty Queen*, the audience expects a comedy and gets a murder, in A *Skull* the audience expects a murder and never gets one.

The joke of the play is that the reader cannot piece together a solution from the literal and more figurative fragments offered. Like Thomas, the audience becomes a failed detective. Despite the lack of evidence, many audience members depart feeling that Mick did it; this feeling, however, seems to rest only on wish fulfillment and on the audience's expectations, based on having seen other McDonagh plays. Viewers become like the town members, echoing Mairtin's sentiments that a murderer is more interesting than a drunk driver. We are implicated and indicted as part of a brutal culture in which blood sells. Mick confesses to Mairtin's murder out of a sense that the town, long ago, cast him in the role of murderer regardless of evidence or the lack thereof: "A pure drink-driving was all my Oona was, as all along I've said, but if it's a murderer ye've always wanted living in yer midst, ye can fecking have one" (*Plays 1* 156). But this is exactly what A *Skull in Connemara* does not ultimately give us—perhaps to our disappointment. The play thus highlights the audience's double bind: the frustration of our desire for blood and gore, along with by our subsequent feelings of disappointment, conflict with our ability to distance ourselves from the world of the play. We are clearly implicated. Just like Mairtin, we look for some violence to spice up our apparently boring lives.

By implicating the audience in this way, the play reveals some troubling contradictions: if the audience's desire for bloodshed is somehow inappropriate, why does McDonagh keep delivering gorier and gorier works? And as he has continued to produce horrific plays, what attitude does that reveal toward his own art and the people who attend his plays? His works seem at least condescending, if not hostile, to his own audience. Lonergan suggests that McDonagh shows a "serious desire to resist the beautification of violence in the works of Wu, Tarantino, and others" by presenting unrelentingly brutal final scenes (" 'Too Dangerous to be Done?' " 73). It seems possible that McDonagh resists the beautification of violence and that this resistance would provide the attractive option of chaining McDonagh's work to a definable and desirable moral objective. However, the scene in *Lieutenant* in which the stage is covered with broken, bloody body parts seems to cater more to an audience appreciative of the camp excesses found in the horror genre—especially slasher films, which tend to approach gore aesthetically—than to be making a "serious point about what happens to human bodies when people are killed" (74). The answer may be closer to that offered in another Lonergan essay: "the solution to the 'McDonagh enigma' does not involve deciding whether his works facilitate the search for truth or the appetite for delusion, but in the acceptance that they facilitate *both*" (" 'The Laughter Will Come of Itself' " 640). These plays critique his audiences' love of violence even while presenting violence aesthetically.

One might wonder, then, if McDonagh's plays frequently violate audience's expectations and, as in *A Skull*'s case, indict viewers as bloodthirsty hypocrites. In fact, his work reveals marked similarities with contemporary horror film in its relationship to its audience. Certainly this twinned impulse to pander to an audience even while implicitly violating that audience also finds expression in Synge's *The Playboy of the Western World* (1907), which is perhaps the most obvious progenitor of this play, as well as in contemporary horror film, which makes a business of fairly explicitly visually violating audience members. All these works, whether Synge's plays or horror films, depend upon shocking or scaring an audience, and they thus must presume a certain basis of common morals or anxieties. For an audience as amoral as McDonagh's characters, these plays would produce nothing and would be terribly boring. They assume an audience whose values can be insulted, and therein lies the pleasure— the scandal and titillation of laughing at the brutal machinations of the very strange people and very strange community of McDonagh's drama. According to Aleks Sierz's research on "In-Yer-Face" theater, works like these attempt to disturb the viewer's "habitual gaze" by violating expectations; shock shakes the audience free of their traditional mores, enabling them to see anew (quoted in Lonergan, " 'Too Dangerous to Be Done?' " 65). All this emphasis on shock and shaking foundations makes it clear that there must be an existing moral foundation for shock tactics to work. Discussing Synge's *Playboy of the Western World*, Christopher Murray makes a similar point:

> the audience's orthodox moral position, which would normally incline towards Shawn's, is undercut and the audience is left little choice but to rejoice with the others on stage at Christy's disclosure. A moral issue is brazenly made fun of and the audience is implicated in the conspiracy. (quoted in Lanters 219)

While, in McDonagh's work, characters who personify some sort of presumed traditional values are quite rare (one exception being Father Welsh in *The Lonesome West*), we should not forget that the play's audience is always there as a moral center, ready to be offended. As José Lanters has stated, "the plays are effective only because they rely on the audience to be able to perceive and feel what the characters do not" (219).

Implicitly, then, all the plays' digs at the Church and the family are directed at the titillating violation of the audience's sacred cows. For both Synge and McDonagh, the spectators are implicitly the object of attack. It is the audience who ultimately becomes the stand-in for traditional, conservative values—for some (however tentative or self-consciously held) faith in the Church and the family—and it is therefore the audience who is violated and implicitly "killed off." This dynamic is the same in the contemporary horror film, which often makes a clear equation between its victims and its audience. Carol Clover argues that horror films consistently terrorize their audiences. As an example of this tendency, she calls attention to the stage directions during Marion Crane's death in *Psycho*: "The slashing. An impression of a knife slashing, as if tearing at the very screen, ripping the film" (199). And as the film implicitly attacks its audience, a transformation of sorts occurs. Clover notes, "It is not only the look-at-the-monster that is at issue here, but the look-at-the-movie. The horror movie is somehow more than the sum of its monsters; it is itself monstrous" (168). And this monstrous inability of the work to be contained properly within the screen or upon the stage, its inappropriate, murderous attitude toward its audience, constitutes perhaps the major reason critics have difficulty with McDonagh's work. Though the violence on the screen is directed toward a variety of characters, the target is, ultimately, the audience. Similarly, the violence in McDonagh's plays, and especially in *A Skull*, ultimately targets the audience, as McDonagh simultaneously caters to and mocks its desire for blood, gore, and murder.

If this violation of the audience—the need to shock it, scare it, and even mock it—was all there was to a McDonagh play, however, one could be excused for wondering why anyone attends his plays. And certainly people wonder the same thing about horror films—why would anyone pay to be implicitly violated and murdered for two hours? Or why pay one hundred dollars a ticket to see McDonagh's most recent play, *The Pillowman*, which features the onstage torture and murder of children? Even a horror film usually kills the monster, reestablishing some sort of moral order by the end—something that McDonagh's works do not tend to do. Lanters suggests that these works "act as agent [*sic*] provocateurs in the national debate," using their "contrariness to accepted pieties" to "raise questions about the representation of identity, including Irish national identity" (222). While her point is compelling, it does not address why audiences would pay to see their "accepted pieties" mocked.

So why does anyone enjoy these plays? Part of the reason is the audience's ability to abject the world of the play, to interpret the world of the play as radically other, as something strange, foreign, and disgusting—something definitely "not like us." An audience can enjoy the violation of its sacred cows, bask in the titillating depictions of violence, and then leave, thinking: "Wasn't that fun? Of course, we're nothing like that." Audiences are able to enjoy the violence of the work because they assume themselves to be removed from it. The world of the play becomes an exaggeration, a farce; the people of the play are monstrous, weird, and crazy. But this attitude puts audiences in a sort of double bind: longing for the titillation that they have come to expect from McDonagh's work while simultaneously distancing themselves from it, falling back on their traditional morals once they leave the theater. This process is problematic. The audience begins the play with a presumed set of moral beliefs, but then the play violates those beliefs. The audience enjoys that violation and is titillated by the violence, until its members leave and write off the play as exaggeration and farce, thereby keeping their presumed values intact. The problem is that such an audience enjoys, even longs for, perhaps expects, the violence and enjoyment of having its morals hit by a poker, slammed over the head with a mallet, or burned in an oven. It tries to have its cake and eat it too. In essence, it is the audience that starts the chain of abjection in McDonagh's work by simultaneously loving the violence and rejecting it as something monstrous, something foreign. And it is, perhaps, the audience members who are finally monstrous and revealed to be a bloodthirsty bunch of voyeurs. McDonagh's work recognizes this dynamic and sometimes attempts to directly critique it, especially in *A Skull in Connemara*.

If the play becomes the abject—something to define one's community against—McDonagh's work, especially *A Skull in Connemara*, tries to resist this perception by implicating the audience in the play's action and revealing its implicit bloodlust. He disrupts the atavistic desire to see and label the monster among us, insisting instead that we recognize ourselves as monstrous, as bloodthirsty, and as terribly flawed.

The central questions in McDonagh's work, of communal cohesion, of monstrosity, of violence, and of identity formation, are all questions broached similarly within the horror and gothic genres, and, indeed, it is partially through his references to horror film that McDonagh foregrounds his interest in monstrosity and abjection. For the horror genre, with its emphases on monstrosity's construction and its results, is uniquely equipped to form a critique of abjection as a basis of personal or national identities. Horror has historically been concerned with national identity because its monsters are often representations of the community's abject. This genre allows for the consolidation of a "national self" through the literary or filmic expulsion of undesirable groups. However, as Luke Gibbons has pointed out, one's construction of monstrosity depends on one's milieu; if the majority can make the minority into a monstrous abject, minorities can also, in their own literary or artistic works, construct the majority as the monster. From either perspective, constructions of monstrosity prop up identity by defining it against an other. The monstrous abject finally emerges as a challenge to just this sort of binary thinking because monsters tend to undermine easy classification. Authors of the "postmodern gothic" such as McDonagh incorporate the horror genre largely in order to expose this paradigm of identity formation as problematic and doomed to failure. This genre emphasizes that monsters are constructed by atavistic nations and communities, sometimes for no better reason than to have an enemy, something against which to define the self or nation. And this point— that monsters are constructed rather than born—has a history as long as the genre itself, reaching back at least as far as Mary Shelley's seminal novel *Frankenstein* (1818). Yet again, McDonagh reveals his dependence on a long and illustrious tradition. Whether using Synge or classic horror films, McDonagh has a talent for cannibalizing and recreating the plots and themes of his predecessors, thereby blending tradition with horrific innovation.

Notes

1 *Psycho IV: The Beginning*—a 1990 sequel directed by Mick Garris—explains Norman's murder of his mother. At one point, she gets the teenage Norman to sleep with her in his underwear, to massage her, and to wrestle with her on the ground. However, when these actions result in an erection, she calls Norman filthy. Her simultaneous forbidden sexual availability and sexual frigidity lead to Norman's twisted desire for her and her subsequent murder.

2 See *The Cambridge Companion to Gothic Fiction* for various definitions and elucidations of the gothic from the eighteenth century to now. The introductory chapter by Jerrold E. Hogle provides a useful introduction to the genre.

3 Certainly there are many critics who might take issue with my assertion that horror and the gothic are, for most intents and purposes, the same. However, for the purpose of most theoretical discussions of monstrosity or audience anxieties —or, at least, for the purposes of this essay—the two are remarkably similar.

4 I do not wish to suggest that critics should take McDonagh at his word and dismiss Beckett and Synge as potential influences on the playwright. As Patrick Lonergan has pointed out, "it is clear that McDonagh's presentation of himself

should not be regarded as accurate" ("'Too Dangerous to Be Done?'" 67). McDonagh is certainly conversant in modern and contemporary drama, despite his protestations. This does not mean, however, that he is not equally conversant in the classics of horror and violent cinema.

5 His reference is to Prince Radian, aka "the Human Torso," who is featured in Browning's film. See Figure 7.2.

6 See Carol Clover's chapter "Her Body, Himself" in *Men, Women, and Chainsaws* for more on the slasher tradition, including the feminized slasher villain and the boyish final girl.

7 See my essay, "Martin McDonagh's Blend of Tradition and Horrific Innovation," for more on the parallels between *The Lieutenant* and the slasher film tradition.

8 Another source that *A Skull in Connemara* seems to use is the life and crimes of Ed Gein, a notorious murderer and grave robber from Wisconsin and the source of the novel *Psycho*, which was written in 1959 by Robert Bloch. Gein was primarily a grave robber; deprived of any natural relationships with women, he would dig them up and take them (or at least parts of them) home with him. The reference to Mairtin using corpses to "to have a good look" at female genitalia, as well as the grave robbing and references to cannibalism, point an alert reader toward McDonagh's awareness of one of the staples of the horror genre tradition—famous serial killers (*Plays 1* 116).

9 *The Lonesome West*'s focus on another kind of scapegoat—the willing sacrifice—is an interesting outgrowth of this very typical McDonagh theme.

10 In addition to Synge's *Playboy*, another Irish dramatic source for this play is Beckett's *Waiting for Godot*. The play's title, *A Skull in Connemara*, comes from Lucky's speech, and the casual violence in the relationship between Pozzo and Lucky seems influential for McDonagh's work.

References

The Cambridge Companion to Gothic Fiction. Ed. Jerrold E. Hogle. Cambridge: Cambridge UP, 2002.

Clover, Carol. *Men, Women, and Chain Saws: Gender in the Modern Horror Film.* Princeton: Princeton UP, 1992.

Douglas, Mary. *Purity and Danger.* 1966. New York: Routledge, 2002.

Eldred, Laura. "Martin McDonagh's Blend of Tradition and Horrific Innovation." *The Theatre of Martin McDonagh: A World of Savage Stories.* Ed. Lillian Chambers and Eamonn Jordan. Dublin: Carysfort P, 2006. 198–213.

Feeney, Joseph. "Martin McDonagh: Dramatist of the West." *Studies* 87.345 (1998): 24–32.

Freaks. Dir. Tod Browning. Metro-Goldwyn-Mayer, 1932.

Gibbons, Luke. *Gaelic Gothic: Race, Colonization, and Irish Culture.* Research Papers in Irish Studies 2. Galway: Arlen House, 2004.

Halberstam, Judith. *Skin Shows: Gothic Horror and the Technology of Monsters.* Durham: Duke UP, 1995.

Hawkins, Joan. *Cutting Edge: Art-Horror and the Horrific Avant-Garde.* Minneapolis: U of Minnesota P, 2000.

Kristeva, Julia. *Powers of Horror: An Essay on Abjection.* Trans. Leon S. Roudiez. New York: Columbia UP, 1982.

Lanters, José. "Playwrights of the Western World: Synge, Murphy, McDonagh." *A Century of Irish Drama: Widening the Stage.* Ed. Stephen Watt, Eileen Morgan, and Shakir Mustafa. Bloomington: Indiana UP, 2000. 204–22.

Lonergan, Patrick. " 'The Laughter Will Come of Itself. The Tears Are Inevitable': Martin McDonagh, Globalization, and Irish Theatre Criticism." *Modern Drama* 47.4 (Winter 2004): 636–58.

——. " 'Too Dangerous to be Done'? Martin McDonagh's *Lieutenant of Inishmore.*" *Irish Studies Review* 13.1 (2005): 65–78.

McDonagh, Martin. *The Cripple of Inishmaan.* London: Methuen, 1997.

——. *The Lieutenant of Inishmore.* London: Methuen, 2001.

——. *The Pillowman.* London: Faber, 2003.

——. *Plays 1 (The Beauty Queen of Leenane, A Skull in Connemara, The Lonesome West).* London: Methuen, 1999.

Miles, Robert. "Abjection, Nationalism, and the Gothic." *The Gothic.* Ed. Fred Botting. Essays and Studies 54. Cambridge: D. S. Brewer, 2001. 47–70.

Modern Gothic: A Reader. Ed. Victor Sage and Allan Lloyd Smith. Manchester: Manchester UP, 1996.

Pilný, Ondřej. "Martin McDonagh: Parody? Satire? Complacency"? *Irish Studies Review* 12.2 (2004): 225–32.

Psycho. Dir. Alfred Hitchcock. Paramount, 1960.

Psycho IV: The Beginning. Dir. Mick Garris. MCA Television Entertainment, 1990.

Se7en. Dir. David Fincher. New Line Cinema, 1995.

Skal, David J. *The Monster Show: A Cultural History of Horror.* Rev. ed. New York: Faber, 2001.

Whatever Happened to Baby Jane? Dir. Robert Aldrich. Warner Bros, 1962.

8   *The Pillowman*: A new story to tell

Brian Cliff

Much of the existing writing about Martin McDonagh reads like a contest between critics who compete to offer the most lavish praise and the most scathing contempt.[1] While his plays are reviewed in the contexts of contemporary, British, and Irish theater, almost all of the scholarship treats him primarily as an Irish playwright, if ambivalently so. This focus has produced some of the most astringent responses to his work; in particular, he has been accused by critics of offering a variety of Culchie or Redneck Orientalism, whether those critics emphasize metropolitan Irish audiences' willingness to see his plays as staging the backwards past they have left behind or whether they emphasize foreign audiences' apparent embrace of the most shopworn Irish tropes.[2] *The Pillowman* (2003), however, is McDonagh's first play not to take place in an explicitly Irish setting, and it has none of the flamboyant stage signifiers of Irishness that have helped make his other plays both so lauded and so contested. It is, for example, probably his least overtly profane play, the one with the least use of "fucking" and "fecking." This relative scarcity suggests, among other things, that the profusion of the word "fecking" in his earlier plays functions as some kind of universal signifier of Irishness for audiences, as if cursing is what the Irish do best.[3] Particularly in light of his reception not just as an "Irish playwright" but as a writer of "plays about Ireland," then, one of the questions about *The Pillowman* is how McDonagh's persistent concerns with violence and humor, described by the other contributors to this volume, function outside of Irish settings.[4] After discussing the play's performance history, plot, and critical reception, this chapter will suggest that *The Pillowman* answers this question by producing what McDonagh's gleefully violent plays have perhaps least prepared his audience to expect: a moment of grace.

The production history

Allegedly the final play McDonagh will stage,[5] *The Pillowman* was first performed in the UK and "in Germany within three weeks of the London premiere" in 2003 (Wallace 665), in Japan in 2004, and in the United

States in 2005, and has since seen a range of international perform-
ances, regional tours, and smaller-market American productions (including
Houston's Alley Theatre, Seattle's ACT Theatre, New Jersey's George Street
Playhouse, and Chicago's Steppenwolf Theatre). Although performances
outside of London in the United Kingdom did get some reviews in the
larger papers, most reviews there were for the initial run at the National
Theatre with Jim Broadbent as Tupolski and David Tennant as Katurian.
Similarly, the Broadway production received widespread reviews in national
papers as well as in regional papers far from Manhattan. This coverage
was no doubt in part because the cast included the well-known film actors
Billy Crudup as Katurian, Zeljko Ivanek as Ariel, and Jeff Goldblum as
Tupolski. As discussed more fully below, both the New York and London
productions of *The Pillowman* provoked particularly divisive reviews, in
part because the play is more dramatically tangled than some of McDonagh's
other works. One irascibly impatient British reviewer, for example, dismissed it as "a hopelessly disorganised play in which the action keeps
grinding to a halt so the main character can read out one of half a dozen
or so interminable short stories. It felt less like an evening at the theatre
than being trapped in a Creative Writing Workshop. I left in the interval"
(Young 66).

   Though received as "new" by reviewers of these performances, *The
Pillowman* dates to McDonagh's now-legendary outburst of initial produc-
tivity, during which he also composed the Leenane and Aran trilogies, and
seems to predate some of those plays. A 1997 profile of McDonagh opens
at "a rehearsed reading" of *The Pillowman*, and describes its earliest form
as "the third play he wrote, but the first he regarded as good" (O'Toole,
"Nowhere Man" N. pag.). At the same time, particularly given the hazily
mythic aura surrounding McDonagh's patterns of composition—Patrick
Lonergan goes so far as to suggest "that McDonagh's presentation of himself should not be regarded as accurate" (" 'Too Dangerous to be Done?' "
67)—it is difficult to ascertain how much the published play was revised
from its earlier forms.[6] Consequently, while the play may have been drafted
before the plays that established his career, *The Pillowman* can also (and
perhaps only) be discussed as a potential capstone on his theatrical career,
whatever its original place in the sequence of his work may have been. In
such a perspective, it is fitting that *The Pillowman* appears deeply and
dramatically interested in the nature of art, and particularly in the possibility that art offers a kind of redemption.

Telling the stories

Given that *The Pillowman* is so far the least widely-known of McDonagh's
plays, and given its departures from his more readily marketable qualities
of humor and Irishness, it requires a brief description.[7] The plot is ornately
knotted, even by McDonagh's hectic standards. It moves beyond his

usually taut structure of reversals to a string of surprises, some of which
risk being overshadowed by his dramatically engaging immoderation, much
as Nicholas Grene has suggested that the "grotesque excess in [McDonagh's]
language [. . .] actually reduces its shock value by taking it out of the
realm of the real" (301). Indeed, if McDonagh's strength on the stage is his
willingness to be excessive, his weakness is his apparent eagerness to be
excessive. Where earlier McDonagh plays like *The Lieutenant of Inishmore*
often quickly revolve around dramatically ironic secrets that the audience
knows but key characters do not, and where the drama of those plays
often lies in the tension between keeping the secret hidden and revealing it,
The Pillowman unfolds layers of reversals, some in non-sequential fashion
and others through the stories told by the central character, Katurian,
stories that come to resemble a Borgesian set of nested narratives.[8]

The Pillowman is set in an unnamed but seemingly Eastern European
country, described by one of the characters as "a totalitarian fucking
dictatorship" (*TP* 23). The central character, Katurian Katurian Katurian,
is a would-be writer and abattoir worker whose name not only evokes the
similarly bureaucratic experiences of Kafka's protagonist, but also offers
something of a joke in its own right, particularly through his initials,
though the play does not call attention to them. The other characters
inhabiting this setting are Michal, Katurian's "slow" or "subnormal" older
brother (9, 24), and two policemen, Tupolski and Ariel. Though several
other actors appear onstage, they function essentially as props in illustrat-
ing Katurian's stories through a series of tableaux.

When the play opens, Katurian is being interrogated because, he
assumes, the state has taken political offense at his stories: "[I]f that's why
you've brought me in here, I can't see what the reason would be, unless
something political came in by accident, or something that *seemed* political
came in, in which case show me where it is. Show me where the bastard is.
I'll take it straight out. Fucking burn it" (7–8). Judging from the evidence
of some reviews, the audiences for the play may have shared his assumption
that the interrogation is politically motivated, a sign of both the powerful
hold such a totalitarian setting exerts on our attention and of McDonagh's
skill at rapid-fire scenes of interrogation, versions of which appear throughout his plays. As McDonagh quickly reveals, however, Katurian and Michal
have been arrested in connection with the disappearance and presumed
murder of three children. The play gradually reveals the specific and graphic
horrors apparently involved in each child's case, horrors lifted directly
from Katurian's stories: a boy whose toes are chopped off and who bleeds
to death; a girl who is force-fed apple slices with razors in them; and a
girl who suffers through a detailed and on-stage re-enactment of Christ's
crucifixion.

Even after Tupolski and Ariel confront him with the dead boy's severed
toes, which they have found in Katurian's house, and even after learning
that Michal has confessed, Katurian clings to his belief that he is being

persecuted for his art. Accordingly, he weaves a paranoid, hubristic web of suspicion about a police conspiracy: "I believe that you are trying to frame us for two reasons. One, because for some reason you don't like the kind of stories I write, and two, because for some reason you don't like retarded people cluttering up your streets" (30). Almost off-handedly, though, Michal soon admits to Katurian that he has in fact killed the children, and insists that he took his brother's stories as instructions for how to treat these children: "I was just testing out how far-fetched they were. [...] (*Pause.*) D'you know what? They ain't all that far-fetched" (50). Once he grasps what Michal has done—though it is not consistently clear whether Michal fully understands it himself—Katurian kills him. Then, in the hope of persuading the police to preserve his stories as part of his file, he falsely confesses to having murdered the children himself. His deception is exposed when he proves mistaken about one child's fate, and just before the play ends he is executed for killing Michal, killing his abusive parents, and lying to the police about the other murders.

"Don't believe everything you read in the papers." (*TP* 40)

As this description demonstrates, *The Pillowman* is less immediately funny on the page and on the stage than other McDonagh plays, although Jeff Goldblum's New York performance as Tupolski did magnify such humor as the play offers, no doubt helping Clive Barnes to review it as proving that "child torture, murder and mutilation" can, in fact, "be funny." In general, however, McDonagh's career has been such that audiences and critics remain likely to approach this work with expectations created by the reception of his other work as Irish, violent, and funny (not necessarily in that order). These are the sorts of expectations that allow Caryn James in *The New York Times* to refer to McDonagh's other plays as "all set in *believable* Irish villages," (N. pag.) an adjective that is no less revealing for being so casual (emphasis added). Indeed, many reviews noted that *The Pillowman* does contain some of the raw ingredients of McDonagh's success with his other works. These ingredients most notably include his mixture of humor and violence, his "scattershot vitriol" (Wolf 48), and his ability to navigate complex plots about hyperbolically dysfunctional families. Because of these strengths, McDonagh's other plays—however substantial their effects and their intentions—allow audiences to walk away with a tear and a smile, or even just a smile.

The Pillowman, in contrast, offers few of the tropes on which such responses have relied and offers no familiar setting to make its violence more readily locatable or containable, no framework of Irishness within which the violence of a play like *The Lieutenant of Inishmore* can be laughed off by audiences so inclined. By removing the Irish setting and going out of his way to remove most contextual signifiers, other than occasional incongruous dialect words like "bloke" (*TP* 96), McDonagh makes the play itself seem determinedly context-free. In place of such context, he leaves a narrative centered on the torture of children; despite his knack for making violence humorous, this narrative inescapably offers less humor than his other plays, violent though those are. Unsurprisingly, some audiences were clearly uncomfortable, at times leaving during the play (McGrath).

Moreover, the play's hints of generalized allegorical meaning about the nature of art combine with its relative scarcity of humor to be unsettling, simultaneously denying the comfort of humor and seeming to signal that the audience should be looking for Big Meanings without giving them much guidance in doing so. Many of the reviews, and particularly the most skeptical ones, focused on this sense that *The Pillowman* wanted credit for a sophistication it had no interest in earning. In the *Guardian*, for example, Lyn Gardner complained that *The Pillowman* "seems like a vanity project about Why Writers Are Very Important People, by a Very Important Writer called Martin McDonagh" (N. pag.). In a more acerbic back-handed compliment, Michael Feingold grudgingly conceded in his *Village Voice* review that, "unlike his 'Irish' plays [. . . this] at least has the dignity of aspiring to be *about* something," (N. pag.) but Charles Isherwood took the opposite view, comparing McDonagh unfavorably to the season's other critical hit, John Patrick Shanley's *Doubt*: "Mr. McDonagh wants merely to tell a story. [. . .] theatrically potent as it is, 'The Pillowman' ultimately has as much to tell us about the darker passages of experience it purports to dramatize as the haunted-house ride at Disneyland does. [. . .] It's Pinter without the point" (N. pag.). Even some more favorable reviews linked similar concerns to the play's form, suggesting that ultimately "McDonagh doesn't present his meaning with much clarity or conviction. His attempts have a dutiful quality that's very different from the vigor and relish with which he presents the tales" (Feldberg N. pag.). Perhaps most pointedly, in an essay about *The Pillowman*, Benjamin Barber has charged that

> McDonagh spins tales within tales about the darkest places in the human spirit without meaning a word of what he says or illuminating any of these sorrowful matters, and our popular culture sinks deeper and deeper into the distancing consolations of irony. [. . .] McDonagh uses [his material] to shock, titillate, excuse, and amuse and proudly teach us nothing. (36, 40)

As these examples suggest, the most heatedly negative of these reviews almost uniformly admitted McDonagh's technical skills, but seemed to resent the play even more, precisely because of those skills.

Despite such reviews, *The Pillowman* met a reception that, particularly in the New York production, was at least generally enthusiastic and at times ecstatic, as evidenced by Clive Barnes's review: "This may not be a play for either the faint-hearted or the unthoughtful, but with it McDonagh

[...] stakes his claim to being the best English-speaking playwright of his generation" (N. pag.). Offering more balanced praise, the *Toronto Star* reviewer found that "It's possible just to go along for the ride here [...] but there's also a lot to be learned about truth and illusion, crime and punishment, repentance and forgiveness" (Ouzounian N. pag.), while the *USA Today* reviewer found *The Pillowman* to be both McDonagh's "most brutal work yet [...] and also his most tender" (Elysa Gardner N. pag.). Much of the warmest praise treated the play as essentially about stories and storytelling, asserting that McDonagh brings an "unexpected freshness and moral ambiguity" to the play's potentially "clichéd-sounding theme" (James N. pag.). Even in New York, however, *The Pillowman*'s success was—unsurprisingly, given its formal and thematic departures from his earlier work—not that of *The Beauty Queen of Leenane*, and its sole Tony Award was for set design.

"I say keep your left-wing this, keep your right-wing that, and tell me a fucking story!" (*TP* 7)

As some of these reviews correctly noted, *The Pillowman* clearly makes the act of storytelling more central than do any of McDonagh's other plays, a centrality emphasized by Katurian's multiple and lengthy storytelling monologues. With its intricate use of Katurian's writing, the play moves through at least two main themes about stories: first, that of the artist in a totalitarian state; second, that of the broader connections between art and suffering, both the myth of the artist made great by his suffering and the myth of the suffering created by violent art. After this perhaps overly familiar beginning, the play develops its own concerns through a curious variant on the desire to find redemption, not so much through Katurian's art itself as through his commitment to the idea of being an artist.

These storytelling themes all flow through Katurian, who seems to have certain similarities with McDonagh, similarities noted and at times over-emphasized by the play's reviewers, one of whom went so far as to assert simplistically that "The supreme and only unquestioned good in the play is the preservation of Katurian's stories from censorship and police destruction; in other words, McDonagh's literary survival, no matter who and how many must die horribly for it" (Simon N. pag.). Katurian not only works in a slaughterhouse (*TP* 9) but also is a writer of promiscuously violent stories, both endeavors (so the logic goes) that seem tidily parallel to the author of *The Lieutenant of Inishmore*, *A Skull in Connemara*, and, most recently, *Six Shooter*, all texts with a seemingly Katurianesque taste for the gratuitous detail, for seeming to take the description of violence one step too far; as one character says of Katurian's stories, they're "something-esque" (18). To be sure, McDonagh has acknowledged some parallels, particularly to Katurian's obsessive writing and to his "arrogance" (McKinley N. pag.), and the play's origins do seem to lie in

Katurian's stories, which McDonagh had written as movie scenarios.[9] And yet, these potentially autobiographical parallels seem finally inexact and limited, little more than one of McDonagh's many red herrings. If they do possess a significance, it may simply be that the cumulative predictability of violence in Katurian's stories indirectly comments on how McDonagh's own drama has been received and on the expectations that have accrued around it. In effect if not intent, then, Katurian may be a version of the vain and violent caricature that quickly defined McDonagh's reputation as "famous not for his writing but for 'telling Sean Connery to fuck off.'"[10]

Semi-allegorical readings such as this one about the author and his character are consistently invited by McDonagh, in his other plays as well as in *The Pillowman*, which "seems to creep toward allegory, but doesn't get there" (McCarter N. pag.), at least not quite. Particularly in his other plays, these characteristically evasive invitations tap directly and profitably into the longstanding tendency of Irish cultural criticism toward national allegory, even as *The Pillowman* simultaneously works to frustrate that same tendency by removing Irish contexts. The most immediately visible of these semi-allegorical themes concerns the image of the writer oppressed by the totalitarian state, an image predicated upon what Michael Billington's review refers to as "the dangerous power of literature" (N. pag.). While this image seems to offer an engagement with art and the nation-state, the play finally does not substantially develop any such engagement. Thus, one reviewer seems almost entirely wrong in asserting that the play "uses a series of killings to reveal how repressive regimes fear the truth-telling ability of art that preserves a civilization's history and connects people to each other and their pasts" (Rosenberg N. pag.). More reasonably, Anne-Marie Welsh, one of the few reviewers to attempt to connect this totalitarian setting to McDonagh's earlier themes, suggests that "the meaningless globalized world" inhabited by his other characters here "has become universal and totalitarian" (N. pag.). Rather than offering a thematic focal point, however, this setting functions primarily as a dramatic mechanism that enables McDonagh to manipulate the audience's sympathies.[11] In particular, the setting in a state where the police—as Tupolski emphatically reminds Katurian (*TP* 23)—are not to be trusted lends temporary weight to Katurian's proclamations of his and Michal's innocence, thereby delaying the audience's confrontation with Michal's guilt and at least temporarily increasing their sympathy for the brothers. This sympathy is in turn essential to the way the play initially seems to present a choice between either prematurely dismissing Katurian as a vain hack or excessively valorizing him through a flawed parable of the artist in a totalitarian state.

After opening the door for both valorization and dismissal, McDonagh quickly shifts to a related theme, that of great art arising from great suffering. This theme is made explicit through the most revealing of Katurian's stories, "The Writer and His Brother," which tells of a boy raised to be a writer by parents who continually torture his brother in the next room. In a nightmarish example of the intentional fallacy gone awry, these fictional parents follow a version of the clichéd theory that great suffering creates great art: by filling their home with ambient sounds of one son's suffering, they hope to make their other son a great writer. This fictional writer discovers the truth when he finds a story by his equally fictional tortured-to-death brother, which, the vain but insecure writer is pained to admit, is "better than anything he himself had ever written" (34). This character tells no one of his discovery, thus preserving his career, and the theme of suffering-into-art becomes instead one of art that uses suffering to its own ends. Where the play initially led the audience to take the persecuted writer's side against the totalitarian state, this story speaks instead to the view of a writer as profoundly vain and self-serving, a view that coincides with some (but not all) of Katurian's behavior onstage. Indeed, as the audience quickly learns, this story of Katurian's is very directly autobiographical, though in an essential and significant departure Katurian kills his parents and, in a choice that resonates throughout the play, saves his brother.

As a corollary to this archetype of the suffering artist, the play also explores the view that art can create suffering, and specifically that violent art is responsible for making people violent. Clearly, Katurian has his own brand of such art; as Tupolski notes, it seems that his "theme" as a writer is " 'Some poor little kid gets fucked up' " (15). While Katurian rejects this interpretation, insisting that he has written less disturbing stories, the play offers little evidence to support him and various characters connect his writing to Michal's violence. Like Tupolski, Michal himself points to Katurian in explaining his own violent actions and denies that his brother has written any pleasant stories: "Like what? Like 'The Face Basement'? Slice off their face, keep it in a jar on top of a dummy, downstairs? Or 'The Shakespeare Room'? Old Shakespeare with the little black pygmy lady in the box, gives her a stab with a stick every time he wants a new play wrote"? Tellingly, Katurian's defensive reply is lame and brief: "He didn't do all those plays himself" (62). This is an ironic response for Katurian, a young writer of 400 intensely odd stories, as well as for a highly successful young playwright like McDonagh. Katurian clearly misses the point, and this exchange reflects how McDonagh's plays achieve much of their humor and their pathos through the characters' incongruously juxtaposed priorities.

More forcefully, Katurian insistently rejects any connection between his stories and Michal's violence, emphasizing instead Michal's own mind as the causal factor: "you're a sadistic, retarded fucking pervert who *enjoys* killing little kids, and even if every story I ever wrote was the sweetest thing imaginable, the outcome'd still be the fucking same" (50–51). Indeed, the play may suggest that Katurian is right: although Michal seems conveniently inconsistent in his intelligence and his moral awareness, and although neither he nor the play quite explains his actions, he does seem to have understood what he was doing: "I know it was wrong. Really. But it was very interesting" (48). Michal's claim that the stories made him do it (50), so aggressively rejected by Katurian and so little supported by the play, is one of many ways of viewing art as a matter of responsibility.[12] Whether progressive or conservative, such views have a long history in Irish culture, a history against which much of McDonagh's career thus far seems to be kicking gleefully. Without framing Katurian's stories in such social terms, however, and without accepting Michal's claim, *The Pillowman* examines how the stories nonetheless serve a purpose for Katurian. Specifically, despite his repeated disclaimers of intentionality and culpability, they reflect his attempt to come to terms with a different, intensely personal obligation—his unique responsibility for his brother.

The play develops its representation of this responsibility through a series of emotional and dramatic reversals that complicate our sense of both Katurian's stories in general and the function of his writing in particular. Thus, while the tone of *The Pillowman* seems fully in keeping with McDonagh's other plays and colored by Katurian's horrific stories, in the final analysis the play departs substantially from that tone. More specifically, the audience is led to expect—by the text as well as by McDonagh's previous work—the play to ultimately reflect Tupolski's assertion that "I don't have a world view. I think the world's a pile of shit. That isn't really a world view, is it? Or is it"? (85). That *The Pillowman* implies an admittedly dark "world view" is clear; however, while Tupolski's earlier assessment of Katurian's "theme" does have a certain validity, the use of these stories in the latter sections of the play moves well beyond simple horror.

One sign of this reversal emerges in "The Little Jesus," a story in which a little girl is crucified and buried alive.[13] Unlike the other stories, "The Little Jesus" works to deceive the audience, which has been led to expect that Michal killed the third child by enacting this story's elaborate details. Instead, Michal has enacted "The Little Green Pig," a comparatively benign story about a green pig who is taunted for being different. Consequently, in one of the most oddly moving moments from McDonagh's plays, the police find not a dead, crucified girl but a strangely happy one who has been painted green and now has three pet pigs she wants to keep (95). McDonagh's plays often have reversals, such as Mairead's shooting of Padraic in *The Lieutenant of Inishmore* (TL 65), or the revelation that the grating gossip Johnnypateenmike saved Billy from his parents' attempt to drown him in *The Cripple of Inishmaan* (TC 110). This reversal, however, is different in the way it pulls back from the horror to reveal something else at once more bizarre, more complex, and more open to the possibility of redemption, a possibility grounded in Katurian's compulsive act of writing.[14]

At first glance, this suggestion of possible redemption seems incongruous with Katurian's earlier, seemingly amoral behavior. From the outset, he is prone to repeated self-centered assertions of his writing's merits: his final words while alive are "I was a good writer. (*Pause.*) It was all I ever wanted to be. (*Pause.*) And I was" (*TP* 101). This seeming vanity runs deep enough that even as he writes out his false confession of unspeakable crimes, he inserts a note in brackets after each story's title: "[Attached.]" (73). Undermining this pride, the play invites a harsher evaluation of his art through the critical comments of other characters, particularly through the contempt of Ariel and Tupolski, and even Michal, who dismisses "The Writer and His Brother." Moreover, unlike the screen test monologue in *The Cripple of Inishmann*, where the Hollywood Irishness mocked by Billy blurs too much into McDonagh's own writing,[15] Katurian's stories do stand out as both less verbally dexterous and more prematurely self-congratulatory—in short, as worse—than the play itself, "gleefully uneven" though it may be (Brown).

At the same time, as already mentioned (see notes 6 and 9), Katurian's stories are apparently based on treatments that McDonagh himself wrote for short films that never came to fruition. McDonagh has also commented that his early stories "didn't work at all—I have no prose style whatsoever."[16] Not only are Katurian's stories not good, then, but also, they are not intended by McDonagh to be good, and by extension Katurian is not meant to be seen as a good writer.[17] Thus, Brantley is not quite right that "Artistic merit [. . .] is irrelevant here," (N. pag.) though one critic suggests that "Katurian's stories get better and better" over the course of the play (Heilpern N. pag.), as if McDonagh recognized that one play can only accommodate so much bad writing before it collapses. In fact, the worse Katurian is as a writer, the more it may be to McDonagh's credit; as Thomas Flanagan has suggested in a favorable review of Patrick McCabe's *Breakfast on Pluto*, "It is not easy to write this badly" (41).

Though much of the dialogue concerns issues of quality and vanity, the play finally establishes these issues primarily as a foundation for Katurian's visceral need to believe his writing is good, good in a way that somehow redeems the torture Michal experienced. After all, if Katurian is the artist that his parents set out to create, then Michal's suffering was still cruel and unjust, but at least it did produce something: Katurian's writing. The play's title story, which suggests this deeply felt responsibility for mitigating Michal's suffering, establishes its strange sense of redemption and its surprising sense of murder bleeding into mercy. "The Pillowman" concerns a giant man made entirely out of "fluffy pink pillows" (*TP* 43), whose mission in life is convincing small children to kill themselves. He does this by showing them the sadness of their impending adult lives, thereby convincing them "how shitty life is" (45). Eventually, miserable himself, he convinces his younger self to commit suicide, only to realize that his own suicide has dragged all those children back into the miserable lives from which they had sought to escape. Although, with a flip dismissal of all such work, Katurian has claimed that "The Writer and His Brother" is his only autobiographical story (76), the Pillowman's parallel to his own killing of Michal with a pillow suggests how he would like to see himself: as performing something between a punishment for what Michal has done and a mercy killing for what he has suffered. "It's not your fault," he tells Michal just before killing him in perhaps the play's most moving moment, "It's not your fault" (67).

It is here, at this intersection of his parents' cruelty with a guilt he owns but did not earn, that Katurian's art—whatever its shortcomings—reflects his sense of responsibility. This responsibility is not directed at his social community, and clearly not at the totalitarian state from which he holds himself apart. Instead, it is centered on Michal, who was damaged by their parents' obeisance to a false allegory of suffering-into-art and who subsequently (even consequently) tortured children, perhaps to reclaim for himself the stories that were written out of his own suffering. This sense of responsibility for Michal, who suffered to make Katurian an artist, is the real reason Katurian so intently seeks to save the stories, not, as Billington suggests, his belief in "the sanctity of literature"; had that been the case, surely Katurian would not have been so willing to "burn" anything in his stories that even "*seemed* political" (*TP* 8). Rather than as an innately human act of expression, Katurian had written as a path to the redemption of his brother's suffering, a redemption that only becomes more pressing after he learns of Michal's violence. When he effectively gives up on that redemption and kills Michal, he becomes even more devoted to the stories, not in their own right but for the possibility of redemption they had come to represent, even though it may already have been lost amidst the torture and the killing. Thus, although Katurian's actions initially register as authorial vanity, they finally signify his grasping at a devotion to something outside of himself. It is not that the stories themselves offer a redemptive uplift, nor that Michal's own violence is washed away, nor that Katurian transforms himself. Instead, deluded though he may be, Katurian seeks to redeem his inherited sins—to re-purpose the stories, to revise his and Michal's lives—through his sheer commitment to the fact of being a writer. For him the stories constitute primarily the evidence of that fact.

Narrating redemption

Clearly, much of the play focuses on Katurian and his stories as the medium for this redemption. In a last reversal, what redemption the play offers is instead enacted after Katurian's death and through Ariel, the policeman who had seemed most irredeemably violent in his anger and least likely to reveal mercy. Though giving this earthy policeman the name of Shakespeare's airy sprite from *The Tempest* may seem to offer an ironic contrast, behind that irony the name suggests that this policeman is both more potentially protean and more the agent of the play's movement toward redemption than he first appears to be. Of course, throughout most of the play, Ariel is profoundly contemptuous of Katurian, both as a

writer and as a suspect in the murder of the children. An ironically revealing typo, however, appears earlier in the published text: immediately after
violently assaulting Katurian without warning, the text has Ariel say with
casually brutal humor, "Oh, I almost forgot to mention . . . I'm the good
cop, he's the bad cop" (12). In performance, however, as clearly makes
more sense in the context, Tupolski instead draws much laughter for utter-
ing this statement. The typographical error of "Ariel" in place of "Tupolski"
effectively gives McDonagh's hand away early, and the conclusion does
reveal Ariel to be "the good cop."

After his own death, the bloodied figure of Katurian makes this reversal
explicit with a speech in which he closes the play by fusing "The Pillowman"
with "The Writer and His Brother." Through this speech, the play offers
something other than what the audience likely expects from McDonagh
and reveals Katurian to be as surprised as the audience may be. "The
story," Katurian says, "was going to finish in fashionably downbeat mode,
with Michal going through all that torment, with Katurian writing all
those stories, only to have them burned from the world by a bulldog of
a policeman" (103). Instead of fulfilling Katurian's vision, however,
McDonagh redirects our attention to Ariel, who disobeys orders and saves
the stories. This act, Katurian concludes, "would have ruined the writer's
fashionably downbeat ending," had he lived to write it, "but was somehow
. . . somehow . . . more in keeping with the spirit of the thing" (104). Rather
than simply dramatizing "the stubborn will of the creative spirit" (Brustein
29), Ariel's choice here is best understood as an act of grace. There may be
little of the divine in him, but he is nonetheless moved by an "influence
which operates [. . .] to regenerate and sanctify, to inspire virtuous
impulses" ("Grace"), and through those impulses to grant Katurian a kind
of reprieve after his death. In place of the "fashionably downbeat" ending
Katurian had envisioned, that is, the play enacts its concerns through
Ariel, who, in an echo of Katurian's effort to save the stories, steps outside
of his own hatred for the stories and gestures toward a redemptive potential.

Ariel's choice carries more weight because it comes without a retraction
of his distaste for the stories, and because it comes without an explanation; he does it "for reasons only known to himself" (*TP* 103). The play
does tentatively suggest that Ariel may identify with Katurian at the end
because, as we learn, Ariel also killed the father who abused him, suffocating
him with a pillow (82), and his own determination to punish those who
hurt children may thus share a common impulse with Katurian's stories
(see 77–78). Though these coincidences verge on the wildly melodramatic,
McDonagh again spikes them with acerbic humor, and does not allow the
play to linger on them or to represent them as definitive. It is thus ironically and finally Ariel—the cruel, pathological, violent cop—who is able to
reveal the play's strange vision of grace, of potential redemption, of the
human qualities that the play's events work to cast in doubt and that he
perhaps more than any of the other characters had seemed so definitively

to lack. It would be both easy and unproductive to exaggerate the scale of his actions here: they are perhaps only "lightly utopian" (Worthen and Worthen 170), and are at times dramatically overshadowed by the Grand Guignol elements of the play. Nonetheless, Ariel's choice to save the stories offers a small glimmer of the grace that constitutes the play's moral and dramatic center of gravity.

As this grace suggests, Katurian's art has proven transformative, not because of its content or its beauty but instead—in a surprisingly delicate way that has few counterparts in McDonagh's drama—because of the redemptive impulse it fosters despite its content, limited and contingent though that impulse may be. With its focus on grace and redemption, this ending runs the risk of overshadowing the torture of children, Michal's death, and Tupolski's weary cynicism, perhaps too quickly and too comfortingly so. Nonetheless, the resulting contrast with Katurian's intended "downbeat" ending both frees the play from depending on the aesthetic success or failure of Katurian's stories and suggests that "the spirit of the thing" is actually, in the play's phrasing, upbeat. This remains a generally incongruous word for McDonagh's drama, and particularly for a play that concerns the torture of children, a word that does not fit easily among the terms in which his work has been received to date. Here, at least, it is an apt one.

Notes

1 Patrick Lonergan has commented extensively on the intensely ambivalent critical response to McDonagh and, particularly regarding *The Lieutenant of Inishmore*, distinguishes insightfully between Irish and foreign audiences' responses ("The Laughter Will Come of Itself" 637–639).
2 In discussing McDonagh and Marina Carr, for example, Victor Merriman charges that their plays "repeat the angriest colonial stereotypes" and that "their appeal to the new consumer-Irish consensus lies in their appearance as ludicrous Manichean opposites—the colonized simian reborn" ("Staging Contemporary Ireland" 253). In contrast, Shaun Richards has mounted the defense that "McDonagh is as engaged in challenging his audiences as were Synge, Molloy, and Murphy" (207). Similarly, Lonergan concludes that "McDonagh's plays certainly do not appear to have facilitated escapism, delusion, or any of the other responses that critics would later attribute to Irish audiences" ("The Laughter Will Come of Itself" 637). Ondřej Pilný has argued against Merriman's claims even more forcefully, referring to them as "profoundly worrying" and as relying on "totalitarian rhetorical patterns" (227, 228).
3 Perhaps ironically, in a review of the Japanese translation of the play, Nobuko Tanaka suggested that the humor diminished in tandem with the profanity: "'The Pillowman' has lost much of its humor in translation [...] . This loss has its roots in language, since the F-words that are so key to the original simply have no Japanese equivalent. Furthermore, the play's deranged cops are also difficult to comprehend by audiences for whom the contemporary police generally have a clean-cut and respected image" (N. pag.).
4 Even before *The Pillowman*, Pilný was asking when McDonagh would "prove his worth on non-Irish themes" (229), as if Irishness somehow provided

McDonagh with a safety net. Indeed, at least one reviewer suggested the play was better for leaving Ireland behind and consequently being "Freed from rusticity" (Rooney 27). A similar point is made by Alastair Macaulay's review.

5 Press reports surrounding his 2005 Academy Award for *Six Shooter* suggested that he would henceforth devote his career to film work. Most accounts refer to one remaining unproduced early play, *The Banshees of Inisheer*, which seems unlikely to be staged, since "McDonagh says, [it] 'isn't any good'" (O'Toole, "A Mind in Connemara" 44). Joan FitzPatrick Dean also refers to the unproduced plays *The Rifleman of Inishturk* and *Dead Days at Coney* (194).

6 Caryn James quotes John Crowley on the origins of *The Pillowman*: "Crowley, who directed both the London and the current Broadway productions and has read the old, pre-'Beauty Queen' version, explained [. . .] that the basics of the play were there from the start: the same characters and story, and much of the same dialogue. But the structure was less complex" (N. pag.). O'Toole usefully describes McDonagh's plays as "conceived" rather than written in 1994, and relates that "after the London run of 'The Lieutenant [of Inishmore],' he returned to his 1994 draft of 'The Pillowman' and began to rework it" ("A Mind in Connemara" 46). Jesse McKinley offers a similar timeline for the play's final writing, reporting that *The Pillowman* "was a script he'd begun years ago, before all the Irish plays, by grafting some of his Borges-inspired short stories—including the story of the poor old Pillowman himself—onto a Pinter-inspired plot. In the fall of 2002 he sent it to the National Theater" [. . .] . (N. pag.).

7 Lonergan ("'Too Dangerous to be Done'?") and Grene offer subtle discussions of the marketing of McDonagh's plays, including but extending beyond consideration of his Irishness.

8 McDonagh has described his early reading of Borges as essential to his work, suggesting it "got [him] going in terms of storytelling" (O'Toole, "A Mind in Connemara" 43). As suggested by the apparent evocation of Kafka in Katurian's name, McDonagh is less an allusive writer than an ironic borrower or shadower of other artists, including the echoes critics have perceived between his work and that of Borges, Shepard, Mamet, Pinter, and Synge (see, for example, Pilný 230).

9 For accounts of Katurian's stories as originating in McDonagh's short stories/ film treatments, see note 6 above, as well as O'Toole, "Nowhere Man"; Terry Grimley N. pag.; and "Profile: Martin McDonagh: The 'greatest' playwright looks forward to Oscar night" N. pag.

10 Lonergan, "'Too Dangerous to be Done'?" 67. Lonergan is quoting O'Toole's article: "Martin McDonagh is famous for telling Sean Connery to f*** off. He also happens to be a brilliant playwright." For details of the play's genesis, see note 6 above.

11 McCarter and Isherwood also see the totalitarianism as a device, but primarily as one that allows McDonagh to telescope Katurian's prosecution (McCarter N. pag.) or to depict more "casually outrageous brutality" on stage (Isherwood N. pag.), while Feingold simply sees it as "a convenient setup for the story."

12 Interestingly, Hana Worthen and W. B. Worthen find in this scene "less a critique of the artist's responsibility for his work than an image of the violence that allegorical abstraction invariably brings to the world of things" (164).

13 Displaying a curious level of comfort, the twelve-year-old actress who was crucified and buried eight times a week during the play's Broadway run told an interviewer that she needed little direction on how to be crucified: "I'm Catholic [. . .] I already knew all about it" (quoted in Hofler 47).

14 Although a number of reviews saw *The Pillowman* as "celebrating [. . .] the raw, vital human instinct to invent fantasies" (Brantley N. pag.), Katurian's parents' horrific behavior means that very little about his writing is instinctual.

15 *TC* 74–76, 88. Lonergan is right to point out this moment in *The Cripple of Inishmaan* as one where McDonagh may be seeking to interrogate "his audiences' willingness to accept such images uncritically" ("'Too Dangerous to be Done'?" 73), but any such subversive potential depends on the marginal or non-existent distinctions between this passage and the rest of the play's language, a marginality that suggests McDonagh must also be implicating himself if he is implicating anyone.

16 Quoted in Lyman. According to O'Toole ("A Mind in Connemara" 43–44), McDonagh was only sixteen when he first wrote one of the central stories in *The Pillowman*, "The Tale of the Town on the River," which Katurian describes as "My best story" and "the only one that was published" (*TP* 19). Michael O'Neill has suggested that *The Pillowman's* last act "gently satiriz[es]" the "sometimes bumbling, derivative components of McDonagh's plays" (690).

17 I am grateful to the undergraduates in my spring 2006 seminar at Montclair State University whose engaged discussion of *The Pillowman* helped shape my sense of the text. Those students disagreed strongly about this point, and some of those who found the play *most* disagreeable were also those who thought the stories were *most* impressive, but all agreed that Tupolski's strange story (*TP* 86–87) is far worse aesthetically.

References

Except where otherwise noted, all electronic sources were unpaginated and were accessed through the Lexis-Nexis database <http://www.lexisnexis.com> at Montclair State University, Harry A. Sprague Library. These and all other electronic references were last accessed in June 2006.

Als, Hilton. "Tears Before Bedtime." Rev. of *The Pillowman*. Booth Theatre, New York. *New Yorker* 25 Apr. 2005. <http://www.newyorker.com/critics/content/articles/050425crth_theatre>.

Barber, Benjamin. "The Price of Irony." *Salmagundi* 148–49 (Fall–Winter 2005): 36–44.

Barnes, Clive. "Dazed & Amused—Brilliant Brit Import Unfolds as Brutal Mix." Rev. of *The Pillowman*. Booth Theatre, New York. *New York Post* 11 Apr. 2005. N. pag.

Berson, Misha. "On Broadway, dark thoughts and deeds in new dramas." Rev. of *The Pillowman*. Booth Theatre, New York. *Seattle Times* 9 May 2005. N. pag.

Billington, Michael. "*The Pillowman*." Rev. of *The Pillowman*. National Theatre, London. *Guardian* 14 Nov. 2003. <http://arts.guardian.co.uk/critic/review/0,,1085217,00.html>.

Brantley, Ben. "A Storytelling Instinct Revels in Horror's Fun." Rev. of *The Pillowman*. Booth Theatre, New York. *New York Times* 11 Apr. 2005. N. pag.

Brown, Scott. "The Pillowman." Rev. of *The Pillowman*. Booth Theatre, New York. *Entertainment Weekly* 18 Apr. 2005. <http://www.ew.com/ew/article/review/stage/0,6115,1049722_9|107236|0_0_,00.html>.

Brustein, Robert. "Prosecution Plays." Rev. of *The Pillowman*. Booth Theatre, New York. *New Republic* 23 May 2005: 27–30.

Clapp, Susannah. "Lost the Plot? You Will." Rev. of *The Pillowman*. National Theatre, London. *Observer* 16 Nov. 2003. N. pag.

Dean, Joan FitzPatrick. *Riot and Great Anger: Stage Censorship in Twentieth-Century Ireland*. Irish Studies in Literature and Culture. Madison: U of Wisconsin P, 2004.

Diehl, Heath A. "Classic Realism, Irish Nationalism, and a New Breed of Angry Young Man in Martin McDonagh's 'The Beauty Queen of Leenane.'" *Journal of the Midwest Modern Language Association* 34.2 (Spring 2001): 98–117.

Evans, Everett. "'Pillowman' goes where others won't; Alley production lives up to the original." Rev. of *The Pillowman*. Alley Theatre, Houston. *Houston Chronicle* 3 Feb. 2006. N. pag.

Feingold, Michael. "Story Horror." Rev. of *The Pillowman*. Booth Theatre, New York. *Village Voice* 19 Apr. 2005. N. pag.

Feldberg, Robert. "Scenes as dark as the most chilling nightmares." Rev. of *The Pillowman*. Booth Theatre, New York. *The Record* [Bergen County, NJ] 11 Apr. 2005. N. pag.

Flanagan, Thomas. "Waking from the Nightmare." Rev. of *Breakfast on Pluto*, by Patrick McCabe. *New York Review of Books* 22 Apr. 1999: 40–43.

Fricker, Karen and Brian Singleton, eds. *Critical Ireland*. Spec. issue of *Modern Drama* 47.4 (Winter 2004): 561–745.

Gardner, Elysa. "'Pillowman' is season's best." Rev. of *The Pillowman*. Booth Theatre, New York. *USA Today* 11 Apr. 2005. N. pag.

Gardner, Lyn. "*The Pillowman*: Playhouse, Oxford 2/5." Rev. of *The Pillowman*. Playhouse Theatre, Oxford. *Guardian* 7 Feb. 2005. N. pag.

"Grace." Def. 11b. *The Oxford English Dictionary*. Second ed. <http://dictionary.oed.com>.

Grene, Nicholas. "Ireland in Two Minds: Martin McDonagh and Conor McPherson." *Yearbook of English Studies* 35 (2005): 298–311.

Grimley, Terry. "Culture: Sleeping Giant of Literature; The National Theatre Brings Its Hit Play *The Pillowman* to Coventry." Rev. of *The Pillowman*. Warwick Arts Centre, Coventry. *Birmingham Post* 1 Mar. 2005. N. pag.

Heilpern, John. "Uh-Oh, Here It Comes . . . McDonagh's Masterly Nightmare." Rev. of *The Pillowman*. Booth Theatre, New York. *New York Observer* 18 Apr. 2005. N. pag.

Hofler, Robert. "Tortured Laughs." *Variety* 18 Apr. 2005: 47.

Isherwood, Charles. "Stories that Tell vs. Storytelling." *New York Times* 6 May 2005.

James, Caryn. "A Haunting Play Resounds Far Beyond the Page." *New York Times* 15 Apr. 2005. N. pag.

Lichtig, Toby. "It must be the way he tells them." Rev. of *The Pillowman*. National Theatre, London. *TLS* 28 Nov. 2003: 20.

Lonergan, Patrick. "'The Laughter Will Come of Itself. The Tears Are Inevitable': Martin McDonagh, Globalization, and Irish Theatre Criticism." Fricker and Singleton 636–58.

———. "Too Dangerous to be Done? Martin McDonagh's *Lieutenant of Inishmore*." *Irish Studies Review* 13.1 (2005): 65–78.

Lyman, Rick. "Most Promising (and Grating) Playwright." *New York Times Magazine* 25 Jan. 1998. N. pag.

Macaulay, Alastair. "Tarantino of the Troubles lays Oireland to rest." Rev. of *The Pillowman*. National Theatre, London. *Financial Times* 15 Nov. 2003. N. pag.

McCarter, Jeremy. "Torture, Vengeance, and Murder? Priceless." Rev. of *The Pillowman*. Booth Theatre, New York. *New York Sun* 11 Apr. 2005. N. pag.

McDonagh, Martin. *The Beauty Queen of Leenane and Other Plays*. New York: Vintage International, 1998.

———. *The Cripple of Inishmaan*. New York: Vintage International, 1998.

——. *The Lieutenant of Inishmore*. London: Methuen, 2001.

——. *The Pillowman*. London: Faber, 2003.

——. *The Pillowman*. Booth Theatre, New York. 11 May 2005.

McGrath, Charles. "Shocked, Amused, and A Little Queasy: *Pillowman* Crowd Not Always Ready for What's Next." *New York Times* 26 Apr. 2005. N. pag.

McKinley, Jesse. "Suffer the Little Children." *New York Times* 3 Apr. 2005. N. pag.

Merriman, Vic. "Staging contemporary Ireland: heartsickness and hopes deferred." *The Cambridge Companion to Twentieth-Century Irish Drama*. Ed. Shaun Richards. Cambridge: Cambridge UP, 2004. 244–57.

——. "'Besides the Obvious': Postcolonial Criticism, Drama, and Civil Society." Fricker and Singleton 624–35.

Morash, Christopher. *A History of Irish Theatre, 1601–2000*. Cambridge: Cambridge UP, 2002.

O'Neill, Michael. "*Mourning Becomes Electra/The Pillowman*." Rev. of *The Pillowman*. National Theatre, London. *Theatre Journal* 56.4 (Dec. 2004): 688–91.

O'Toole, Fintan. "Martin McDonagh is famous for telling Sean Connery to f*** off. He also happens to be a brilliant playwright." *Guardian* 2 Dec. 1996. N. pag.

——. "A Mind in Connemara: The Savage World of Martin McDonagh." *New Yorker* 6 Mar. 2006. 40–47.

——. "Nowhere Man." *Irish Times* 26 Apr. 1997. N. pag.

——. "Spellbinding mix of horror and wit." Rev. of *The Pillowman*. The Lowry, Manchester. *Irish Times* 15 Mar. 2005. N. pag.

Ouzounian, Richard. "Bleak, funny *Pillowman* jolts you awake." Rev. of *The Pillowman*. Booth Theatre, New York. *Toronto Star* 5 May 2005. N. pag.

"*The Pillowman* by Martin McDonagh." Rev. of *The Pillowman*. Booth Theatre, New York. National Theatre, London. Complete-Review.com. <http://www.complete-review.com/reviews/dramauk/mcdonm1.htm>.

Pilný, Ondřej. "Martin McDonagh: Parody? Satire? Complacency"? *Irish Studies Review* 12.2 (2004): 225–32.

"Profile: Martin McDonagh: The 'greatest' playwright looks forward to Oscar night." *Sunday Times* [London] 5 Mar. 2006. N. pag.

Rees, Catherine. "The Good, the Bad, and the Ugly: The Politics of Morality in Martin McDonagh's *The Lieutenant of Inishmore*." *New Theatre Quarterly* 21.1 (Feb. 2005): 28–33.

Richards, Shaun. "'The outpouring of a morbid, unhealthy mind': The Critical Condition of Synge and McDonagh." *Irish University Review* 33.1–2 (Spring–Summer 2003): 201–14.

Roche, Anthony. "Contemporary Drama in English: 1940–2000." *The Cambridge History of Irish Literature, Volume II: 1890–2000*. Ed. Margaret Kelleher and Philip O'Leary. Cambridge: Cambridge UP, 2006. 478–530.

Rooney, David. "*The Pillowman*." Rev. of *The Pillowman*. Booth Theatre, New York. *Daily Variety* 11 Apr. 2005: 27, 39.

Rosenberg, David A. "*The Pillowman*." Rev. of *The Pillowman*. Booth Theatre, New York. *Back Stage* 14 Apr. 2005. N. pag.

Simon, John. "Exquisite Corpses: *The Pillowman* revels a bit too much in its own brilliance and repulsiveness." Rev. of *The Pillowman*. Booth Theatre, New York.

New York 25 Apr. 2005. <http://newyorkmetro.com/nymetro/arts/theater/reviews/
11755/>.

Tanaka, Nobuko. "Satire booms in dark dramatic fantasies." Rev. of *The Pillowman*.
Parco Gekijo, Tokyo. *Japan Times* 17 Nov. 2004. N. pag.

Wallace, Clare. "Irish Theatre Criticism: De-territorialisation and Integration."
Fricker and Singleton 659–70.

Welsh, Anne Marie. "McDonagh shows mastery of his craft; 'Pillowman' an
imaginative work." Rev. of *The Pillowman*. Booth Theatre, New York. *San Diego
Union-Tribune* 29 May 2005. N. pag.

Wolf, Matt. "Martin McDonagh on a Tear." *American Theatre* 15.1 (Jan. 1998):
48–50.

Worthen, Hana and W. B. Worthen. "*The Pillowman* and the Ethics of Allegory."
Modern Drama 49.2 (Summer 2006): 155–73.

Young, Toby. "Shock Tactics." Rev. of *The Pillowman*. National Theatre, London.
Spectator 22 Nov. 2003: 66.

9 "Never mind the shamrocks"— Globalizing Martin McDonagh

Patrick Lonergan

A psychopathic killer is on the loose. Bodies are turning up in strange places. The police are developing elaborate theories but getting nowhere. And the killer has been given a catchy nickname—"The Pillowman." To those familiar with Martin McDonagh's works, this passage might seem a loose description of his 2003 play *The Pillowman*. It is, however, a sketch of an episode from Salman Rushdie's 1999 novel, *The Ground beneath Her Feet*, in which a serial killer called Cyrus Cama is responsible for murders in Mysore, Bangalore, and Madras. Unable to "stand the anonymity" brought by his nickname, Rushdie's Pillowman sends "a boastful letter to all the relevant police chiefs, incriminating himself while insisting that he would never be caught by such duffers as they" (136). He is later captured and incarcerated, but proves popular with his guards.[1]

There are obvious differences between McDonagh's play and Rushdie's novel, as well as some interesting parallels. The most amoral moments of violence in *The Pillowman* are performed by Michal, who acts out his brother Katurian's grim tales of infanticide, apparently unaware of the moral consequence of doing so. He is caught rather easily by the police and, unlike Rushdie's character, lacks the mental capacity to take responsibility for his actions. And although he displays some pride in his achievements—"I'm getting quite good at it," he tells Katurian—he cannot be described as boastful (*TP* 49).

What both texts have in common is their characters' need to be recognized for their achievements: Katurian is willing to sacrifice his life in the hope that his stories will survive, while Cyrus Cama appears to view incarceration as an acceptable price for being recognized as the killer that he is. And there is, of course, the use of the same name—the Pillowman— in texts that in both cases focus on actions that are "profoundly disordered, utterly immoral and highly dangerous" (Rushdie 137).

When confronted with these details, it is possible to form erroneous conclusions about who is influencing whom here. Rushdie's novel appeared four years before McDonagh's play premiered in London, so one might assume that McDonagh's use of the "Pillowman" name is an example of his tendency to quote gleefully from a wide range of cultural sources or, as

Christ Morash (borrowing from Baudrillard) puts it, to produce "copies that have forgotten their originals" (269). Yet McDonagh told Fintan O'Toole that his play was written in 1994 (O'Toole, "A Mind in Connemara" 44) and we also know that *The Pillowman* was first performed by Druid Theatre in a reading in Galway three years later[2]—long before Rushdie's novel appeared. On the other hand, it is reasonable to assume that Rushdie was not borrowing from McDonagh's text, given that its existence was not widely known until 2003; it is impossible that McDonagh was quoting from Rushdie. We can only conclude that both authors, writing around the same time, happened to use the same name—which appears nowhere else—in stories that describe similar events. In short, the affinity looks like a strange, but interesting, coincidence.

This resemblance points to the difficulty of dealing with such issues as influence, intention, and intertextuality in McDonagh's plays—issues that become particularly problematic when they are considered outside the parameters of the Irish dramatic tradition. We know that McDonagh borrowed the title of *A Skull in Connemara* from Beckett's *Waiting for Godot* (1955) and *The Lonesome West* from Synge's 1907 drama, *The Playboy of the Western World* (Beckett 43, Synge 65). Additionally, the first play in *The Leenane Trilogy*, *The Beauty Queen of Leenane*, shows traces of both Tom Murphy's *Bailegangaire* (1985) and Beckett's *Endgame* (1956), while *The Pillowman* bears some interesting resemblances to Gary Mitchell's *The Force of Change* (2000), another text written after McDonagh's play, but published before it. McDonagh has, however, refuted suggestions that he was influenced by the Irish dramatic tradition when he wrote *The Leenane Trilogy*, and has tended to reject attempts to link his work with that of other Irish writers. McDonagh explains that, although his work can be compared to Synge's, his composition of the *Leenane* plays was not influenced by that writer:

> [a]s soon as I started writing the first scene [of *A Skull in Connemara*], I realised it was completely fresh for me and I wasn't harking back to anything I had seen or read. I can see similarities now. I read *The Playboy of the Western World* and the darkness of the story amazed me. I thought it would be one of those classics that you read in order to have read, rather than to enjoy, but it was great. At the time, though, I didn't know it at all. (quoted in O'Toole, "Nowhere Man" 1)

Notwithstanding McDonagh's denial of having been influenced by Synge, he has been compared to that writer more frequently than to any other (cf. Richards, Lanters, Vandevelde).[3]

As McDonagh acknowledges when he states that "I can see similarities now," the comparison of his work to Synge's is certainly valid—but comparison to other authors and forms is also possible. For example, a feature of four of McDonagh's six produced plays is the reappearance of characters who are presumed dead by the audience: Mairtin in *A Skull* (*Plays 1* 118), Billy in *The Cripple of Inishmaan* (*TC* 61), the mute girl in *The Pillowman* (*TP* 95), and Wee Thomas in *The Lieutenant of Inishmore* (*TL* 56). There is certainly a parallel between these reappearances and the "resurrection" of Old Mahon in Synge's *Playboy*, particularly in the case of Mairtin in *A Skull in Connemara*. Yet we could also compare this feature of McDonagh's plays with elements of other cultural forms—with, for example, the surprising return of apparently dead characters in soap opera (such as Harold Bishop in the Australian serial *Neighbours*, "Dirty" Den Watts in the BBC's *Eastenders*, or Bobby Ewing in the American soap *Dallas*). It might also be compared to a scene in Quentin Tarantino's *Reservoir Dogs* (1992), in which Mr. Orange (a character presumed to be unconscious by the audience) shoots Mr. Blonde. Yet, whereas McDonagh denies being influenced by Synge, he has consistently spoken of his indebtedness to Australian soap and Tarantino.

Just as critics have shown themselves generally unwilling to explore the influences that McDonagh himself acknowledges, so too have they ignored his desire to avoid being categorized as an Irish dramatist. Only Victor Merriman has attempted to broaden analysis of McDonagh's works, but does so only as a mode of negative criticism, suggesting that *The Leenane Trilogy* offers "a kind of voyeuristic aperture on the antics of white trash whose reference point is more closely aligned to the barbarous conjurings of Jerry Springer than to the continuities of an indigenous tradition of dramatic writing" ("Staging Contemporary Ireland" 254). Most other critics attempt to define McDonagh's importance in national terms—to consider his place in the Irish literary canon or to present him as an example of the British style of "in-yer-face" theater (Sierz 219–225).

Yet McDonagh himself resists the attempt to categorise him as either Irish or British:

> I always felt somewhere kind of in-between. . . . I felt half-and-half and neither, which is good [. . .]. I'm happy having a foot in both camps. I'm not into any kind of definition, any kind of -ism, politically, socially, religiously, all that stuff. It's not that I don't think about those things, but I've come to a place where the ambiguities are more interesting than choosing a strict path and following it. (quoted in O'Toole, "Nowhere Man" 1)

The attempt to relate McDonagh's works to nationalized categories tends to lead critics into frustration. For Mary Luckhurst, he is a turncoat Irishman, "selling out" to the British—a "thoroughly establishment figure who relies on monolithic, prejudicial constructs of rural Ireland to generate himself an income" (40). Quoting from a selection of McDonagh's media interviews, Luckhurst presents the anti-Irish responses to *The Lieutenant* from the British press as evidence that the playwright is deliberately "forging speech patterns and representations that build on prejudicial constructs [in Britain] of the Irish as little more than boneheaded buffoons" (38).[4] Many others have attacked McDonagh on similar grounds, and the debate about whether his work has value—or whether it can be seen as "really" Irish (whatever that is) or "actually" English—continues to have a polarizing effect on scholars of his work.

It could be argued that, in provoking such responses as these, McDonagh's work can indeed be related to other Irish plays: for example, Luckhurst's critique of *The Lieutenant* seems eerily similar to Brendan Behan's self-referential response to similar attacks on his own work in *The Hostage* (1958):

Soldier: Brendan Behan, he's too anti-British.
Officer: Anti-Irish, you mean. Bejasus, wait till we get him back home. We'll give him what for for making fun of the Movement.
Soldier: [To the audience] He doesn't mind coming over here and taking your money.
Pat: He'd sell his country for a pint. (204)

The accusation that McDonagh is "selling out" to the British—or, as Behan has it, "coming over here and taking your money"—means that his work can be located not in an Irish literary tradition, but rather in an Irish critical tradition, in which scholars express concern about the reception of Irish plays abroad. In such criticism, there is a tendency to conflate authorial intention with audience response, to assume that if McDonagh's works are received in ways that give rise to anti-Irish stereotyping, the author must himself be deliberately "cashing in" on the existence of such prejudice. No evidence exists to suggest that this is the case, however.

In part, this confusion between intention and reception arises because such scholars place excessive weight on comments made by or attributed to McDonagh in press interviews, which are frequently full of inaccuracies, exaggerations, omissions, and inconsistencies. For instance, Mimi Kramer, writing for *Time Magazine* in 1997, reported correctly that the performance in the West End of *The Leenane Trilogy* and *The Cripple of Inishmaan* made McDonagh "the only writer this season, apart from Shakespeare, to have four plays running concurrently in London" (71). This report was transformed quickly into the ludicrous assertion that McDonagh was the first playwright *since* Shakespeare to have four of his plays running in London, a claim first made by Sean O'Hagan which has appeared subsequently in many venues (32). Moving from inaccuracy to inconsistency, it is also notable that many different dates have been given for the composition of McDonagh's plays. For example, Liz Hoggard reports that McDonagh wrote *The Lieutenant of Inishmore*, "after the failure in 1996 of the first

IRA ceasefire" (12). Yet (as I discuss below) Penelope Dening suggests that its composition predates that of *The Cripple of Inishmaan* (12), while O'Toole claims that the play was written in 1994, simultaneously with McDonagh's five other produced plays ("A Mind in Connemara" 44). When scholars are confronted with such obviously exaggerated claims—or with the existence of so many apparently contradictory statements by McDonagh—they seem to have concluded that the writer himself might be something of a fraud.

The problem, however, appears to arise from the conditions under which theater journalism is commissioned and received in UK and Irish daily newspapers. Many, though of course not all, of the writers commissioned by newspaper editors to interview McDonagh seem to know little about drama, with one of them characterizing him as "the perfect playwright for People Who Dread Theatre" (Hoggard 11). The presentation of McDonagh in this way may, as Luckhurst argues, have helped to market his plays; perhaps, however, it reveals better the attitudes of commissioning editors to theater, which, in the case of McDonagh, reveals a tendency to focus on those elements of medium that are assumed to be of interest to a non-theatergoing audience: violence, the deliberate provocation of controversy, iconoclasm, and an air of not taking oneself too seriously. In any case, it reveals the need to be cautious about using McDonagh's media interviews as a way of interpreting his plays.

Furthermore, it is surprising, given the intensity of debate that surrounds his work, that critics have been reluctant to explore McDonagh's statements about the writers and artists that actually have influenced him. In part, this neglect arises because at the beginning of his career, McDonagh sometimes spoke dismissively of others' work. For instance, Richard Eyre reports that, when McDonagh was asked what he thought of the 1997 opening of David Hare's *Skylight*, he replied "well, I didn't write it so it's crap" (364)—a comment that encapsulates well the tone of his remarks at that time.[5] Critics' objections to this (apparent) arrogance may explain their unwillingness to take McDonagh more seriously; certainly, his dismissal of other writers has tended to overshadow his discussion of those dramatists whom he admires. However, he spoke in his first interviews about his indebtedness to American dramatist David Mamet and the British writer Harold Pinter; indeed, he told Fintan O'Toole that his use of the "Irish" voice in his first plays arose from a deliberate decision to disguise the influence of those two writers ("Nowhere Man" 1). At that time, he also referred to his high regard for such plays as Mamet's *American Buffalo* (1975), Pinter's *The Birthday Party* (1958), Sam Shepard's *True West* (1980), and Tracey Letts's *Killer Joe* (1993), and the influence of such texts may be found in *The Leenane Trilogy* in particular. In 2001, McDonagh spoke frankly about the influences he had drawn on for *The Lieutenant of Inishmore*. He describes that play as "much more in the Joe Orton tradition than in any tradition of Irish drama"—a statement that seems accurate if the play is considered in relation to Orton's *Loot* (1965) in particular – adding that *The Lieutenant* can be seen as an expression of his desire to get "as much John Woo and Sam Peckinpah into the theater as possible" (quoted in Rosenthal 10). And throughout his career to date, he has spoken consistently of how his work has been informed by his admiration for others' work: for the films of not only Peckinpah and Woo, but also those of Tarantino, Martin Scorsese, and Terrence Malick; for Australian soap opera; for the music of the Pogues, the Clash, Nirvana, and the Sex Pistols; for the fictions of Nabokov and Borges.

What is notable about McDonagh's range of influences is its eclecticism. For instance, he reads Argentinean fiction, saying of Borges that, "it's from him I began to appreciate the importance of telling a story" ("New Druid Playwright is a 'Natural.'" 23).[6] He enjoys independent cinema from the United States and Hong Kong and moves easily from Pinter to Kurt Cobain to *Neighbours*. In citing such influences, he is far from unusual; indeed, the popularity of his works arises partially because audiences share a similarly broad range of cultural interests and are conversant with the wide array of forms from which he quotes.

It is worth recalling that Irish playwrights have always pointed out the importance of international culture to their work. The influence of Ibsen on Shaw, Synge, and O'Casey is very apparent, and much has been written of Yeats's use of Japanese Noh theater. Tom Murphy has stated that as a young writer he felt that "anything Irish is a pain in the arse," and instead sought out the work of Lorca and Tennessee Williams (quoted in *Talking about Tom Murphy* 94). Younger writers such as Mark O'Rowe and Conor McPherson in general resist attempts to relate their work to that of the canonical Irish dramatists, Synge and O'Casey, instead citing Mamet, Pinter, and Arthur Miller as their influences; and, although Marina Carr acknowledges being influenced by Synge, she appears most indebted to Tennessee Williams.[7]

It could be argued that McDonagh is different from other Irish dramatists in that his work crosses more easily the boundaries between high and low cultural forms, but again he is not unusual in this respect. O'Rowe draws liberally from Asian cinema in such plays as *Made in China* (2001) and *Howie the Rookie* (1999). McPherson's *The Weir* (1997) and *Shining City* (2003) depend for their impact on audiences' enjoyment of old-fashioned ghost stories and appeared at a time when supernatural plot twists were being made popular by such filmmakers as M. Night Shyamalan in *The Sixth Sense* (1999). And Brian Friel makes extensive use of popular American song in his works, notably in *Dancing at Lughnasa* (1990) and *Wonderful Tennessee* (1993). It seems fair to suggest therefore that to attempt to consider such writers' work in an exclusively Irish context is to overlook many important features of their writing, both in terms of the composition of their work and Irish audiences' familiarity with the internationalized cultural forms on which these authors draw.

The difficulty for scholars who attempt to come to terms with such elements of McDonagh's work is that existing analysis of it is grounded in a national literary model. As such, our methodology presupposes a stable "Irish" tradition in which McDonagh's plays may be located and further assumes that inclusion in that tradition should be determined by literary value. How then can we accommodate such issues as the influence of Tarantino, Pinter, and Mamet—or the impact of "low" cultural forms such as soap opera—on McDonagh's work?

One solution might be to see McDonagh's work as part of a "world" literary tradition, but this conception, too, creates to problems. McDonagh may be considered in relation to a vast array of other writers, from Synge to Borges to Rushdie—and no doubt, the list of other writers who might also be considered is infinite. However, there is an obvious impracticality in studying his writing without regard for literary or national boundaries. "What can one make of such an idea"? asks Claudio Guillen, describing the possibility of studying world literature as "a wild idea, unattainable in practice, worthy not of an actual reader but a deluded keeper of archives who is also a multimillionaire" (38). As the striking similarities between *The Pillowman* and *The Ground beneath Her Feet* illustrate, a consideration of McDonagh's work in an international context—which would indeed be possible only for a deluded multimillionaire archivist— can at best alert us to interesting coincidences. Furthermore, notions of a world literary system make the same presupposition as national literary systems: that inclusion in the canon or system is determined by notions of physical space and an author's ability to meet set criteria about literary or artistic worth.

I want to suggest, then, that the problems created by critics' attempts to categorize McDonagh in terms of Irish drama arise because of a clash between the assumptions underlying literary criticism on the one hand and the globalized quality of much contemporary cultural production and reception on the other; that is, we are attempting to use a nationalized discourse to critique work that has transcended national boundaries. I would suggest that Martin McDonagh's drama needs to be understood not in relation to an international or world literary system, but rather in relation to a globalized framework, grounded in Ireland but engaged with ideas from other cultures. Doing so will allow us to consider more fully the issues of hybridity, intertextuality, and aesthetic value in McDonagh's plays, while also pointing us toward new ways of understanding the works of other dramatists, both Irish and international. To make this case, I want to consider McDonagh's drama in relation to some of the influences he has himself cited, considering how a criticism that styles itself as national—as both Irish and British dramatic criticism currently does—may be used to understand the work of such globalized writers as McDonagh.

"Everybody needs good neighbours": McDonagh and soap opera

When considering the Irish qualities of McDonagh's work, it seems useful to begin with the issue of setting. All of McDonagh's Irish plays are set in identifiable locations—in Leenane, a small town in the north of County Galway (and the location for the shooting of the Irish film *The Field*), and on the Aran Islands, which lie off the coast of the same county. The setting of *The Pillowman* is by comparison quite vague: "Kamenice," as Werner Huber notes, "is a very common place-name in the Slavonic settlement areas of East Central Europe. Thus, we find, for example, Česká Kamenice (in Bohemia, Czech Republic), and also Saska Kamenice (in Saxony, where the German form is 'Chemnitz')" ("From Leenane to Kamenice" 285). It is possible, therefore, to relate the settings of each of McDonagh's plays to existing locations.

He has stated, however, that his decision to choose such settings has largely been arbitrary. Speaking to Penelope Dening about the composition of *The Lieutenant of Inishmore*, McDonagh claims that the play was set on the Aran Islands only because "for plot purposes, [he] needed 'a place in Ireland that would take a long time to get to from Belfast.' Inishmore fitted the bill. Three Aran Islands prompted the idea of a trilogy" (Dening 12). This decision about the setting of *Inishmore* in turn led to McDonagh's *The Cripple of Inishmaan* and the unpublished, unproduced *Banshees of Inisheer*.

The arbitrary manner in which these places were chosen implies that, for McDonagh, plot rather than setting is of primary importance: he does not seek to provide an authentic representation of any of the places that he portrays, but instead chooses locations that are appropriate to the stories that he wishes to tell. Hence, in the case of Leenane, we are told that (as is true in almost every Irish town) there is a church and graveyard, but we are given no sense of their location in relation to the homes of the characters, or to other places in the town. Similarly, we are told that Father Welsh from *The Lonesome West* "drowned himself in the lake last night" (*Plays 1* 177), which seems rather unusual, given that the largest body of water in or near Leenane is not a lake, but Kilary Harbour, an area of great natural beauty that dominates Leenane but which is never mentioned in *The Leenane Trilogy*. We might also note that it is not the practice of the Irish police to station its members in the towns where they were brought up, which makes it extremely unlikely that Tom Hanlon in *A Skull in Connemara* would be posted to Leenane. It is also worth noting that the real police station in Leenane is staffed only two or three days a week by police based in the nearby town of Clifden.

Likewise, we learn little about the Aran Islands from *The Cripple* or *The Lieutenant*. The running joke in the latter play about Davey's pink bicycle (*TL* 4) presumably arises from McDonagh's knowledge that cycling is the principal mode of transportation on Inishmore, but there are few accurate references to the local geography—to the prehistoric forts, the stone walls, or the windswept character of foliage and shrubbery. The plotting of *The Lieutenant* also reveals a marked lack of interest in geographical accuracy. Padraic arrives on Inishmore at night, meeting Mairead by "moonlight" (32), after which Donny and Davey go to sleep at five in the morning, or "early blue dawn" (36). Padraic does not arrive at his father's house until seven hours later, at "twelve noon," according to the stage directions (38). Given Padraic's concern for his cat, one would assume that he would go immediately to his father's house; yet, because the entire island of Inis Mór is just under nine miles in length, it seems strange that it takes Padraic at least ten hours to travel there from the island's harbor (the entire journey from Northern Ireland to the Aran Islands could be completed in about seven hours). And of course, we never get any reference in either of the published Aran Islands plays to Irish, the first language of the islanders. Indeed, the language used by all of McDonagh's characters fails to display any of the regional variations that would be evident in the speech of people from different parts of Ireland, so that although we are told that Christy, Brendan, and Joey "all have Northern Irish accents" in *The Lieutenant* (27), this is not evident in the script, and was not made evident in its premiere RSC performance in 2001.

This lack of geographical authenticity is also a feature of McDonagh's only non-Irish play. *The Pillowman* offers us no insight into the kind of society that Katurian lives in: we are told that it is a totalitarian state, but it is unclear what form of totalitarianism is in operation. The references to the city's Jewish Quarter do not provoke any of the expressions of anti-Semitism that might be expected in a fascist European state (*TP* 26) and, because the power of the "Little Jesus" story arises from its breaking of religious taboos, the setting seems unlikely to be a communist country. Indeed, it seems most likely that the decision to set the play in a totalitarian state arises simply from McDonagh's desire to raise the dramatic stakes, by making the possibility that Katurian will be executed for his writing seem credible to his audience—another example of his prioritization of plotting over geographic authenticity.

Indeed, there is little reference to contemporary politics in any of McDonagh's plays: we get brief allusions to the Yugoslav Civil Wars of the early 1990s in *The Lonesome West* (*Plays 1* 173), but have no sense of how politics functions within the Ireland being presented onstage. This absence of political awareness is particularly notable in *The Lieutenant of Inishmore*, a play ostensibly attacking certain strands of Irish political thought that makes no reference to any of the figures actually involved in Irish republicanism. The only real people referred to in the play are instead victims of the Northern Ireland Troubles. McDonagh includes "jokes" in his play about the Guildford Four (*TL* 33), wrongly convicted of involvement in terrorism; he invites us to laugh at the victims of the Bloody Sunday shootings by the British Army in Derry in 1972 (28). And his characters also allude to four victims of IRA violence: Timothy Parry and Jonathan Ball, the children (aged twelve and three respectively) killed by the 1993 IRA bombing of Warrington, England, and Stephen Melrose and Nicholas Spanos, two Australian tourists shot dead in the Netherlands in 1990 when they were mistaken for off-duty British soldiers by the IRA.[8] That the deaths of these people are used for humorous purposes, while their murderers are satirized only in general terms, reflects very poorly on McDonagh, and reveals how the politics of *The Lieutenant* are related only superficially to the conflict in Northern Ireland.

This discussion reveals that taking McDonagh's plays literally can lead only to absurdity—the places that he uses may all be found on a map, but local knowledge of these places is not displayed by the author, required of the audience, or communicated by the plays. Accordingly, it seems fruitless to attempt to consider these plays in the context of other Irish treatments of place. To require of McDonagh's work such features as authenticity and accuracy in the presentation of political and social facts is to miss the point of his works entirely: McDonagh's Leenane, Inishmore, and Inishmaan should not be thought of as similar to O'Casey's or McPherson's Dublin, Friel's Ballybeg, Mitchell's Belfast, or Murphy's Tuam. Rather, place in McDonagh's works functions to aid international audiences' understanding of the plays. This, I argue, constitutes not an example of McDonagh's indebtedness to Irish drama, but rather an example of how his works may usefully be considered in relation to soap opera.

Much has been written of McDonagh's interest in this form of television. "We'd get up at 12:00, 1:00," John McDonagh told the American media in 1997, describing the lifestyle he shared with his brother in their London home in the early 1990s: "We'd have breakfast; we'd watch Australian soap operas on the television; and then he'd go to his room, and I'd go to mine, and we'd twiddle our thumbs, and maybe we'd write something, and then come down and have something to eat at 6:00, and start watching television again" (*Today Show*). Comments like these have often been quoted in discussion of McDonagh's work and used as evidence to support the claim that the playwright learned his dramatic craft not from the great authors of world theater but from watching such Australian soap operas as *Neighbours* and *Home and Away*. Such claims have tended to be asserted rather than explored; I therefore want to consider whether they have any validity.

A number of important studies of soap opera in Britain, Australia, and the United States have been published in recent years, appearing mostly in the field of cultural studies—with the result that scholarship in this area has tended to explore the relationship of the genre to such issues as gender (Blumenthal, Brundson, and Mumford), ethnicity (Gillespie), and social class (*Remote Control*). As yet, few studies have attempted to explore the relationship between soap opera and literature. Where comparisons are made, the tendency is to state that soap opera draws on such literary forms as melodrama (Ang) and the nineteenth-century realist novel (Hobson 28), but little work has appeared suggesting that literature might draw on soap operatic conventions.

Treatment of this issue in McDonagh's work has tended to be superficial, being explored in most detail by the Australian media when *The Leenane Trilogy* was produced in Sydney in 1998. In an article headlined "Aussie Soaps: McDonagh Comes Clean," the *Sydney Morning Herald's* Joyce Morgan asked a question that was preoccupying the Australian press at that time: "did he really learn to write plays by watching *Neighbours*"? The answer to that question proves somewhat inconclusive. Morgan tells us that while in Australia McDonagh was "amused to keep hearing the rumour that he learned how to write plays by [watching] Australian soap," but he "acknowledges there's a spot of truth" in the rumor. "I was unemployed for a long time and when you are unemployed in England all you do is watch soaps and television and most of them are Australian," McDonagh stated, before asking, "hey, you don't know when they're on here, do you"? (27). *The Leenane Trilogy's* director Garry Hynes was also asked for her views on the subject. "Australian soaps entertain a lot of people, otherwise they wouldn't be as popular as they are," she told the Sydney *Daily Telegraph*, further noting, "Martin entertains people, so the connection is quite apt really." This might seem a rather weak link, but later in that interview, Hynes states explicitly that "Australian soaps have made a very big contribution to these plays, and to the writer generally" (quoted in Chisholm 45). This relationship was made even more explicit when Maggie Kirkpatrick—best known in Ireland and the UK for her role in the Australian soap *Prisoner, Cell Block H*—starred in a 1999 touring Australian production of *The Beauty Queen of Leenane* directed by Hynes. I have suggested above that there is a need to treat newspaper reports on McDonagh's writing with caution, so it seems unwise to take these comments as a definitive statement on the matter: after all, neither Hynes nor McDonagh elaborates on what kind of "big contribution" Australian soap might have made to his works. There is, however, a clear similarity between McDonagh's plotting and use of place, discussed above, and the way these techniques function in soap opera.

All of the major international soaps are set in broadly identifiable geographical locations: *Eastenders* and *Brookside* are set in the English cities of London and Liverpool, respectively; *Neighbours* takes place in Brisbane, Australia; and one of the most successful soaps of all time is *Dallas*, set in Texas. These settings do not provide a representation of a place that its inhabitants will recognize as their own or perform a localized culture for audiences living elsewhere. Rather, these locations give audiences a sense that the stories being presented are credible because the action is situated in an ostensibly authentic setting that will be recognizable to audiences. Such recognition is provided not by viewers' knowledge of the real locations of London, Brisbane, or Dallas, but instead by program-makers' inclusion of local markers that are understood both nationally and internationally to refer to those places. Just as McDonagh provides picture-postcard representations of Ireland that have no purchase on geographical realities, soap opera makers provide landscapes or cityscapes that conform to outsiders' expectations, as seen in the use in *Coronation Street* of an iconic row of terraced houses to represent the north of England, in *Eastenders* by the use of a map of London, or in the perennially good weather of *Home and Away*'s Summer Bay and *Neighbours*' Brisbane. Likewise, accent tends to be of a generic regional variety (London speech in *Eastenders*, the Texan tones of J. R. Ewing in *Dallas*), using a homogenized form of English peppered with easily understood local slang and pronunciations, ensuring that the dialogue is both localized and easily understood across regional and national boundaries.

The use of settings that are simultaneously recognizable and exotic or "other" accounts for the popularity of soap opera across national boundaries, a phenomenon related to the genre's capacity to allow viewers to identify selectively with characters, themes, and storylines without needing localized knowledge to do so. As Dorothy Hobson notes, soap opera is thus a "universal form":

> Audiences bring their own experience, knowledge, preferences and understanding to every television text they watch. They interpret the text according to what they choose to take from it and this may change according to their own circumstances and experiences. [...] [V]iewers always highlight areas which have interested them and discuss the programme in a way which is driven by their specific interest. [...] This is not just a negotiated reading or a polysemic understanding, but rather an active choice of what aspects of the programme they wish to take. They subconsciously edit out stories and themes that are not of interest, and they see in every work aspects which are of interest to themselves. (166–67)

This process of selective identification is enhanced by the emphasis on storytelling in the genre. Soap operas tend to involve occasionally outrageous plotting, with the return of characters presumed dead a relatively regular phenomenon, which, as mentioned above, is also a recurrent feature of McDonagh's writing. Such storylines function within the genre by the creation of rules of internal credibility, which is aided by the relative stability of character development, whereby the moral parameters of the soap opera environment are delineated by the consistency of characters' responses to the events presented. Characters in soap opera thus tend to represent single character traits (the lustful villainy of J. R. Ewing in *Dallas* or Dirty Den in *Eastenders*, the down-to-earth decency of every soap's patriarch or matriarch), or to embody a single issue of social importance (homosexuality, single parenthood, drug abuse, etc.). The movement of soap opera plotting is thus not teleological, as is the case in much drama or prose fiction, but circular: since a soap opera can be continued indefinitely, it is essential that its primary characters remain relatively unchanged— their circumstances may alter but their character traits must remain firmly in place.

We can see many of these features in the work of McDonagh. As stated earlier, his work reproduces many of the staples of soap opera plotting: unrequited love (as between Billy and Helen in *The Cripple* and Girleen and Father Welsh in *The Lonesome West*), domestic discord (as between Mag and Maureen in *Beauty Queen* and Coleman and Valene in *The Lonesome West*), and unfulfilled ambition (Tom's desire to be promoted within the Irish police in *A Skull*, Billy's trip to Hollywood in *The Cripple*). Similarly, McDonagh's action is centered on the development of plot rather than character, with the result that none of the people he presents ever changes. Valene and Coleman and Ariel and Tupolski in *The Pillowman* will continue to bicker and Billy will resume life on Inishmaan (perhaps with tuberculosis), as will most of the surviving characters in Leenane. Indeed, the reference in *The Lonesome West* to the brutal behavior of the under-twelves' football team suggests that the population of the town is trapped in a cycle of eternal recurrence, with the children behaving much as the adults do (*Plays 1* 168). And, no doubt, Wee Thomas will not wait long after the conclusion of *The Lieutenant* before setting off on another "two-day bender chasing skirt the length of the island" (*TL* 48). The only alterations to the circumstances of the characters arise through death, as in the case of Mag and Father Welsh in *The Leenane Trilogy*, Mad Padraic in *The Lieutenant*, and Katurian and Michal in *The Pillowman*, or emigration, as with Mairead in *Lieutenant* and Pato in *Beauty Queen*. And, most important, McDonagh's Ireland relates closely to the Brisbane of *Neighbours* or the London of *Eastenders*: the place being presented is not one that corresponds to geographical, political, or social realities, but rather one that is presented to affirm audiences' presuppositions about those locations.

McDonagh's use of place to generate a process of selective identification closely links his works to soap opera. As I have written elsewhere, one of the notable features of McDonagh's work is the variety of ways in which it is received by audiences in different places. For example, although McDonagh presents Leenane and the Aran Islands as identical, the responses of audiences in both places to his plays diverge interestingly: audiences in Leenane itself were reportedly uncomfortable with the references to the Irish language in *Beauty Queen*, for instance, while audiences in the Aran Islands found the same line hilarious (Lonergan, "Druid's *Leenane Trilogy* on Tour" 199). Similarly, *The Lieutenant of Inishmore* has been received as a condemnation of terrorism in Turkey but was also presented as a condemnation of the Australian government's involvement in the "War against Terrorism" in Sydney (Lonergan, "The Laughter Will Come of

Itself" 640). This variety of interpretations exemplifies the reflexive quality of McDonagh's works, which are successful not because they are universal or local, but instead because they are sufficiently open to interpretation to be understood in multiple ways by different audiences. To that extent, they can be compared to soap opera, whose viewers "interpret the text according to what they choose to take from it [. . .] [which] may change according to their own circumstances and experiences," as Hobson puts it (166).

It should be noted that this feature of McDonagh's plays might also be observed in other cultural forms to which he has referred. In order to develop this discussion, I want therefore to turn to an examination of the impact of one of those forms—1990s cinema—on McDonagh's work.

Shallow graves or gravely shallow? McDonagh and 1990s cinema

The relationship between McDonagh's work and cinema has received some attention to date, which has focused principally on the intermediality of *The Cripple of Inishmaan*, extensive references to Robert's Flaherty's 1934 documentary film *Man of Aran*. Robin Roberts, for example, argues that McDonagh's play, together with Marie Jones's drama *Stones in His Pockets* (1999), "use[s] the US film industry to represent the corrupting and dangerous influence of American media on Ireland" (111). Although this is an intriguing argument about the play, it neglects to explore McDonagh's consideration of how Irish filmmakers and actors (and Irish playwrights) might be complicit in the media representation of their country. In contrast to Roberts, Werner Huber sees *The Cripple* as an example of how "McDonagh metaphorically and rather cynically uses *Man of Aran* as a general emblem of the 'crisis of representation' and as a broadside targeted at various images of Ireland." He goes on to suggest that the play should be seen as an example of meta-cinema ("Contemporary Drama as Meta-Cinema" 14)—its main achievement formal rather than thematic.

While Roberts and Huber draw different conclusions, both make clear that *The Cripple of Inishmaan* in particular can be seen as an attempt by McDonagh to use theater as a means of commenting on the composition and reception of films about Ireland. I do not wish here to rehearse these arguments, but rather to broaden them, to move from considering what McDonagh's plays might say about certain films to discuss what certain films might reveal about McDonagh's plays.

The film that appears most closely to resemble McDonagh's works is, interestingly, not one he has mentioned in any interviews: the 1994 British movie, *Shallow Grave*, directed by Danny Boyle. This film appeared shortly before *The Beauty Queen* premiered, and was released during the period when most of McDonagh's plays were composed, if we are to believe the statements made by McDonagh to O'Toole in his 2006 *New Yorker* interview. Like *The Lieutenant of Inishmore*, *Shallow Grave* features intensely disturbing scenes of dismemberment, with the mild-mannered accountant David presented in Boyle's movie with his "right arm [. . .] moving briskly back and forth accompanied by a vicious sawing noise" (*Shallow Grave* 45). Similarly, in McDonagh's play a character named Davey (and not "David" as in *Shallow Grave*) will, together with Donny, "hack away" at body parts, turning them into what McDonagh calls "sizeable chunks" (*TL* 55). As in *The Pillowman*, *Shallow Grave* features a pair of police officers investigating murders, who act to "disconcert and destabilise" their suspects with "asinine nonsense" (82).

There is also a similarity between McDonagh's plays and this film in terms of setting and accent: *Shallow Grave* is set in Scotland, offering occasional moments of local color that are not relevant to the plot (men in kilts, a traditional dance) and features characters who will be broadly recognizable to middle-class audiences throughout the West—an accountant, a doctor, and a journalist, each of whom speaks in a homogenized but mildly accented form of English. In a similar fashion, McDonagh's plays also present characters speaking in an English that is non-standard but easily understood, and who also occupy broadly recognizable social or familial roles—as shopkeepers, a priest, a pair of warring brothers, a dysfunctional mother and her daughter, and so on. He also uses location to provide local color but not local knowledge, as I have discussed earlier. I would suggest, however, that the principal impact of the film on McDonagh's work has been in the area of reception, particularly in Britain. Together with Irvine Welsh's novel *Trainspotting* (1993)—which was adapted first as a play (1994) and then as a film also directed by Boyle in 1995—*Shallow Grave* was instrumental in creating the trend in British culture for darkly humorous but intensely violent works of fiction. It also helped to cultivate audiences for the new wave of so-called "in-yer-face" dramatists that emerged in Britain from 1996 onwards, one of whom was, as Aleks Sierz argues, McDonagh himself.

The resemblance of McDonagh's work to this British film is worth highlighting because the area to which McDonagh's works are most frequently compared is the genre of gangster movies, particularly those from the United States. Some interesting similarities emerge in such a consideration. For example, in a 2004 episode of the mafia serial *The Sopranos*, two members of Tony Soprano's crew travel to a farm in rural New Jersey to dig up the corpse of one of their victims, who was murdered many years before. The pair bring the remains to an outhouse where, using wooden mallets, they smash the victim's bones into powder, before placing them in a sack and dumping them in a river ("Cold Cuts"). This moment recalls McDonagh's *A Skull in Connemara*, which features an almost identical set-up, with two characters "battering the shite" out of skeletons before "eas[ing] them into the lake" (*Plays 1* 103). This correspondence demonstrates how readily McDonagh's works may be compared to the genre of

American films and television focusing on gangsters (particularly the Mafia) whose ethnicity as well as their behavior marks them as different from mainstream American society.

McDonagh's plays were, of course, composed long before *The Sopranos* was first aired, but he has often cited Scorsese and Tarantino as influences—though, again, he has not elaborated on how they have influenced his work. He has, however, spoken explicitly about the resemblance of his work to the films of Tarantino:

> I suppose I walk that line between comedy and cruelty [which is evident in Tarantino's films] because I think one illuminates the other. And, yeah, I tend to push things as far as I can because I think you can see things more clearly through exaggeration than through reality. It's like a John Woo or a Tarantino scene, where the characters are doing awful things and, simultaneously, talking about everyday things in a really humorous way. There is a humour in there that is straight-ahead funny and uncomfortable. It makes you laugh and think. (quoted in O'Hagan)

McDonagh's comments on the similarity between himself and Tarantino offer a useful way of thinking about his own works. In particular, Tarantino's earliest films, *Reservoir Dogs* (1992) and *True Romance* (1993), can provide a template for analyzing McDonagh's plays, particularly in relation to the self-referentiality of Tarantino's movies and his use of cultural forms that are regarded as either aesthetically or geographically peripheral.

Reservoir Dogs opens famously with a discussion of the meaning of a song by a popular cultural icon—Madonna—and posits a number of possible meanings for her early hit "Like a Virgin." It's "all about a girl who digs a guy with a big dick," says Mr. Brown in the film's opening line (Tarantino, *Reservoir Dogs* 3). This discussion of a woman's sexuality quickly moves into consideration of other women: of Vicki Lawrence, the "cheatin' wife [who] shot Andy," and of the waitresses serving the gang of criminals their pre-heist breakfast. "Waitressing," says Mr. White, "is the number one occupation for female non-college graduates in this country. It's the one job basically any woman can get, and make a living on" (10). This comment contrasts interestingly with the discussion of Madonna that has just concluded.

The movement in this scene is from the cultural to the social: from the representation of a woman as a sexual agent in Madonna's song to a discussion of the grim realities of life for women not unlike those described in some of Madonna's earliest work: the urban working class. By making the opening scene of his film move along this arc, Tarantino instantly highlights two important themes to his audience. The first is the extent to which any form of culture—the pop song, in this case—can be a subject of debate, analysis, and multiple interpretations. The second is the manner in which the representation of people in popular culture diverges strongly from their social roles, particularly insofar as gender and social class are concerned. The film is, after all, centered on the interpretation of performances—of the credibility of undercover cop Mr. Orange's performance as a gangster, for example—and it also draws attention to the need for audiences to relate cultural representations to their sources in society. Tarantino thus uses this opening scene to provide audiences with the interpretative tools needed to understand and appreciate his film fully.

McDonagh's works operate in similar ways. His use of Flaherty's *Man of Aran* in *The Cripple of Inishmaan* provides audiences with an extended tutorial in how to interpret Irish culture. The same is true of Billy's audition for a Hollywood movie. The audience is moved by the apparent death of Billy in a Hollywood motel: "I fear I'm not longer for this world, Mam," he says, before launching into a lengthy list of Irish clichés about banshees and fair colleens (*TC* 52). Audiences are being prepared to receive this inauthentic representation of Ireland as if it were an integral part of the plot of *The Cripple*: indeed, McDonagh appears to assume that they will react emotionally to the action's sentimental qualities. Those audiences will then be embarrassed by the discovery that what they had taken to be reality was a screen test for a Hollywood movie, and that Billy was not only unsuccessful in his attempts to gain the part for which he had been auditioning, but also contemptuous of the "arse-faced lines they had me reading for them" (63). McDonagh thus draws audiences' attention to the need to avoid accepting mediated images of Ireland uncritically, which is an important interpretative tool for his own plays.

Similarly, *The Lieutenant of Inishmore* draws repeatedly on existing modes of representation of Irish terrorism in popular media. The serious intent of the film, *In the Name of the Father* (1993), is undercut as McDonagh proposes that it might be a suitable date movie for Padraic and Mairead, while Padraic's assertion that "there's no boy-preferers involved in Irish terrorism" (*TL* 33) can be read as a reference to Neil Jordan's *The Crying Game* (1993). As I suggest elsewhere, the play also alludes and makes direct reference to Irish rebel songs, to the presentation of republicanism on the Irish stage, and to media representations of terrorism in the UK (Lonergan, " 'Too Dangerous to be Done'?"). As such, *The Lieutenant* can be seen as offering audiences an opportunity to consider the validity and authenticity of previous representations of Irish terrorism: the play, therefore, is again a tutorial of sorts on how Irish culture might be understood.

This didactic pattern may also be identified in McDonagh's other works. As has been observed often by critics, McDonagh's plays set in Ireland draw on existing modes of theatrical representation of the Irish to focus on issues of interpretation and analysis—about who killed whom, about the meaning of words such as "unbear" in *The Lonesome West* (*Plays 1* 183), about whether "splinter group" is one or two words in *The Lieutenant* (*TL* 45), and about how Ireland is understood by American tourists. *The Pillowman*, his only non-Irish play, also deals with issues of interpretation by considering the issues of intention and responsibility in relation to artistic production, contrasting Katurian's apparently disingenuous assertion that "the only duty of a storyteller is to tell a story" (*TP* 7) with the way that his actions are motivated by many different senses of duty, particularly toward his brother.

Another similarity between McDonagh and Tarantino lies in the area of idiom and cultural influence. Tarantino's use of the word "nigger" in his films has brought a significant amount of criticism his way, notably from Spike Lee, who used part of his film *Bamboozled* (2000) to satirize a scene in *Pulp Fiction* (1993) in which a character, played by Tarantino himself, uses that racial epithet several times. Tarantino's films also generally feature wide usage of African-American idiom, often by white characters. This pattern is also notable in *True Romance*, which features a character called Drexl: "a white boy, though you wouldn't know it to listen to him," Tarantino tells us (7). This is borne out in the script:

> *Why you trippin'? We jus' fuckin' with ya. But I wanna ask you a question. You with some fine bitch, I mean a brick shithouse bitch . . . and you say "Bitch, suck my dick." And then [she] says "First things first, nigger, I ain't suckin' shit till you bring your ass over here an' lick my bush!"* (9)

Objections by Lee and others to such usages are easily understood. Drexl (played in the film by British actor Gary Oldman) is white, and uses African-American slang and intonation to express desires that are extraordinarily sexist and aggressive. The white character here is not just appropriating African-American speech; he is doing so to make statements that are extremely objectionable, implying that there is an association between the acts themselves and the manner in which they are articulated.

The use of this idiom and of racialized epithets throughout Tarantino's movies works in a similar fashion: Jimmy, the white character played by Tarantino himself in *Pulp Fiction*, gives us the following rant in the film:

> *What's on my mind at this moment isn't the coffee in my kitchen, it's the dead nigger in my garage. . . . Now let me ask you a question, Jules. When you drove in here, did you notice a sign out front that said, "Dead nigger storage"?—Answer the question. Did you see a sign out in front of my house that said, "Dead nigger storage"? . . . You know why you didn't see that sign? . . . Cause storin' dead niggers ain't my fuckin' business!*

The callous manner in which these comments are uttered—and their delivery by Tarantino himself—suggests strongly that the epithet is being included solely for the purposes of provocation.

Yet Tarantino has explicitly countered such accusations. "The word 'nigger' is probably the most volatile word in the English language," he states, arguing,

> Should any word have that much power? I think it should be de-powered. But that's not my job. I don't have any political agenda in my work. I'm writing characters. The use of the word "nigger" is true to Ordell [a character in *Jackie Brown*]. To not have him say that would be a lie. (quoted in Keough N. pag.)

Tarantino thus presents himself as a storyteller, whose first duty is not to anyone's "political agenda," but rather to his own plotting and character-ization. His use of African-American slang might also be compared to the use in his films of cultural forms that are regarded as in some respects marginal in his films: blaxploitation pictures, pulp fiction, Hong Kong martial arts films, and others.

McDonagh has been attacked on similar grounds. Victor Merriman sees his work as presenting a range of "theatrical freaks" to present a version of rural Ireland as a "benighted dystopia" ("Settling for More" 59) and he argues that the purpose of these presentations is to allow middle-class audiences to avoid facing their responsibilities for the genuinely marginalized members of Irish society. He goes on to suggest that McDonagh is pre-senting a version of Irish "nature" that can act as a form of reassurance to middle-class audiences concerned about being perceived as "culture[d]" ("Decolonisation Postponed" 315). He adds that McDonagh's success in Ireland can be explained by his appeal to the sensibilities of middle-class and *nouveau riche* urban audiences:

> The decision [by McDonagh and other Irish playwrights] to populate the stage with violent child-adults repeats the angriest colonial stereo-types as a form of communal self-loathing. The *dramatis personae* of these plays specifically mark out figures of the poor which are over determined by their Irishry. Gross caricatures with no purchase on the experience of today's audiences, their appeal to the new consumer-Irish consensus lies in their appearance as ludicrous manichean oppo-sites—the colonised simian reborn. In each belly laugh which greets the preposterous malevolence of its actions there is a huge cathartic roar of relief that all of this is past—"we" have left it all behind. ("Settling for More" 60)[9]

The "caricaturing" of Irish people referred to by Merriman is principally in the area of speech, with the backwardness of McDonagh's characters being represented by an inarticulacy that is closely related to their Hiberno-English idiom. A case in point is Pato's speech of exilic longing in *Beauty Queen*—"when it's there I am, it's here I wish I was [...] . But when it's here I am ... it isn't *there* I want to be, of course not. But I know it isn't here I want to be either" (*Plays 1* 22). In performance, this speech can be quite moving—but its pathos is communicated precisely by its simplicity, by Pato's inability to express with elegance thoughts that are complex and deeply felt. And it is worth observing that while this inarticulacy can be found in all of McDonagh's Irish plays, it is present in *The Pillowman* only in the speech of Michal, which would support the suggestion that McDonagh's plays seem to portray Irishness and mental disability as interchangeable categories.

For McDonagh, however, his use of Irish speech was a simple matter of aesthetics:

> I wanted to develop some kind of dialogue style as strange and heightened as those two [Mamet and Pinter], but *twisted* in some way so the influence wasn't as obvious. And then I sort of remembered the way my uncles spoke back in Galway, the structure of their sentences. I didn't think of it as structure, just as a kind of rhythm in the speech. And that seemed an interesting way to go, to try to do something with that language that wouldn't be English or American. (quoted in O'Toole, "Nowhere Man" 1, emphasis added)

His presentation of Irish speech as a "twisted" form of English or American diction gives his plays the rhythm that he desired. Just as Tarantino denies that his use of African-American diction has any function within a "social agenda," McDonagh similarly sees his use of Hiberno-English as a simple matter of storytelling.

A difficulty arises from the disparity between authorial intention and reception, however: once Tarantino and McDonagh's works are viewed by an audience they enter a social forum in which their use of idiom becomes problematic. As discussed above, the issue of accent and social marginalization is also a feature of soap opera, and of films other than American heist, Mafia, and gangster movies. The discussion of *Shallow Grave* earlier reveals that the resemblance in McDonagh's work to particular cinematic styles is not (as has been suggested) to the genre of gangster film; nor is it exclusively a matter of he and Tarantino both using postmodern pastiche in their works. Rather, all three forms discussed thus far—1990s cinema, McDonagh's plays, and the soap opera genre—have in common their ability to travel across international boundaries with ease, despite their use of regional or marginal idioms, settings, and forms. How, then, do these three forms function within a global context?

Core and periphery in global culture

I have suggested that McDonagh's work may best be understood in a global context, and that the same is true of Tarantino's films and soap opera. This section considers how a framework for such an understanding may be developed, exploring how and why the Irishness of McDonagh's plays functions in a global context. I conclude by asking what the consequences of this understanding of McDonagh's works might be for nationalized forms of literary and dramatic criticism.

Literature and other "high arts" have tended toward internationalization since the nineteenth century or earlier. The concept of a world literature (*weltliteratur*) was originally mooted by Goethe, and developed by Marx and Engels: the avant-garde, as well as the educated elite, of most countries have always tended toward the cosmopolitan. How then does globalization represent a new departure for world literature?

The impact of globalization on literature is manifested in the deterritorialization of the relationship between core and periphery in literary production. Although Pascale Casanova and Franco Moretti reach different conclusions, both argue that the current world literary system should be distinguished from those that existed in previous eras because it is founded upon a relationship of core and periphery: that it is a unitary system, but comprised of unequal parts. As Moretti writes, the system is "*one* and *unequal*: with a core, and a periphery (and a semiperiphery) that are bound together in a relationship of growing inequality" (56, emphasis in original). In the area of theater, Rustom Bharucha also argues that globalization involves an unequal relationship between core and periphery. He focuses on countries in the developing world, pointing out that the transfer of cultural productions in the West is governed by copyright and involves authorship and (usually) the payment of royalties. He contrasts this practice with the "cultural piracy" that has led to aspects of peripheral cultures being assimilated into the core. Examples of such "cultural piracy" in the present context might be the use by McDonagh of received images of Irishness and by Tarantino of African-American idiom.

While the insights of Bharucha, Casanova, and Moretti are useful, there is a risk in each case that their insights may lead us to overlook the extent to which the relationship of core and periphery is no longer simply geographical or physical. As Bharucha shows, geography remains an influence on the distribution of power; however, core and periphery are also formed within national boundaries. Examples of "cultural piracy" between core and periphery certainly involve a movement from the developing world to the West, as he argues, but such movements also occur within core cultures. Examples of this movement include the commodification of African-American urban youth culture by United States multinationals (not to mention its usage by Tarantino and others), or the assimilation of feminist rhetoric into mass entertainment (see, for example, Gilroy 242–78 and McNair 113–28 respectively). Core values are much the same through-out the globalized world, but values may differ from one peripheral locality to another; the formation of core and periphery hence operates on a cul-tural and conceptual level, with one of them always privileged on a deterritorialized basis.

One of the principal causes of the formation of core and periphery is the impact of mobility on the production of culture. The relationship of core to periphery should be understood in terms of the mobility of cultural products within conceptual spaces. The cultural "core" of a globalized society is defined by the mobility of the products within it. Although all peripheral spaces are necessarily different, any periphery will be character-ized by the inhibition of that mobility. Globalization thus involves an increase in the movement of people across national boundaries, but the relative status of business executives and tourists on the one hand, and displaced peoples, economic migrants, and asylum seekers on the other, varies considerably. Refugee, tourist, and executive may share ethnicity, gender, level of education, religion, and nationality: the inequality between the three exists in their entitlement to move across national boundaries. Mobility thus is the "most powerful and most coveted stratifying factor" (9) in contemporary society, as Zygmunt Bauman suggests. The growing importance of mobility means that, in Bauman's words, "the freedom to move, perpetually a scarce and unequally distributed commodity, fast becomes the main stratifying factor of our late-modern or postmodern times" (3).

McDonagh's works can thus be seen as operating within the core because of their mobility; in contrast, other forms of Irish dramatic writing become peripheral because of their being immobile: examples of the latter category including (*inter alia*) plays in the Irish language and, perhaps, the works of Tom Murphy, which depend for their impact on audiences' appreciation of a range of references that are specific to Ireland.

I would suggest that McDonagh's work achieves such mobility because of its use of a peripheral cultural idiom—the stereotypical rural Irish speech and setting—to achieve recognizability across national boundaries. As I discuss elsewhere (Lonergan, "The Laughter Will Come of Itself"), McDonagh's construction of Irishness operates as a commodified abstraction—or a brand—that can operate globally, being received reflex-ively, and selectively, by localized cultures. This conception allows us to understand better the notion of hybridity in his works. He uses techniques that allow for cross-national mobility – such as received notions of Irishness, an emphasis on plot rather than setting, stable characterization, and reflex-ivity – and combines them with the authenticating characteristics of Irish settings and idioms. In a similar fashion, Tarantino's works are mobile because of his use of the same techniques, with authentication being pro-vided by reference to a range of decontextualized pop culture references. And soap opera, as noted above, uses the imagined spaces of Brisbane,

London's East End, or Dallas to anchor stories that are received selectively by international audiences.

These "authenticating" markers also allow for plays to be "branded" as representing particular modes of culture—a development that may have arisen from the impact of mass media entertainment such as cinema on the production of theater. Walter Benjamin argues that "any thorough study proves that there is indeed no greater contrast than that of the stage play to a work of art that is completely subject to, or like the film, founded in mechanical reproduction" (223). However, while the presence of live actors before an audience means that important differences between cinema and theater remain, the structures that determine how, when, and for whom cinematic, televisual, and theatrical products are produced are increasingly convergent. The common ground between theatrical and cinematic production now lies in the concept of reproducibility. Benjamin observes that in older art forms such as painting and theater, "the presence of the original is the prerequisite to the concept of authenticity," so that "the original preserved all its authority" (223). In a theatrical context, authority and authenticity were vested in the presence of a live audience and performers. In film, however, "man has to operate with his whole living person, while foregoing its aura. For aura is tied to presence: there can be no replica of it. The aura which, on stage, emanates from *Macbeth*, cannot be separated for the spectators from that of the actor" (223).

A theatrical performance is incapable of being mechanically reproduced, as Benjamin observes. The use of branding means, however, that the site of authenticity and authority—the "aura" of the production—has been removed from the live performance and made conceptual: the authenticity of a cultural product is now grounded in the recognizability of its cultural sources, as I have suggested in relation to soap opera and McDonagh's use of Leenane and the Aran Islands. With a "branded" cultural product, one does not experience a performance, but identifies oneself with a concept—with the Irishness or "in-yer-face" quality of McDonagh's plays, with the hip postmodernity of Tarantino's blend of various pop styles, and with the sense of community and familiarity fostered among audiences of soap operas. A theatrical performance cannot be reproduced and thus remains recalcitrant to the centralized management required for mass-mediation. But a brand may be controlled centrally and reproduced infinitely without a loss of authenticity.

This possibility explains producers' emphasis on the brand over the performance. If a show is internationally distributed, then actors, sets, and performances must change. A brand can be used everywhere, however, so that, for example, the construction of *The Lieutenant of Inishmore* as a satire on terrorism allows audiences in Turkey and Australia to interpret it in the context of localized experiences of terrorism and its consequences. Globalization thus creates the conditions under which it became possible to think of theater as a mass-mediated form of entertainment, with the brand functioning as a form of manageable reproduction that is not mechanical but conceptual. The transformation of cultural production from mechanical to conceptual is another example of a deterritorialization of power and of how changing perspectives on space are altering the organization of institutions and products.

This alteration in the construction of culture allows us to understand better the relationship between McDonagh, Australian soap opera, and Tarantino. All three draw on cultural forms that are geographically peripheral—either in terms of regional speech, social marginalization, or geographical isolation—but present them within frameworks that may be internationally diffused. Thus there is now a divergent relationship between the cultural core and geographical periphery: artists who can offer what might be called a "tourist's gaze" on peripheral cultures—working-class London, rural Ireland, or the subcultures of Los Angeles—can achieve an international success that places them at the core of cultural production.

Work by writers such as McDonagh, therefore, should be seen not as local or national—or even as international in the sense that Goethe envisaged world literature—but instead as functioning according to a globalized cultural model. This model encourages audiences to respond to his plays' universal qualities and dilemmas (the desire to be elsewhere, inter-familiar strife), while receiving its usage of Irish idiom and setting as markers of authenticity that "brand" the experience as valuable. In a similar fashion, Tarantino's movies make use of the authenticating markers of peripheral cultures (Kung Fu films, soul music, blaxpoitation movies) in order to provide a geographical rooting for plot-driven tales that have such universal qualities as a focus on father-son relationships, "true romance," or revenge quests. And soap opera resembles both McDonagh's plays and Tarantino's films in its ability to use plot to encourage audiences to identify themselves with imagined communities.

This interpretation is not meant to suggest that the national, the local, or indeed the international have become obsolete as categories of literary analysis; on the contrary, the rise of globalized cultural forms makes it essential that suitable levels of attention are paid to peripheral cultural forms, particularly localized ones. Instead, the emergence of global networks of mass communication—the internet, cinema, international news corporations, and the international theater network—has resulted in the development of new forms of culture that use specific strategies to transcend (rather than crossing) national boundaries. McDonagh's work is one of the strongest examples in contemporary theater of this new kind of culture.

It might be suggested that, for scholars, the emergence of work by writers such as McDonagh requires us to adopt again the methodologies of world or comparative literatures. It is, however, important to note that academic scholarship has itself been the subject of globalization and its attendant processes of branding, deterritorialization, and homogenization. The differentiating effects of mobility and their impact on academic discourse and formation are evident in many ways, all of which involve the promotion of the ideology that academic disciplines and pedagogical skills should be easily transferable across national boundaries. The impact of globalization on academic formation may therefore lead to what Peadar Kirby, Luke Gibbons, and Michael Cronin have termed "ideological franchising." This process involves "wholesale import of concepts and analyses from a power-ful centre . . . and their application in a Proecrustean fashion to the local society" (*Re-inventing Ireland* 14). Antonio Hardt and Paulo Negri are particularly useful in their treatment of postmodernity in this context. While pointing out that postmodernity has produced huge benefits in the West, influencing the development of feminism and other important move-ments, they suggest that "the postmodern epistemological challenge to the 'Enlightenment'—its attack on master narratives and its critique of truth—also loses its liberatory aura when transposed outside the elite intellectual strata of Europe and North America" (155). Referring to developments such as the establishment of a Forum for Truth and Reconciliation in South Africa, they point out that

> establishing and making public the truth of the recent past—attribut-ing responsibility to state officials for specific acts and in some cases exacting retribution—appears here as the ineluctable precondition for any democratic future. The master narratives of the Enlightenment do not seem particularly repressive here—on the contrary! (248)

As the comments by Kirby, Gibbons, and Cronin and Hardt and Negri suggest, the attempt to promote one methodology as a way of understand-ing the globalization of literature needs to be based on an awareness that the academy is itself one of the most globalized institutions of the world, and that there is therefore an attendant risk of prioritizing one set of responses to a play or film over others. To consider the impact of globalization on one locality—Ireland in the present case—requires an awareness of the need to resist the totalizing impulses inherent in consid-erations of globalization.

An important consideration for scholars of McDonagh must thus be to establish an appropriate mode of considering the impact of globalization on theater, which will be founded on an awareness of both local and global elements of that consideration. It also seems valid to want to broaden the range of inquiry beyond genre, form, and national boundaries. The rise of "creative industries" means that theaters now conduct their business using models that apply across all forms of culture, rendering distinctions of genre, form—and perhaps between avant-garde and kitsch—obsolete (cf. Caves, 5–27)

An Irish resident whose attendance at a play by Martin McDonagh has a series of cultural and social consequences will necessarily receive the play in a particular way. Audiences elsewhere will have necessarily different responses. It is vital that we avoid falling into the trap of authenticating one kind of response while deriding the other—to see Irish audiences' responses to McDonagh's play as "accurate" or to see the response of London critics to his plays as an adequate method of understanding the meaning of the play in itself.

It is, however, equally vital that critics bring an awareness of how local preoccupations shape their understanding of globally diffused plays. I would suggest, therefore, that theater studies in Ireland, Britain, and elsewhere do not need a new paradigm ("globalization theory"), but a new framework. The risk is that, by popularizing globalization theory, we will merely be rebranding existing modes of scholarship designed for international diffusion, such as postcolonial or postmodern theory, presenting "new and improved" critical terms that will do little to elucidate the actual conditions under which Irish theater is made and received, not only in Ireland, but also throughout the world. We must, in short, bring local knowledge into a global conversation, with an awareness of how Irish plays mean different things, to different audiences, in different parts of the world.

Notes

1 I wish to thank Dr. Karen Fricker of Trinity College Dublin for pointing out Rushdie's use of this character to me.

2 The reading took place at Druid's Chapel Lane Theatre on April 20, 1997, as part of the Cúirt International Festival of Literature, Galway. Thanks to Maura Kennedy of Cúirt for confirming this information.

3 I point out elsewhere (Lonergan, "Druid's *Leenane Trilogy* on Tour" 198) that, although McDonagh claimed not to have read Synge when he wrote *The Leenane Trilogy*, he had certainly done so before *A Skull in Connemara* and *The Lonesome West* were first staged. I also suggest that many of the echoes of Synge, Beckett, and John B. Keane in McDonagh's work may be traced to the influence of Garry Hynes, who directed *The Leenane Trilogy*.

4 While I admire much about her article, I am generally unpersuaded by Luckhurst's critique of *The Lieutenant*. She provides an accurate account of the London print media's response to the play, which certainly did feature quite a lot of anti-Irish sentiment (this reaction, it must be said, is not an unusual response from that sector to Irish culture, whether in traditional, popular, or literary form). However, she attempts to present this response as evidence that McDonagh is cynically exploiting such prejudice by using his "ability to conjure monolithic English notions of Irishness" (40). No direct evidence is provided to support this assertion. For example, she presents McDonagh's indifference to the status of productions of his plays outside of the United Kingdom as evidence of his mercenary tendencies, quoting his comment that "I just count the money" (35) to support that assertion. However, this comment was *not* made about productions "in the States, in Scandinavia and in Germany" as Luckhurst claims (35), but instead was made in response to the question of whether "he is [. . .] interested in finding out whether, as sometimes happens to other British dramatists, European directors have tinkered with the plays' settings or tweaked the endings" (Rosenthal 10). When viewed in the context in which the remark was actually made, McDonagh's comment seems less mercenary; read in conjunction with his other interviews it seems an example of arrogance born of defensiveness, rather than greed. The issue of whether McDonagh is responsible for the many different responses his plays provoke is a complicated one, as I discuss

elsewhere (Lonergan, "The Laughter Will Come of Itself"). However, I do not believe we can make inferences about authorial intention from the responses of London critics to one production of a play that has appeared in many countries other than England, or from comments overheard by Luckhurst at one production of the play in the same country. Her article is, however, an excellent example of how remarks made by McDonagh in media interviews have tended to provoke strong responses to the plays from commentators, and it also acts as a useful reminder of the context in which Irish plays are sometimes received in London.

5 It should also be noted that McDonagh's statement was made in private to Nicholas Hytner, who passed it on to Eyre. It is not made clear whether he made this comment sincerely or in jest.

6 I wish to thank Joan Dean for making a copy of the *Galway Advertiser* article available to me.

7 Mark O'Rowe provided this information during a pre-show talk before the Gate Theatre Dublin's production of *Crestfall* on May 30, 2003, and Conor McPherson confirmed it during a pre-show talk before Eugene O'Brien's *Eden*, at the Peacock Theatre, Dublin on January 25, 2001. For Carr on Williams, see *Reading the Future* 56.

8 "You never see the INLA shooting Australians" states Davey (*TL* 55), while Mairead's mother sends the following message to her: "good luck and try not to go blowing up any kids" (57).

9 While I agree with Merriman's analysis of the reception of the plays in Dublin, I have suggested elsewhere that it would be wrong to see the response of audiences in Ireland's capital as an indicator of how the plays were received throughout Ireland in its entirety (Lonergan, "Druid's *Leenane Trilogy* on Tour" 211).

References

Ang, Ien. *Watching "Dallas": Soap Opera and the Melodramatic Imagination*. New York: Routledge, 1985.

Bauman, Zygmunt. *Globalization: The Human Consequences*. Cambridge: Polity P, 1998.

Beckett, Samuel. *Complete Dramatic Works*. London: Faber, 1986.

Behan, Brendan. *The Complete Plays*. New York: Grove P, 1978.

Benjamin, Walter. *Illuminations*. Ed. and trans. Hannah Arendt. London: Fontana, 1992.

Bharucha, Rustom. *The Politics of Cultural Practice—Thinking Through Culture in an Age of Globalization*. London: Athlone P, 2000.

Blumenthal, Dannielle. *Women and Soap Opera: A Cultural Feminist Perspective*. New York: Greenwood P, 1997.

Boyle, Danny, dir. *Shallow Grave*. John Hodge, screenplay. MGM, 1994.

Brundson, Charlotte. *The Feminist, the Housewife and the Soap Opera*. Oxford: Oxford UP, 2000.

Casanova, Pascale. *La République Mondiale des Lettres*. Paris: Éditions des Seuil, 1999.

Caves, Richard E. *Creative Industries: Contracts between Art and Commerce*. Cambridge and London: Harvard UP, 2000.

Chisholm, Caroline. "Three of a Kind." *The [Sydney, Australia] Daily Telegraph* 5 Dec. 1997: 45.

"Cold Cuts." *The Sopranos*. Season 5, Episode 62. Dir. Mike Figgis. DVD. Warner Home Video.

Dening, Penelope. "The scribe of Kilburn." *The Irish Times* 23 April 2001: 12.

Druids, Dudes and Beauty Queens: The Changing Face of Irish Theatre. Ed. Dermot Bolger. Dublin: New Island, 2001.

Eyre, Richard. *National Service*. London: Bloomsbury, 2003.

Gillespie, Marie. *Television, Ethnicity and Cultural Change*. London: Routledge, 1994.

Gilroy, Paul. *Against Race*. Cambridge, MA: Harvard UP, 1999.

Guillen, Claudio. *The Challenge of Comparative Literature*. Chicago: U of Chicago P, 1993.

Hardt, Antonio and Paulo Negri. *Empire*. Cambridge, MA: Harvard UP, 2001.

Hobson, Dorothy. *Soap Opera*. Cambridge: Polity P, 2003.

Hodge, John. *Shallow Grave*. London: Faber, 1995.

Hoggard, Liz. "Playboy of the West End World." *The Independent* 15 June 2002: 10–13.

Huber, Werner. "Contemporary Drama as Meta-Cinema: Martin McDonagh and Marie Jones." *(Dis)Continuities: Trends and Traditions in Contemporary Theatre and Drama in English*. Ed. Margarete Rubik and Elke Mettinger-Schartmann. Trier: Wissenschaftlicher Verlag Trier, 2002: 13–24.

——. "From Leenane to Kamenice: The De-Hibernicising of Martin McDonagh"? *Literary Views on Post-Wall Europe: Essays in Honour of Uwe Boker*. Ed. Christopher Houswitsch. Trier: Wissenschaftlicher Verlag Trier, 2005: 283–94.

Jordan, Neil, screenplay and dir. *The Crying Game*. Lions Gate, 1992.

Keough, Peter. Rev. of *Jackie Brown*. *Boston Phoenix* 1 May 1998. N. pag. 13 May 2006 <http://www.filmvault.com/filmvault/boston/j/jackiebrown2.html>.

Kramer, Mimi. "Three for the Show." *Time Magazine* 4 Aug. 1997: 71.

Lanters, José. "Playwrights of the Western World: Synge, Murphy, McDonagh." *A Century of Irish Drama: Widening the Stage*. Ed. Stephen Watt, Eileen Morgan, and Shakir Mustafa. Bloomington: Indiana UP, 2000: 204–22.

Lee, Spike, dir. and screenplay. *Bamboozled*. New Line, 2000.

Lonergan, Patrick. "Druid's *Leenane Trilogy* on Tour." *Irish Theatre on Tour*. Ed. Nicholas Grene and Christopher Morash. Dublin: Carysfort P, 2005: 193–214.

——. " 'The Laughter Will Come of Itself. The Tears Are Inevitable': Martin McDonagh, Globalization, and Irish Theatre Criticism." *Modern Drama* 47.4 (Winter 2004): 636–58.

——. " 'Too Dangerous to be Done'? Martin McDonagh's *Lieutenant of Inishmore*." *Irish Studies Review* 13.1 (2005): 65–78.

Luckhurst, Mary. "Martin McDonagh's *Lieutenant of Inishmore*: Selling (-Out) to the English." *Contemporary Theatre Review* 14.4 (2004): 34–41.

McDonagh, Martin. *The Cripple of Inishmaan*. London: Methuen, 1997.

——. *The Lieutenant of Inishmore*. London: Methuen, 2001.

——. *The Pillowman*. London: Faber, 2003.

——. *Plays 1 (The Beauty Queen of Leenane, A Skull in Connemara, The Lonesome West)*. London: Methuen, 1999.

McNair, Brian. *Striptease Culture: Sex, Media, and the Democratisation of Desire*. London and New York: Routledge, 2002.

Merriman, Vic. "Decolonisation Postponed: The Theatre of Tiger Trash." *Irish University Review* 29.2 (Summer 1999): 305–17.

——. "Settling for More: Excess and Success in Contemporary Irish Drama." *Druids, Dudes and Beauty Queens* 55–71.

——. "Staging Contemporary Ireland: Heartsickness and Hopes Deferred." *The Cambridge Companion to Twentieth-Century Irish Drama*. Ed. Shaun Richards. Cambridge: Cambridge UP, 2004: 244–57.

Morash, Christopher. *A History of Irish Theatre, 1601–2000*. Cambridge: Cambridge UP, 2002.

Moretti, Franco. "Conjectures on World Literature." *New Left Review* 2.1 (Jan./Feb. 2000): 54–68.

Morgan, Joyce. "Aussie Soaps: McDonagh Comes Clean." *Sydney Morning Herald* 8 Jan. 1998: 27.

Mumford, L. S. *Love and Ideology in the Afternoon: Soap Opera, Women, and Television Genre*. Bloomington: Indiana UP, 1995.

"New Druid Playwright is a 'Natural.'" *Galway Advertiser* 11 Jan. 1996: 23.

O'Hagan, Sean. "The wild west." *Guardian Weekend* 24 Mar. 2001: 32.

O'Toole, Fintan. "A Mind in Connemara: The Savage World of Martin McDonagh." *The New Yorker* 6 Mar. 2006: 40–47.

——. "Nowhere Man." *The Irish Times* 26 Apr. 1997, *Weekend Supplement*: 1.

Reading the Future: Irish Writers in Conversation with Mike Murphy. Ed. Cliodhna Ni Anluain. Dublin: Lilliput P, 2000.

Re-Inventing Ireland. Ed. Peadar Kirby, Luke Gibbons, and Michael Cronin. London: Pluto P, 2002.

Remote Control: Television Audiences and Cultural Power. Ed. Ellen Seiter et al. London: Routledge, 1991.

Richards, Shaun. "'The outpouring of a morbid, unhealthy mind': The Critical Condition of Synge and McDonagh." *Irish University Review* 33.1–2 (Spring/Summer 2003): 201–14.

Roberts, Robin. "Gendered Media Rivalry: Irish drama and American film." Spec. issue of *Australasian Drama Studies: Performing Ireland*. Ed. Brian Singleton and Anna McMullan. 43 (Oct. 2003): 108–127.

Rosenthal, Daniel. "How to Slay 'Em in the Isles." *The Independent* (London) 11 Apr. 2001: 10.

Rushdie, Salman. *The Ground beneath Her Feet*. London: Vintage, 1999.

Scott, Tony, dir. *True Romance*. Quentin Tarantino, screenplay. Warner, 1993.

Sheridan, Jim, dir. Terry George and Jim Sheridan, screenplay. *In the Name of the Father*. Adapt. from Gerry Conlan's *Proved Innocent*. Universal, 1993.

Sierz, Aleks. *In-Yer-Face Theatre: British Drama Today*. London: Faber, 2001.

Synge, J. M. *Complete Works*, Vol. IV. *Plays: Book II*. Ed. Ann Saddlemyer. Gerrards Cross, UK: Colin Smythe, 1982.

Talking about Tom Murphy. Ed. Nicholas Grene. Dublin: Carysfort P, 2002.

Tarantino, Quentin. *Pulp Fiction*. London: Faber, 1999.

——, screenplay and dir. *Pulp Fiction*. Miramax, 1993.

——. *Reservoir Dogs*. London: Faber, 2000.

——, screenplay and dir. *Reservoir Dogs*. Miramax, 1992.

——. *True Romance—The Screenplay*. London: Faber, 1995.

Today Show. "Playwright Martin McDonagh Takes Broadway by Storm." WNBC, New York. 16 Apr. 1998.

Vandevelde, Karen. "The Gothic Soap of Martin McDonagh." *Theatre Stuff: Critical Essays on Irish Theatre*. Ed. Eamonn Jordan. Dublin: Carysfort P, 2000. 292–302.

Appendix: Chronology of Martin McDonagh's life and works

1970:	McDonagh born March 26, 1970, the second son of working-class Irish parents in the Elephant and Castle neighborhood of London.
1970s–1980s:	McDonagh and his brother John attend Catholic schools in London with students of mostly Irish descent and are taught mainly by Irish priests. The brothers spend summers with their parents and father's family in Connemara, western Ireland. Family moves to the Camberwell area of London.
1982:	Loses his Catholic faith and begins to listen to punk rock, especially the Clash and the Pogues.
1984:	Attends the theater for the first time and sees American playwright David Mamet's *American Buffalo*.
1986:	Returns to the theater to see Martin Sheen in Larry Kramer's *The Normal Heart*.
1986:	Leaves school at sixteen, shirks work, and lives on the dole (welfare). He tells his brother a narrative about a man who cuts a boy's toes off and feeds them to the rats, which later becomes one of the stories in *The Pillowman* (2003).
1987:	Works at a supermarket as a stockboy, then quits and goes back on the dole.
1988–1992:	Works part-time as an administrative assistant in the Department of Trade and Industry.
1992:	Father retires and parents return to Ireland. Lives with his brother in the family house in Camberwell, London. Begins sending his roughly 150 stories written since sixteen to film companies, but none are produced. Writes radio dramas, film scripts, and stage plays over the next two years.
1994:	Brother John wins fellowship in screenwriting to the University of Southern California. Martin quits his job at the Department of Trade and Industry and begins writing every

morning, producing drafts of seven plays in nine months, including the unpublished, unproduced *The Banshees of Inisheer*. Watches soap operas in the afternoons, which hones his dramatic gifts.

1995:   Garry Hynes, director of Druid Theatre, reads *A Skull in Connemara*, contacts McDonagh, and buys the rights to all three plays in *The Leenane Trilogy* (*The Beauty Queen of Leenane*, *A Skull in Connemara*, and *The Lonesome West*).

1996:   *The Beauty Queen of Leenane* opens on February 1 at Town Hall Theatre, Galway. Co-production of Galway's Druid Theatre and London's Royal Court Theatre. Curses Sean Connery in November shortly before receiving the "Most Promising Playwright Prize" at the London *Evening Standard* Theatre awards ceremony. Incident spurs scandal in the British tabloids.

1997:   *The Cripple of Inishmaan* opens on January 5 on the Cottesloe stage of London's Royal National Theatre.

1997:   *A Skull in Connemara* opens on June 4 at Town Hall Theatre, Galway. Co-production of Druid Theatre and Royal Court Theatre. *The Lonesome West* opens one week later, on June 11, again co-produced by Druid/Royal Court.

Late 1990s: Druid, Royal Court, and the National all refuse to stage *The Lieutenant of Inishmore*, offended by its graphic violence and fearful that the play's critique of republican terrorism in Northern Ireland could endanger the peace process in the province. McDonagh announces in the press that he will submit no new plays to any theater until *The Lieutenant* is staged.

1998:   *The Beauty Queen* opens at the Walter Kerr Theatre in New York on April 23. It is nominated for the 1998 Tony Award for Best Play and wins the 1998 Drama Desk Award for Outstanding New Play.

1999:   *The Lonesome West* opens at the Lyceum Theatre on Broadway on April 27. It is nominated for the 1999 Tony Award for Best Play.

2001:   *The Lieutenant* opens May 11 at The Other Place, Stratford-upon-Avon, produced by The Royal Shakespeare Company.

2003:   *The Pillowman* opens November 13 on the Cottesloe stage of the Royal National. *The Lieutenant* opens September 29 at the Olympia Theatre, Dublin, as part of the 2003 Dublin Theatre Festival.

2005:   McDonagh's 27-minute film short, *Six Shooter*, about a bereaved man who meets a psychopath on a train, first broadcast by the Irish Film Board/Film Four/*A Missing in Action Film*/Funny Farm Films. *The Pillowman* opens at the Booth Theatre on Broadway on April 10. It wins a New York Drama Critics Circle Award for Best Play (Foreign) and receives Outer Critics Circle, Drama Desk, and Tony nominations for Best Play.

2006:   *The Lieutenant* opens at the Lyceum Theatre on May 3 and is nominated for the 2006 Tony Award for Best Play, as well as the 2006 Drama Desk Award for Outstanding Play. *Six Shooter* wins Oscar for best live-action short film. Begins work on first full-length feature, *In Bruges*, about two hit men hiding in Bruges, Belgium after accidentally murdering a child.

Index

Note: page numbers in *italics* denote photographs